IRS: A VIEW FROM THE INSIDE

IRS: A VIEW FROM THE INSIDE

YVONNE WILEY-WEBB

Kroshka Books
Huntington, New York

Senior Editors:	Susan Boriotti and Donna Dennis
Office Manager:	Annette Hellinger
Graphics:	Wanda Serrano
Information Editor:	Tatiana Shohov
Book Production:	Latoya Clay, Cathy DeGregory and Lynette Van Helden
Circulation:	Anna Cruz, Ave Maria Gonzalez, Ron Hedges and Andre Tillman

Library of Congress Cataloging-in-Publication Data

Wiley-Webb, Yvonne.
    IRS : a view from the inside / Yvonne Wiley-Webb.
        p.   cm.
    ISBN 1-56072-846-9
    1. United States. Internal Revenue Service--Management. 2. United States. Internal Revenue Service. 3. Tax administration and procedure--United States. I. Title.
HJ2361.W545   2000   CIP
336.24'0973--dc21   00-061951

DEDICATION

This book is dedicated to my family. To my husband for his support and encouragement and to my children as they lived with me during most of the years in which I experienced those things I have written about.

Contents

ACKNOWLEDGMENTS XI

CHAPTER ONE: INTRODUCTION - THE BEGINNING 1

The introduction furnishes the reader with an overview of IRS as seen from the inside by an employee. The insights will be provided starting from the professional position of Revenue Officer and covering twenty five years of a career ending in the top level position of the Chief, Collection Division of the largest Collection Division in IRS nationwide.

CHAPTER TWO: CLIMBING THE CAREER LADDER 7

My climb up the career ladder happened during a time when IRS was required to accept women in positions historically believed to be "for males only" positions. Even the public had difficulty accepting women in revenue officer jobs. IRS has been and still is having difficulty sharing authority and power with women and minorities. Incredible deficiencies of the organization will be discussed in this chapter

CHAPTER THREE: EXTRA CURRICULAR ACTIVITIES 47

Aside from collecting taxes and or managing those who collect, IRS employees day to day work lives reflect that of the outside. While IRS employees are supposedly held to higher standards because of the nature of their jobs, you will read of executive level directors abusing sick leave and vacation privileges. Some of these executives retired after more than thirty years and used little or no sick leave or annual leave to take vacations. The public might be interested in knowing that these executives get paid lump sums for all unused accrued annual leave upon retirement. This topic along with situations regarding sexual harassment and many other maladies infecting IRS employees will be discussed in this chapter.

CHAPTER FOUR: IRS HIERARCHY   **93**

Few people know or understand the structure of the IRS. This chapter will describe the organization and will discuss the basic collection job as seen on the inside. It will also describe specific situations regarding IRS enforcement including seizures and threats of seizures. It will enable citizens to recognize danger signs alone the way when enforcement actions are in the process of being implemented.

CHAPTER FIVE: REVENUE OFFICER TRAINING   **101**

Training is provided over extended periods of time for new employees; however, many times it is substandard as a result of last minute approval of funds from Congress. Inferior training has significant impact throughout an employee's career resulting in potential nightmares for taxpayers. Examples of this inferior training will be provided in this chapter.

CHAPTER SIX: IRS - A VIEW FROM OUTSIDE   **125**

In an effort to attempt to provide objectivity, a view of IRS from the outside will be provided by a former IRS employee, the author. This view was experienced while working fourteen months in a private firm that represents taxpayers with IRS collection problems. The most interesting facet of this situation is that the author has had the experience of sitting on both sides of the table having twenty-five years of IRS employment.

CHAPTER SEVEN: ADDRESSING CONCERNS EXPRESSED DURING 1997 IRS HEARINGS   **147**

Horrors shared by taxpayers during the 1997 IRS Congressional Hearings will be discussed based on IRS experiences as well as allegations highlighted in a popular nationally recognized magazine regarding a currently employed IRS manager. The author experienced several years of working with this manager who is currently on administrative leave while the allegations are being investigated.

CHAPTER EIGHT: INCREASING COLLECTIONS   **155**

The pressure to increase collections comes from a double-edged sword in IRS with employees expected to collect taxes in a manner acceptable to IRS, taxpayers, and congress. The use of quotas to increase collections has been done and will continue under the current pressures.

CHAPTER NINE: LABOR/MANAGEMENT RELATIONS 181

The resources utilized in labor management situations in IRS is unbelievable. Substantial human resources are consumed by people hired as front line employees who are taken under the wings of the union as soon as performance problems are identified. Management in most districts is not in control of the organization. Management authority at the national level of IRS has been abdicated to the union. Many managers have thrown in the towel as a result of feeling fear and intimidation from the union and abandonment from executive level management. Examples can be seen by an employee being given the approval to observe Halloween as his religious day because he claims to be a warlock.

CHAPTER TEN: EMPLOYEE OUTREACH EFFORTS 223

Yes, IRS has this horrible reputation, some of which is deserved; however, many employee hours are spent providing assistance to those citizens not able to afford to pay to have their income tax returns prepared. Also, many hours are spent in "stay in school" programs for students. Readers will have the opportunity of observing another side of IRS employees.

CHAPTER ELEVEN: IRS TODAY 233

The IRS of today, while undergoing significant changes, continues to face the old challenges. Just how IRS will be able to treat taxpayers the way they and Congress expects while collecting delinquent taxes remains to be seen.

EXHIBITS 237

ACKNOWLEDGMENTS

My heartfelt thanks to the many IRS employees who gave me their best during my career years. While they are too numerous to name they know who they are. They are the ones who were always loyal and trustworthy, providing daily support. They will always remain in my fondest memories.

I am truly grateful to my sisters and brothers and to my many friends who have provided me with their ultimate confidence in my success in this endeavor.

Many thanks to the various IRS employees nationwide, who although they wished to remain anonymous, shared with me their many career experiences.

My undying gratitude goes to Nova Science Publishers, Inc. for publishing my first writing endeavor.

Chapter One

INTRODUCTION - THE BEGINNING

INTERNAL REVENUE, those very words strike fear in the hearts and minds of many, many taxpayers. Stories run amok every year of IRS' misuse of power and abuse of taxpayers, especially during the income tax filing season. In addition, the media becomes consumed with IRS stories anytime one of the major political powers decide to take on IRS as a result of taxpayers complaints hitting the fan or in the case of an IRS whistleblower becoming front page news.

Did you know that IRS has the power to seize homes, businesses, automobiles, and most other personal properties belonging to citizens? This power is reserved for IRS employees and they do not have to request approval or authorization from a court.

Employees with two years or less employment are able to make decisions that can and often do destroy lives.

Fear, intimidation, secrecy, Gestapo tactics, secret policies, are all descriptions used by the public to describe the much feared and hated IRS. The very symbol IRS strikes fear in the hearts of taxpayers. Even IRS employees are fearful of the organization, especially when it relates to their personal income tax situations.

Employees experience a grave sense of dread when faced with the possibility of being audited even when they know everything on their tax return can be accounted for. Executive level managers of IRS have been known to say they have held back certain deductions they were legally entitled to just in case IRS found a problem with something on their return. They would then be able to use the previously withheld item to offset any potential liability.

Are these fears valid? Does IRS misuse power granted by Congress? Are taxpayers abused by IRS employees? The answer is a resounding Yes! While these abuses are not done on a wholesale basis by every employee and it is not part of a planned IRS conspiracy, it does happen. When it happens it can be devastating. How do I know it happens? Well, I can be considered somewhat of an expert on IRS policies and practices, particularly with those of the Collection Division.

I retired from IRS in January 1996 after 25 plus years in the IRS Collection Division, the last eight as the Chief, Collection Division in Laguna Niguel, California. Just prior to my retirement IRS implemented a major re-organization endeavor, separating districts. However during my tenure, IRS Laguna Niguel Collection Division was the largest in the nation with 1000 or more employees when fully staffed.

I ended my career in one of the most powerful positions in IRS nationwide. While there were those in the executive ranks above me, anyone responsible for a large Collection Division was considered by IRS to be in a power position. The position was powerful because of the extensive absolute approval authority to conduct seizures, file liens, and levies, and basically to determine the fate of many taxpayers' lives.

Throughout my career IRS was always regarded as the best managed government agency in the United States. The idea that this statement was and still may be accurate is tremendously frightening. The idea was frightening to me even as a revenue officer trainee and remained so throughout my career. This feeling was shared by my peers as well as my fellow managers while I worked there.

In 1972 I would have made the A list of those ignorant of the laws regarding the IRS tax system. I was recruited from the U. S. Post Office for a job as a revenue officer in the IRS Collection Division of the Los Angeles District. Today, after retiring I remain as amazed as I was in 1972 at the veil of secrecy and intimidation surrounding the inner workings of IRS.

I researched libraries and book stores and could not find one book written by an IRS Collection Division employee detailing personal experiences with IRS from inside the Collection Division. Apparently retirement does not provide sufficient courage for former employees to publicly discuss their IRS employment. By and large, many, many employees are unhappy working inside IRS, including first line managers, top level managers, as well as executives who obviously do not feel loyal to the organization, yet fear prevents them from sharing their experiences.

As a young Black female, I was very proud to be selected to work for IRS in 1972. During that time IRS was probably at its peak in terms of receiving respect from citizens. Even though few people looked forward to paying taxes, many people had a sense of respect for IRS employees and their power. Most people had a sense of responsibility and obligation to file and pay taxes. That respect started to erode at a fast pace around the time of the Vietnam conflict. Citizens began to question government at all levels and refused to blindly accept authority.

The primary divisions during my career in IRS were Collection, Examination, and Criminal Investigation Division. Throughout my entire career Taxpayer Service Division has been in and out of vogue dependent upon budgetary issues, congressional pressures, and level of concern regarding taxpayers rights.

Taxpayer Service Division, the one division supposedly interested in providing good customer service was part of the Collection Division at the time I started working for IRS. It then became a separate division and then guess what, it has now gone back into one of the other divisions. This is always a signal to IRS employees that the organization is downplaying the importance of quality customer service to taxpayers. It also signals that the collection of taxes has once again become a priority over customer service. The rights of taxpayers then become of secondary concern in the minds of employees.

Availability of counter service assistance provided by Taxpayer Service Division for walk-in taxpayers has come and gone through the years and it is interpreted by employees as a sure sign of the importance of or lack thereof for providing quality customer service.

My first position in IRS as a revenue officer required seizure of homes, closing businesses, levying on wages, bank accounts, and even seizing automobiles out of taxpayers' driveways as they watched from their doorway. The owners/taxpayers did not know whether or not I had the approved authority to take their property. Most just stood by upset; however, a few became angry and verbally abusive.

On occasion some taxpayers threatened physical violence. On those occasions I called the police or when desperate, IRS special agents. Most revenue officers would do anything they could rather than call on the special agents for protection. Special agents from Criminal Investigation Division were a big joke in IRS. One special agent shot himself in the foot over twenty years ago and it is still joked about among the remaining old timers who remember the incident. Also, it was often said special agents only had one bullet in each office so look out if you need their help.

At any rate, back then the general public did not know what IRS employees could and could not do. Can you imagine that in today's world the general public still does not really know what authority IRS employees have. The veil of secrecy is still there and seems to be impenetrable.

Most people don't even know the difference between revenue agents and revenue officers. Even the media refers to most IRS employees as agents, yet revenue officers are the employees who wield the more observable significant enforcement power. They are the ones who conduct seizures, taking taxpayers' property.

Revenue officers were my employees in the Collection Division. Revenue agents work in the Examination Division and they are the ones who perform audits - actions containing its own power and intimidation.

I ended my career with IRS providing overall approval and authority for the hundreds and hundreds of seizures of personal and real property. Thousands and thousands of Federal tax liens were filed with thousands and thousands of levies executed by my subordinate employees.

A lien is an interest or encumbrance that one person has on the property of another. It is security for a debt or obligation. A Federal tax lien attaches to a taxpayer's property and rights to property owned during the life of the lien. The lien also provides the authority for IRS employees to levy upon or seize taxpayers' property. As an encumbrance on property included, but not limited to, are liens against real property, judgments secured against creditors, or third parties interest in property given as collateral.

The Federal tax lien provides the authority to IRS employees to secure payment of delinquent taxes by levy. A Form 668-A, Notice of Levy, is used to attach funds belonging to (or owed to) taxpayers which are in the control of a third party. The most common of these being bank accounts and accounts receivable.

As a revenue officer I personally experienced the pressure of seizure quotas. The subject of seizure quotas is something that has always been vehemently denied by IRS national level management during all senate hearings and to any and all media questions, of course this is the big lie. Throughout my career major competition existed between managers and revenue officers in taking property belonging to taxpayers. Sometimes the competition was so strong there were contests conducted between groups.

As a manager I had the opportunity to witness and receive pressure from local district, regional, and national executives in an effort to increase dollars collected. Increasing dollars collected ultimately means increased seizures.

The subject of seizure quotas was discussed at an IRS senate hearing in the 1980's. At that time a union official who also happened to be a revenue officer, testified that collection groups in IRS posted signs showing seizure statistics, which was a definite no, no as statistics were not supposed to be maintained by managers.

In addition, this union official testified that motivational signs were displayed in groups with one in the building where he worked saying, "Seizure fever, catch it". Of course executive level IRS management denied knowing about the statistics and signs. They then turned around and came down heavy on first line managers threatening to take drastic action against them if any signs or statistics were found in any group.

With IRS being as large as it is, it is obvious executive level management cannot know everything that goes on daily; however, mid-level, top level, and executive level management make frequent visitations to the various offices so that it is near impossible to believe no one knew about the items prior to the Hearings.

As you read this book you may wonder why I spent 25 years in an organization I seem to have such little respect for. To set the record straight I want to be sure it is understood that some of the finest people I have ever known work for IRS. Some became employed there because they needed a job at a point in time when jobs were available in IRS. Some because at one point in time the jobs were believed to be honorable opportunities to serve the government.

One of the major problems is that once an employee has started to ascend the pay scale, most of them cannot afford to leave and so, many remain and attempt to do the job in the best manner possible. Overall, most government jobs are thankless ones what with everyone always ready to take pot shots, lumping all government workers into one category.

The revenue officer job has to be one of the most thankless and stressful positions in the government. During my training year as a revenue officer, there was a running joke that few revenue officers live to retire because of the pressure. Those who do live to retire generally end up with health problems resulting from stress such as high blood pressure, strokes, and/or heart attacks.

Included in my objectives for writing this book is a desire to provide taxpayers with some insight into the power wielded by IRS employees. It is my belief that every taxpaying citizen should know the rights they are entitled to when confronted with IRS employees and potential enforcement action. To know what IRS has the power to do and how IRS operates inside is the best insurance for being able to pull back the menacing veil of secrecy and to feel confident in staring down the enemy, in this case, the IRS.

Chapter Two

CLIMBING THE CAREER LADDER

To understand my ascent up the career ladder, the vehicle that enabled me to experience the things I am writing about, it is important to know the basic structure of the IRS organization. In addition to the following, the structure will be discussed in more detail in Chapter Three - IRS Hierarchy.

IRS districts vary in size with small districts' structure varying from that of large districts. During most of my career there were small, medium, and large districts throughout the nation. My career was spent in two of the largest districts in IRS, Los Angeles and Laguna Niguel, California. The Los Angeles district became so large it had to be divided with its territory becoming part of three districts, one already existing at the time, the San Jose District, and the third, the newly created Laguna Niguel district.

I was selected as a GS-7 Revenue Officer in 1971. This was at a time when women and minorities were few and far between in IRS. The job was considered to be a law enforcement position; therefore, in the 1970's it was not considered the type of job women were suitable for.

Most revenue officer groups have an average of 12 revenue officers per group. At the time I joined IRS, there was a group that consisted of nine female revenue officers. These new revenue officers had completed their training class a year prior to mine. The group manager of this new group, a white male, an old timer, made the job virtually impossible for the females so that by the time I was hired a year later all but one had been fired or had resigned.

During those early years there was a definite feeling among IRS managers and employees who happened to be mostly male, that females simply could not do the job. Now mind you, there was an element of danger that existed for revenue officers; however, the requirements for the job consisted of brain power, not brawn power.

Revenue officers are required to make field visitations on cases received in their inventory. Sometimes the visitations need to be made to homes and sometimes to businesses. Sometimes the areas to be visited leave much to be desired and sometimes the address may be that of a bar, even nude bars. These visitations are to be made during regular working hours which are generally no later than 4:30 to 5:00 pm.

I made field visitations to bars during my revenue officer days and I found some bars opened as early as 10:00am and customers were in there drinking at that early hour. While I did not run into any harm I did have to endure sexist remarks made by the almost all male customers. Many men did not think women could handle that kind of situation and so in their paternalistic mode they felt it would be better for women to not be hired as revenue officers. If women were stubborn and insisted on being hired IRS had plenty male managers willing to do what was best for the females, fire them.

During my training year I was assigned to the Los Angeles Federal Building in downtown Los Angeles. I was one of two women (one white and one black) in a group of all white males. I had a very successful training year, probably because I was a mature adult in my mid-thirties and could not be intimidated easily.

The classroom training was conducted in the regional training center in Van Nuys, California. My classroom training group consisted of about sixty trainees, two full classrooms of thirty each. Trainees from throughout the region attended the training in Van Nuys including two trainees from Guam. Specific details regarding training problems are discussed in Chapter Five, Revenue Officer Training.

Los Angeles Collection Division was experiencing a tremendous backlog of delinquent employment tax cases when I first arrived in the group. My fellow trainees and I all had inventories of two hundred plus taxpayer cases.

In an effort to collect the taxes in an expeditious manner, procedures known as "knock and lock" had been implemented and were in full force. The rule was that you knocked on the door of a delinquent business, made a demand for full payment, and failing to receive payment in full, immediate action was taken to lock the door. Locking the door meant seizing the business and having a locksmith change the locks to prevent the taxpayer from accessing the premises. Once a business was seized the next step was a sale of that business.

Many, many seizures were made under the knock and lock system. Employees were actually promoted and given awards based on the number of enforcement actions they took, especially if those actions were seizures.

I personally conducted the largest seizure in my training group, seizure of a lumber company, delinquent in employment taxes. All of the assets including three trucks, a Volkswagen automobile, all supplies, and equipment were seized. The company then became the property of the federal government.

The seizure was somewhat uneventful, if a seizure can ever be uneventful. The sale however, was a different situation.

My original coach during training was a wonderful, very smart, efficient young man. Because he possessed those qualities just mentioned, he was offered several promotional opportunities for positions in other areas. He left before the training year ended for a promotion in another state.

My replacement coach was a man who while he was extremely strait laced, was okay with me, but to an outsider he gave the appearance of being very arrogant and officious, demonstrating those characteristics to the maximum degree in the presence of the public.

A group of Los Angeles businessmen commonly referred to in a derogatory manner by IRS Revenue Officers as "the forty thieves", attended all IRS sales and they were generally successful in their bids for taxpayers' assets. They asked a lot of questions, as might be expected, and at my sale of the lumber company they approached the coach and asked questions regarding the equity of the taxpayer in the seized assets. The coach referred them to the IRS manual stating, "We are only selling the taxpayers right, title, and interest in the assets".

Repeated questions received the same answer over and over again. The bidders became so frustrated with the coach one cussed him out. They were, however, very courteous to me and actually helped me be successful with my first sale. While I don't remember the exact dollar amount I received for the sale of the assets, I do remember it was enough to pay the taxpayer's liability in full which was not always the case with IRS sales.

After all of these years the things that stand out most vivid in my mind deal with examples of IRS' uncaring, hard-line collection activities demonstrated during my training year. The most significant one being when I was assigned a Taxpayer Delinquent Investigation (TDI) to secure a delinquent return from a man about 90 years old. He had a household employee and he had failed to file and pay all required employment tax returns.

If a taxpayer fails to file a tax return, the IRS Service Center sends several notices to the taxpayer advising that the return is delinquent and that it must be filed immediately. Failure on the taxpayer's part to file the return results in the Service Center issuing a Taxpayer Delinquency Investigation (TDI) to a revenue officer.

When I made the field visitation to the elderly man's home I realized he was delinquent because of his frailty and what appeared to be forgetfulness. I had to make several visitations to his home to secure the return. I actually ended up preparing the return for him, something we were told not to do. I prepared the return because it was very easy to do and because even as a trainee it seemed ridiculous to me to waste time waiting on the return while continuing to harass this old gentleman.

In the meantime I was being pressured by my coach to close the TDI by securing the return and full payment, so on my third and last visitation the taxpayer finally had his records together, I prepared the return and asked for payment. I asked for payment, I didn't demand it as we were supposed to do. The taxpayer was clearly unable to handle much stress; however, he insisted on writing his own check and signing the return. His writing was very shaky and barely legible. However, I was able to close the TDI with full payment.

The taxpayer died that night. I found out he had died because I had to call his home the next day for some additional information. When I found out that he had died I told the coach and his lack of feeling and sensitivity were amazing. Since I was a relatively new employee it would have made me feel better about the organization if the coach had made an effort to assure me I had nothing to do with the taxpayer's death.

However, I was teased for some time for having gone the limit to close a case. Comments were even made that I killed the old man to get a full pay. It became a laughing matter that I did not find humorous. The coach's primary interest was in getting the case closed. He did not voice any concern over the death of the taxpayer.

Also during my training year, the overall IRS organization demonstrated an uncaring attitude in the area of sexual harassment which at that time was an unknown term. There were no laws, rules, nor regulations regarding the subject. However, it was being committed in daily lives and it was going on in at least one group in IRS that I knew of.

A female revenue officer in the adjoining group told me her manager was known for openly making sexual remarks in the group. He had even gone so far as to pat her on the behind. She said it was known by all of the women in her group that you never turned your back on this group manager in an elevator.

This was the same manager who often went and sat on the floor, in the corner, during meetings conducted by his manager. This is also the same man who retired and shortly thereafter attempted suicide by shooting himself in the head. The bullet evidently missed the mark he was aiming for and disfigured his face for life. He finally died a few years ago in what I have been told was a very disturbed state.

The strangest thing about this entire situation was that top level management knew this man was unstable, yet this is the man who ultimately made hundreds of decisions of whether taxpayers' assets should be seized and sold. All of this took place during the "knock and lock" period with a lot of seizure activity taking place. Many times I wondered whether something was wrong with my thinking because a lot of situations like this seemed to go unnoticed by many employees and management.

As a result of the foregoing, the level of respect for management was zero during my first few years in IRS and to make matters worse division level management ruled with an iron fist. The aforementioned "knock and lock" procedures were implemented as requirements from the division chief's office.

The author of the "knock and lock" procedures, the division chief's assistant was referred to by revenue officers as the "chief's henchman", a cold, cruel man capable of doing anything to intimidate taxpayers and employees.

The so called henchman had such a horrendous reputation the "dirt" on him always preceded him into the many districts he worked on his way up the career ladder. Employees in the district he was leaving always saw to it that the employees in the new district were provided with as much history of his heinous actions as possible. IRS had a phone system where employees all across the nation could call each other with the call appearing to be a business call. The phone lines sizzled each time the "henchman" left a district.

Upon my arrival in the IRS Los Angeles district I was advised by senior employees that the road to success was paved with seizures, sales, full payments, and no questions asked. This was in part due to the well known agenda and expectations of the "henchman".

In addition to the extremely hard-line attitude of top level management, part of the basis for so much disrespect for division level management was the result of the employees belief of what happened at the management off-site meetings held each quarter during the year.

These meetings were held for all first line managers and above. The employees referred to the meetings as "love ins" and they were discussed by employees all the way down the line. At taxpayers expense this group of highly paid officials went off-site to a vacation resort area for three or four days each quarter. Rumors ran amok that the division chief was using the meetings to prey on the female managers.

While I am not sure of the validity of these rumors, I do know for certain that a division chief in power during that time did use his power to prey on his female employees. I was a friend of one of his staff assistants and she let me listen in on a phone conversation in which it was very clear he was propositioning her.

In addition, after he left the Los Angeles District for another district he arranged a temporary assignment for this staff assistant to work in his new district. She ultimately transferred there for a permanent position. She told me that he had "hit on her". She never actually said they had an affair; however, the temporary assignment she was offered was at the same level of the position to which she was already permanently assigned so there wasn't any advantage in accepting it.

Near the end of my career, the above mentioned off-site meetings came under close scrutiny and were virtually banned regardless of whether they made sense from a financial standpoint or not. IRS received very negative publicity anytime it was known that meetings and/or conferences were held in vacation type resort areas.

As a result of the negative publicity, very poor management decisions were made from the top down on many issues, many of which should have been just your every day common sense decisions. Rather than be placed in a position where it was possible to receive negative press, decisions would be made that were of tremendous financial cost to the organization.

In the case of the off-site meetings, rather than allow off-site meetings in resort areas off season with off season prices, the decision was often made to have them at local hotels in cities where the cost was twice that of off season resorts. To be fair however, IRS management was placed in a no win situation.

Organizations as large as IRS have the need to bring all managers together from time to time. However, if they went to a resort anytime of the year and the press heard about it, the media vehicles would highlight IRS' abuse of taxpayers' money without explaining the low cost.

During my time as an Assistant Chief, the district held an off site meeting for all managers at Lake Arrowhead, California. Lake Arrowhead is located in the mountains and can be a very stressful drive to get there. A group of female managers in my division got together and decided to hire a limousine to take them to the off season resort as they were very nervous about trying to make the drive themselves. The powers to be above me quickly advised me to tell them they could not arrive at the resort in a limousine as it could create very negative publicity for the organization.

This decision was made even though the managers' expenses would have been the same if they drove their own personally owned automobiles. Finally, the district accepted the fact that some of the managers were apprehensive about driving the steep mountains and a bus was rented for those wanting to ride it. The bottom line was that the limousine was out.

During off season periods rooms are available in abundance in resort areas such as Palm Springs, California in very nice hotels for rates as low as $50.00 a night. However, IRS being IRS, during the clamp down, management off-site meetings were held at city hotels with rates almost twice as high.

All of this was done to avoid the wrath of Congress and the public. Heaven forbid that sound management decisions be made.

Congressional control and bickering over the budget left few funds to get the job done. In addition to the funds being less than what was needed, they were always being held in abeyance until the two major parties, democrat and republican, decided to agree sufficiently enough for the budget to be approved.

The approval of the budget was almost always given well after the beginning of the new fiscal year. It is virtually impossible for a big business to operate successfully under those circumstances and regardless of how anyone chooses to look at it, IRS is a big business.

The man who was the division chief during the "love in" period mentioned above eventually became a district director in a large district. He ruled that district with an iron fist and came close to destroying it. He was the district director who destroyed the career of a gay division chief discussed in the chapter on Extra Curricular Activities.

During his reign of terror he established many ridiculous rules including one that forbade married employees from working in the same branch, yet he had his girl friend transferred from out of state to work as his right hand person in his district. By the way he was married, a fact known by all of his employees. The girl friend worked directly under his supervision.

According to employees in the district, watching the director and his girl friend operate on a daily basis was like looking at a soap opera. They actually thought they were operating discreetly, however, employees from the secretarial ranks to the highest level of management in the district were well aware of this director's hypocritical farce. This director was encouraged to retire after almost wrecking the district. Details of his detrimental actions in the district are explained in the chapter on Extra Curricular Activities.

Collection Division employees have a very difficult job and Congress and circumstances are consistently making the job even more difficult. An example was seen during my training year when revenue officers were assigned Tax Delinquency Accounts (TDA's) for telephone taxes.

After a balance due tax return has been filed if full payment does not accompany the return, the tax delinquency is assessed by the IRS Service Center, notices are sent to the taxpayer asking for payment and advising of potential enforcement action if payment is not made. Continued failure to pay results in a TDA being issued to a revenue officer to collect the taxes.

TDA's were assigned to revenue officers for delinquent telephone taxes during the Vietnam Conflict. The telephone taxes were used to finance the Vietnam Conflict and many taxpayers who protested the war refused to voluntarily pay the tax. Therefore, it became a task for IRS revenue officers to collect the tax.

Most of the assessments were approximately $10.00 or so yet the taxpayers/Vietnam protesters ended up paying $30 or $40 more for each assessment as the taxpayers refusal to pay resulted in levy's being placed on their bank accounts or wages. The banks, always interested in making a buck, charged significant amounts to the taxpayers for having to process the levy. As a revenue officer I worked many of the telephone tax TDA's and had to collect all of the payments by serving levies to attach funds in the taxpayers' bank accounts. I was successful in closing most of my cases promptly and most by securing the delinquent returns and collecting full payment. This success enabled me to obtain a transfer to an office closer to my home after completing my training year.

A case I worked in the new office will always remain in my memory. I had a TDA on a barber shop for delinquent employment taxes. The taxpayer's case was coded "R" which meant he was a repeater of employment tax delinquencies. The "R" code made this taxpayer a prime candidate for "knock and lock" procedures.

However, the taxpayer was in luck because I made an independent decision to give him twenty four hours notice. I did this because I was required to have an assisting revenue officer in order to conduct the seizure and all of my co-workers were out of the office at the time I made the field visitation to the barber shop.

If I had been interested in adding numbers to the seizures I had conducted for the month I could have waited until someone came in the office to accompany me for seizure of the barber shop. My case inventory was very large, somewhere between 150 and 200 taxpayer cases, therefore, I was never desperate for seizure numbers. Many of my cases always met the district's requirement for immediate seizure.

In an effort to stay on top of my inventory, I made the field call to the barber shop and made a "demand for full pay". This was what revenue officers were expected to do according to top management, "Demand immediate full pay!", not ask for it - but demand it.

As I expected, the taxpayer said he didn't have the money and I gave him twenty four hours to pay in full or I was going to close his business the next day. He said he didn't have the money and that if he had to pay by the next day he would have to use money he had to feed his children. I had to be honest with him and I told him while I didn't make it a practice of talking about my personal life, it really came down to his children or mine because if I failed to close his business my job might be in jeopardy.

He followed me to my car and held the door so that I couldn't close it. He started to cry, actually sobbing, and begging for more time. I told him he had twenty four hours, until 10:00 a.m. the following day to bring the full payment to my office or I would be back at his business in the afternoon with a locksmith to change the lock. I finally persuaded him I was serious and he turned the door a loose. I received the full payment at the allotted time the following day.

Revenue officers, including me, who experience situations of this nature, convince themselves that the taxpayer can pay at the time of the demand and are just procrastinating to get additional time. This kind of thinking makes the job easier to do and helps to justify doing something basically distasteful.

In my example of the owner of the barber shop, the taxpayer did come up with the money. Where he got it was not my concern. I was able to close my case full paid. A definite plus for me.

Although I always attempted to remain positive and unafraid while in the field, on a few occasions I experienced frightful situations that raised my level of fear considerably. The most frightening one of all occurred while making a field visitation to a residence in Torrance, California. I knocked on the door of the front house located at the address of my assignment. A woman answered and when I asked for the taxpayer she told me he lived in the back house. I thanked her and started to walk away when she said, "Dear, you should be very careful of his dog."

Now, nothing is more frightening to me than an unknown dog and particularly a big one. My heart immediately started pounding and apparently this woman saw the fear and panic on my face and she offered to walk me to the back house. I accepted her offer and she proceeded to escort me.

She left me at the front door and I knocked on the door. A somewhat unkempt bearded young man came to the door. His appearance alone was frightening enough, but all I could think of was the dog. The taxpayer invited me in. Immediately upon entering the house I saw this huge dog laying on the floor. Once inside I advised the taxpayer I was there about a delinquent tax account. To be honest I have to admit I said it as nice as I could, nicer than I had ever said to any other taxpayer.

The taxpayer told me he couldn't pay the taxes and I told him that being the case I needed to get some financial information from him. We proceeded to go over the financial statement and just before we finished the phone rang. When the phone rang the taxpayer got up from the couch where we were sitting and went to the phone. The dog stood up and started to bark as loud as he could. The taxpayer said, "Be quiet WOLF." WOLF didn't pay him any attention and I felt as though I was going to have a heart attack.

Here I was with a taxpayer who not only couldn't pay, but he was somewhat frightening in his appearance, and his disobedient dog WOLF was barking loudly and blocking the front door. Finally, the taxpayer got off the phone and I said as nonchalantly as possible, "Well, I have as much information as I need so I will go back to the office and I will contact you later after I have a chance to review the file." He said, "Fine, what do you think is going to happen?"

Since I pride myself on being nobody's fool I have to admit I half lied. I said, "We have a procedure that allows us to write off certain taxes if the taxpayer can't pay and it appears you may fit into this category." I already knew from the information he had given me that he could pay the taxes, but since I am not crazy there wasn't any way I was going to tell WOLF's master he had to pay anything. I eased on out of the door after he had pulled, and I do mean pulled WOLF away from the door. All of my future contacts with that taxpayer were done by phone and mail. I did ultimately receive a full payment, but only after I had levied on his wages.

Another somewhat frightening situation came about when I was accompanied by a senior revenue officer on a field visitation to demand payment, again for delinquent employment taxes. I went to a business office in Torrance, California and while I can almost see the people involved and the inside of the office I don't remember the nature of the business.

At any rate, the taxpayer was not there, but his secretary was there and her boy friend was visiting her. I had previously given the taxpayer his notice and the first official demand for payment and he was supposed to have the money the day of my visitation. I had told him I would be in the area and would pick it up. Evidently the taxpayer was trying to avoid me and the inevitability of the seizure by being away from the office that day.

I told the secretary I was going to close the office and her boy friend jumped in and said "No, you're not" directing his words to the male revenue officer with me. I advised the boy friend, "This is my case and you should address your comments to me. However, you are treading dangerous waters by getting involved in a tax matter that isn't any of your business." I also advised him, "You will have to vacate the premises as a lock smith is on his way."

The boy friend continued to direct his hostile remarks to my co-worker telling him, "I'd like to meet you in a dark alley some night". We were finally able to get the secretary and her boy friend to leave the office without incident and I seized the business and all available assets, had the lock changed and locked the door.

I believe the secretary's boyfriend continued to divert his tirade towards my co-worker because he would have been uncomfortable being verbally abusive to a female. Remember, this was back in the days when women were just being provided opportunities for law enforcement type jobs and the revenue officer job is definitely a law enforcement position.

In addition, the job of a revenue officer is a thankless one. While someone has to collect delinquent taxes, everyone outside of the job can find fault with those who do it. Most people don't even realize that in the case of delinquent employment taxes IRS is dealing with what is known as trust fund taxes. Trust fund taxes are those funds withheld from wages by employers and are supposed to be paid over to the Social Security Administration.

Many taxpayers are unaware that money withheld from their wages never reached the appropriate destination of Social Security Administration until years later when they are applying for Social Security benefits. Many taxpayers are unaware of this important issue because they do not understand how the system works. I sincerely believe some negative attitudes towards IRS employees might be altered if the average citizen knew and understood the various impacts IRS actions have on their lives.

The revenue officer who is criticized for seizing and closing a taxpayers' business is trying to collect employment tax funds that should have gone to the Social Security Administration for all employees working for that taxpayer. My first hand knowledge of IRS actions has allowed me enough information to wonder about the appropriateness of IRS employees' actions on some occasions; however, before citizens start to judge and criticize IRS actions they need to be sure they are aware of everything that has happened. Many times the criticism is deserved, but many times it is not.

Taxpayers need to know that during the times when IRS criticism is deserved, the taxpayer has the right to discuss the problem situation with the employee's manager. The taxpayer has the right to take the problem all the way up the line if necessary, discussing it with the highest level manager in the district, which is usually the District Director.

Failure to resolve an issue in the district can lead to taxpayers making complaints to their political representatives and/or to the taxpayer advocates working in IRS. While the advocates work for IRS they are not assigned to the district, therefore, they have more appropriate objectivity when looking at a complaint.

Even though revenue officers have to operate at a very high level of stress and potential danger most of them attempt to operate with care and concern for the rights of the taxpayers; however, for the most part it is not appreciated by the taxpayers and understandably so. Anytime a taxpayer has a problem understanding what is going on when a revenue officer contacts them they should first attempt to discuss it with the revenue officer and when all else fails the problem should definitely be elevated upwards through the management chain.

As a division chief I welcomed comments from taxpayers regarding the actions of my employees. I welcomed the comments for several reasons including my wanting to know any problems in the division so that I could correct them. In addition, it was always better for me to know about the problems before my boss heard about them. I sincerely worked hard to improve the division and I was open to constructive comments from anyone even if they had to come in the form of complaints.

There were many taxpayers who were kind and courteous to me even while I was in the process of taking enforcement action against them. There were also many who were nasty and threatening.

I can remember seizing and closing down a taxpayer's business and having the taxpayer thank me when I handed them the seizure document. Obviously the taxpayer did not want me to close the business, but there were times when the taxpayer was in clearly over his/her head.

Many times it was obvious the taxpayers did not know how to get out of the hole they were in. A few taxpayers told me that even though my seizure actions were devastating to them at the same time there was somewhat of a sense of relief. The decision of whether or not they should remain in business had been taken out of their hands.

I always tried to be professional and courteous to all taxpayers regardless of how they responded to me. I made sure not to appear nonchalant about what was going on and to be sure not to display any type of humor when dealing with the serious matter of delinquent taxes.

I always tried to keep in mind that most people owed taxes as a result of bad personal decisions, including mistake, misfortune, ignorance, and poor business management to name a few. While there are taxpayers who just simply refuse to pay voluntarily, most of those who end up owing taxes do so through no deliberate fault of their own.

There is a significant percentage of taxpayers who are trying to beat the system any way they can. However, this does not justify harassment or harsh treatment on the part of the revenue officer, but years and years of dealing with similar situations can make employees become callused and hardened. It then becomes imperative that management provide appropriate oversight and involvement in cases to assure positive customer service is provided.

Management also needs to establish plans to provide relief for employees who are experiencing burnout. The employee who is hired as a revenue officer and works until full retirement (thirty years) needs to be provided an occasional opportunity for relief from the case inventories that require constant lien, levy, seizure, and sale actions. Occasional relief will provide substantial benefits to the revenue officer as well as the taxpayers they are required to deal with. They should be able to return to the case inventory with a refreshed, more positive attitude.

After a successful period as a revenue officer and numerous acting assignments in management I applied and was accepted in the IRS Collection Division Management Program. My first two management assignments were very busy and somewhat stressful dealing with the sheer number of cases I was responsible for. Both of the assignments were in what was known as the Office Group.

In Office Group I was responsible for employees whose primary duty was to attempt to contact taxpayers by phone and/or paper notice. In addition, they were responsible for a walk-in counter available for taxpayers to respond to notices received from the Office Group employees or from an IRS service center anywhere in the nation.

My assignment to Office Group was during a time when the philosophy of the customer always being right was foreign to IRS employees. During this time the IRS employee was always right and the taxpayers were always wrong and simply owed the money as far as IRS was concerned. IRS did not have a taxpayers' advocate during that time and the Taxpayers Bill of Rights was unheard of. It was cut and dry and much easier for the employee, but far worse for the taxpayers.

The Office Group employees phoned or wrote and made demands for payment by a deadline date. The taxpayer paid up in full or immediate levy action (attachment of bank accounts, wages, etc.) was conducted. If full payment was not received the case was sent to the field for knock and lock procedures on businesses, and immediate seizure of homes, automobiles, liquor licenses, rental income, you name it, for income taxes.

In spite of what the public may think today, enforcement action twenty years ago was much swifter and harsher. Increased media access makes it seem as though IRS has been worse in the recent past. Not so! I know from personal experience that cases requiring enforcement action are not being worked timely nor effectively in accordance with IRS manual procedures. Nor are cases being worked timely nor effectively in accordance with IRS executive management expectations.

Those "good old days" were the days when revenue officers seized and locked up businesses on Friday morning and remained in the field until time to go home. This was a punishment for the taxpayer. Even if the taxpayer came up with the money to pay the tax liability later in the day he would not be able to contact the revenue officer until Monday, therefore, he could not get his business open until Monday at the earliest.

After two years in Office Group on two assignments, one as a first line manager responsible for a section and the other as the Chief, Office Group responsible for the entire office (three sections), I was promoted out to a field group manager position. It was now my time to go out and oversee those revenue officers in their lien, levy, seizure and sale actions.

This was my welcome to the real world of Collection Division management. Although I had worked in the field as a revenue officer, being a part of field management was somewhat of a cold dash of water in my face. I had been successful in my former managerial positions; however, I was totally unprepared for the cut throat tactics of the employees union representatives and for the hard line, "kick ass" philosophy of the branch chief, my immediate manager.

My first assignment was in an office that was known to be extremely difficult, if not impossible, to manage, as the union and management were at war. The union officials and stewards made life difficult if management took any kind of action towards attempting to get employees to do the job they were hired for, including treating taxpayers with a modicum of dignity.

In subsequent years after I left that office some of those union representatives who utilized the cut throat tactics were found to be doing illegal acts strictly prohibited by the IRS Code of Conduct. Some were fired after working many years as a revenue officer. One in particular was found guilty of travel voucher fraud. He had charged the government for travel expenses for travel that was totally unrelated to the job. While some were ultimately fired they made life on the job hell for management while they were there.

My first encounter in a one on one meeting with a union steward was horrifying. The meeting had been scheduled at my request to discuss a grievance filed by the union on behalf of an employee. In this office employees seldom had the chance to take the initiative to file a grievance. The union filed grievances as a form of harassment against management whether the employee wanted them to or not.

Many employees were too intimidated to stand up to the union as they were afraid they might need the union's representation in the future. Several employees told me they did not want to be a member of the union, but they had been told by union representatives if they were not dues paying members they would have to stand alone should they ever have problems with management. The union representatives were consistently spewing hateful statements about management and employees didn't know whether to believe them or not. To be on the safe side the employees joined the union and followed its direction.

The day of the scheduled meeting, the steward and I met behind closed doors in a conference room in the office. As soon as the meeting started the steward stood up and raised his voice to a shouting level. This very large man then proceeded to pound on the table as he walked around it, ranting and raving. He told me, "The District Director would be very unhappy with you if he knew how you are treating your employees".

The issue at hand was a review I had completed on an employee, I had provided constructive criticism to the employee for not following IRS manual guidelines. The steward could not find anything specifically wrong with my review other than he was determined to prevent employees from receiving any negative comments whether they deserved them or not.

I sat at the table in amazement listening to the steward's ranting and raving. After a couple of minutes I stood up and told him, "You are out of line and I am not going to allow you to speak to me in that manner". He was shocked that I stood up to him. Here you had a large man well over six feet tall and I am only five feet, one inch tall. His size alone could be intimidating.

Although I am small in stature, I refused to be intimidated by anyone. My size and the fact that I am female, was very young, and looking even younger than I was, had led the steward to believe he could easily intimidate me. This particular steward played a significant role in numerous problems IRS experienced in trying to get employees to earn their pay on a daily basis. More detail regarding this area has been discussed in Chapter Nine on Labor - Management Climate.

The animosity demonstrated towards me by the union after I failed to cave in to their demands was unbelievable. The best example I can give regarding the animosity relates to the Agreement between IRS and management in which management was required to notify the union in advance of any meetings held with employees.

Union stewards always attended those meetings and were free to challenge management in a friendly or non-friendly way. As a result of my relationship going sour with the union I was targeted and all of my meetings became almost unbearable.

Every time I made a statement advising the employees of something they needed to do or of some new procedure, I was asked by the union where I had gotten the authority for that advisement. It became so bad on one occasion I told the union steward he had to leave a group meeting I was conducting as he had become totally disruptive. All hell broke out as a result of that. Top level management had taken the position that no matter what, the steward had the right to be in the meetings.

I admit I over reacted in telling the union steward he had to leave; however, even though I had complained to my branch chief of how near impossible it had become to be able to have group meetings with my employees, management had not found it appropriate nor necessary to intervene and help me even though I was very inexperienced. After all this was my first field management position.

As it turns out the way I was being treated was not the way white male managers were being treated even when they had serious disagreements with the union. One of my employees who was a member of the union did not agree with how I was being treated and he told the union that and he also told me. He said the chapter president told him women should not be managers and especially black women. This employee happened to be a white male also, but he always tried to do the right thing and he supported me whenever he thought I was doing the right thing. He was one of a very definite minority of group members who had the nerve to go against the union.

To make matters worse my branch chief while I was in this office actually hated both the union chapter president and the steward assigned to Collection

Division. He hated them to the extent he told me that my number one priority was to fire the chapter president as he was assigned to my group.

The branch chief did not care whether the union official deserved to be fired or not. He wanted him fired regardless. He told me no matter how successful I might be in other things in the group as far as he was concerned I would not be successful if I did not fire the chapter president.

There was bad blood between the union and this branch chief because the branch chief had been responsible for removing the chapter president from a former management position he had performed in. The union had gone to the director to complain about the branch chief and even though the director had not reversed the branch chief's decision the branch chief was furious about the complaint. This branch chief was known to hold grudges and to never forget when someone had crossed him. He had made his effort to get rid of union personnel his number one priority above everything else.

Even though the chapter president was very, very difficult to manage he did just enough work as to not justify being fired. Needless to say, he was still in the group when I left. The management position I was in was upgraded and I was not qualified for the grade so I was reassigned out of the branch. Otherwise I would have had tremendous problems getting promoted as the branch chief was very serious about his firing priority. He visited me in my office every week and he always made it a point to ask for an update on my firing plan.

The manager who was promoted to the position I had held in that office prior to the upgrade, told me she had received the same marching orders that I had received regarding the firing of the chapter president. She failed also. Some years later the chapter president was fired for an illegal matter rather than for failure to work his cases as the branch chief had wanted.

Ironically, a few years after I had left that office, the chapter president visited me in my office to ask me to help him in a case where he was representing an employee. He wanted me to provide some positive statements regarding this employee. The employee was very near retiring and had been caught cheating on his travel reimbursement report. This was an employee who had worked hard along with the chapter president to make my life miserable. This was also an employee I had thought all along might be misusing his time in the field.

I found it very humorous as well as ridiculous that this chapter president would come to me for help. I actually laughed in his face while I told him, "I can't believe you are stupid enough to think I would help you. You never demonstrated one ounce of respect for me in my managerial position and now you are seeking my help? Get out of my office before I call security and have you thrown out". He looked at me as though I had lost my mind and he quickly gathered his belongings and left. When I think back on it I sometimes think I might have lost it for a second or so because that was totally out of character for me to act like that.

Numerous, frivolous grievances were filed against me after the conference room episode although the steward subsequently advised me, "My behavior during our conference wasn't personal, it's just the mode in which I choose to perform while performing my union duties." Although I did survive those days and moved on to other group manager assignments until this day I remain amazed at the tremendous waste of human and monetary resources as a result of the unbelievable actions that were allowed to go on in that office.

Finally, I was promoted to a GS-13 Group Manager position and was reassigned to another office in the district. In that office I met a union steward who was the epitome of corrupted human beings. He made the other union crew almost seem like angels. He has been discussed in detail in the Chapter on Labor -Management Climate.

Before I move on to other examples it is important for the reader to know that two of the worse union stewards in the first office were former managers who had been removed involuntarily from their managerial positions. One of them had been a terror to both employees and taxpayers in his managerial position, yet he filed grievances against management for issues far less serious than things he had done as a manager.

While he was in the management position he required employees to look in taxpayers' refrigerators while on field visitations to their residences. The viewing of the inside of the refrigerator was supposedly to provide the revenue officer an opportunity to counsel the taxpayer if too much food was found. The employee was supposed to tell the taxpayer he should be using some of the food money to pay taxes.

The directives of this then manager were put in writing and disseminated to employees in the group. When the branch chief discovered this memo he rescinded it and tried to pull back all copies. Revenue officers are notorious for keeping copies of documents management tries to rescind. These documents are held for years and shared down the ranks with new employees. It is an effort to embarrass management.

I know this because before I became a manager I received memos in which management requested the return of documents that reflected negatively on the Service. As employees we always complied with management's request after we had made our own personal copy for the file we maintained at home.

In addition to the revenue officer looking in the taxpayers' refrigerator, the manager went over financial statements provided by taxpayers with a fine tooth comb. When taxpayers are asked to full pay their delinquent tax accounts if they state they are not able to pay in full, employees are required to have the taxpayer complete what is called a Collection Information Statement.

This statement lists the taxpayer's assets and liabilities. The employee then makes a determination based on the statement as to whether the taxpayer can pay or not. If not a full pay, then monthly payments may be considered. Collection Information Statements showing the taxpayer's inability to pay provides the opportunity for the revenue officer to determine the taxpayer's case a hardship one. Once the case has been coded hardship, collection of the liability will be placed in abeyance until a later date should the taxpayer's financial situation improve.

The chapter president/former manager made demands to taxpayers to cut down on their utility bills, food, clothing, or any area he chose. He then told them if they cut down in those areas they should be able to pay their taxes. This was clearly an infringement of the taxpayer's rights and was not in accordance with IRS policy.

Well, when the branch chief heard of this stupid act he immediately took this man out of management. Thus, the beginning of the union - management war in that office.

After working on my second group manager assignment for a year I had the opportunity to be reassigned to an office closer to home. I was once again working with the branch chief I had worked with in the first office. He was a man from the old school and his philosophy, to be used daily, was "kick them in the ass and they will do what you want them to do". This applied to employees, managers, and taxpayers alike.

On this new assignment I was assigned to a brand new group that had to be completely set up which is very time consuming. My newly selected secretary did not have any secretarial skills nor experience in the position. She simply applied for the job and was selected because she met the job grade requirements for promotion to the next level. She was selected prior to my arrival, therefore, I had no say in the selection. She was a nice person, but again, not qualified in experience for the job.

The first month in the group she had made an error while inputting case closures into the computer system. This resulted in very few closures being shown on the computer generated report for the group's first month. When I discovered the error I worked with her to correct it, but it was too late for that month.

The next month, near the end of the month when month end reports were due, I found that the group had done a fantastic job considering it was a new group. The employees had closed a significant number of cases with lots of payments having been received. This was the name of the game, money and case closures. I was so pleased I had a special cake made for the group to thank them for their efforts. Morale was high and we were in a celebrating mood.

Before we were able to complete the month end reports and send then to the branch chief, his highness himself, the branch chief made a visitation to the group. Branch chiefs' offices were not in the outlying offices, they were all headquartered in the downtown Federal Building. The branch chief told me he wanted to speak to me in the conference room in private.

We went into the conference room where he told me, "I am disappointed in the closure results from the month before and what you need to do is to kick ass and get the cases closed". I was very upset, however, not too intimidated, not even by the branch chief, so I told him, "I don't believe in treating employees that way and kicking ass to increase productivity is not my style." I further told him, "Had you asked to see the reports for the current month this visitation would not have been necessary." For once he was speechless and I wasn't sure whether it was because of the news of the increased productivity of the group or my stand up and be counted attitude.

Now don't get me wrong, I wasn't totally fearless; however, I had decided a long time before that incident that I would always do what I thought was the right thing no matter how afraid I might be. I pretty much lived by that decision most of my life including today. In addition, I knew he couldn't fire me immediately with all of the government seniority I had under my belt. He could, however, have made my life miserable and taking it one step at a time he could have taken actions to terminate me if production had not improved. I was one step ahead of him because I already knew the better than required improvements had already started.

That branch chief never had that attitude with me again; however, he rode other managers for many years with an attitude that loudly said he expected employees to close cases through full pay regardless of how many seizures and sales it took. He once lambasted a manager at an all managers meeting in front of the entire division as a result of low productivity. Is it any wonder revenue officers and managers sometimes operate the way it is alleged they do?

The message from the top all through the years has been productivity, productivity. In the later years as productivity became an ugly word, executive level management stopped using it but believe me the expectations never changed. If a manger did not get with the program and meet productivity goals he/she would be embarrassed by the reports generated nationwide and by visitations and reviews conducted by visiting regional and national analyst.

During my days as a manager on this my last group manager assignment, the message from the division chief's office was the same as the one from the "kick them in the ass" branch chief. At one point when TDI closures were down, the assistant chief of the Collection Division advised at an all managers meeting that instead of managers being concerned about end of year merit pay bonuses, we should be worried about our basic pay because if we didn't get the TDI's closed we'd be out of a job.

IRS continues to state emphatically that the organization has never rated employees based on statistics yet during this time the division was definitely counting closures. The assistant chief was subsequently fired in another district as a result of travel expense fraud.

I personally never had a problem with believing that the Collection Division should be productive. The major problem was that while management preached productivity to employees that goal was being denied when confronted by the media, public, or congress.

While enforcement numbers were never to be used in year end appraisals for employees or managers, it was virtually impossible to be given positive recognition or an award if the numbers were low. Everyone knew this was the unwritten rule although everyone denied it. You can rest assured that any employee receiving a work performance award only received it if they had closed a lot of cases, received a lot of money, and had conducted numerous seizures.

After working in my final group manager position for two years I was given the opportunity to act in my branch chief's position during his absence on extended sick leave. There was a written rule regarding higher graded pay for employees temporarily assigned to higher graded duties. The position I was temporarily assigned to was a higher grade than my permanent assignment; however, I wasn't given the higher pay.

At the time I wasn't aware that it was a personnel requirement under certain circumstances to pay employees the additional money. I learned early on in IRS that unless you knew all of the rules you were sure to be shortchanged many times while working there. It was rare for anyone to advise you of your rights, particularly if you were in management. Since I didn't really know all of the rules I just worked hard and concentrated on doing the best job possible.

I was grateful to have the opportunity to show what I could do in a higher level job as I was very ambitious and eager for promotion. My branch chief returned within a few months but I was allowed to continue acting because the Los Angeles District had started the process of splitting the district into two districts with a plan for part of the original district ultimately becoming part of a third district.

Two districts, Los Angeles and San Jose became three with the establishing of the Laguna Niguel District in southern California. With Los Angeles District in the middle of the three, Orange County, San Diego County, Riverside County and a small portion of southern Los Angeles County made up the new Laguna Niguel District.

At the same time the District was splitting Los Angeles hired over 300 revenue officers, some of whom were to be assigned to Laguna Niguel and the balance to make up an additional branch for Los Angeles. I was selected for the new branch chief position with responsibility for groups in Carson, Lawndale, and Bakersfield, California.

This permanent assignment gave me a front row seat in the division office where all branch chiefs were housed. I was able to see first hand just where the pressures were coming from and also to feel there direct hit. At that time inventories were huge with revenue officers having anywhere from 100 to 200 cases each. The marching orders were to close cases, collect money.

Pressure was on the division chief and her assistant to reduce the inventory and increase collections. Both the chief and her assistant were Hispanics and were in positions relatively new for minorities and particularly female minorities. Immediately upon being selected as division chief, the female Hispanic became the butt of many cruel jokes and the target for the union. The union even went so far as to give her a disrespectful nickname and to publish it in their newsletter on a regular basis along with scathing criticism of how the division was being managed. Los Angeles District was completely out of control at that time.

The assistant chief had been selected for his position through a special acceleration program which caused major concern on the part of several white male branch chiefs who had been waiting in line for the assistant chief position. At least two of them had virtually claimed the position and were sure they would be selected.

One of the white male branch chiefs who thought the job was his was my former "kick them in the ass" branch chief. He did not take losing easily for two reasons. One reason was that he was at an age where he knew he had probably had his last opportunity for promotion and secondly and more importantly he had difficulty dealing with the fact that someone he felt was inferior to him had beaten him out in the competition for the job he desperately wanted.

He set out on what was an apparent plan to sabotage division level management. Although he had known the division chief for a long time, he made her his target also. He apparently felt she betrayed him by not selecting him to be her assistant.

Knowing what I know today, I feel fairly sure the division chief was not given the authority to make the selection. She had to agree with the selection and make the best of it because her boss, the director, probably told her that was the way it was going to be. Many times that's the way things are done in IRS, particularly when the person supposed to be in charge did not have much clout.

While I was working for the "kick them in the ass" branch chief, our branch was given the responsibility for planning and coordinating one of the quarterly all managers meetings. This was a two to three days meeting and responsibility was rotated each quarter. Rumors were running rampant that the division chief and her assistant had failed in the job and were on their way out.

Looking back now I'm not sure if this was true or whether this was one of those wild rumors that seem some how to become true once they start to circulate.

Even though no official announcement had been made regarding the fate of the chief and her assistant, my branch chief had a banner prepared for the all managers meeting showing the division chief running after an airplane that had already taken off and he had the union's nickname for her printed in big bold letters. He claimed he had it prepared as a joke but even with my limited experience I recognized it as a cold cruel shot at the chief.

This was a form of introduction for me as to how the big boys played the game. Sure enough the rumors became truth and both the chief and her assistant were eventually reassigned to other positions. The chief who was an attorney left Collection Division and went to an IRS legal counsel position. The assistant chief was eventually taken out of his job, downgraded, and transferred to a district out of state. It has been alleged that he was later fired as a result of travel expense fraud. At any rate, he left the organization before he was eligible to retire.

It was a known fact that they both lost their positions because the division did not collect enough money nor close enough cases. This was a perfect way to get the message across to all managers that the name of the game was collecting money and closing cases. Everyone knew how to achieve the objective. All it took was seizures, levies, liens, and more seizures. Remember, these were delinquent accounts for taxpayers who had failed to pay voluntarily.

The two branch chiefs who were disgruntled about not being selected for the assistant chief position virtually stopped supporting the division and one of them was up front and vocal about it by saying that since the chief and assistant had been selected to manage the division he was going to see how successful they could be without his help. Well, they were not successful although I'm not sure how much of their failure can be attributed to the sabotage tactics of the unhappy branch chief.

When I was selected for the branch chief position there were two grade levels for the position. New branch chiefs were selected into the GS-13 position. Upon completion of that grade the person then qualified for the GS-14 position. As I was already a GS-13 manager, I was laterally assigned to the position at the GS-13 level which was fine for me at the time. I just wanted to get my foot in the door. Also I was still somewhat naïve. Although I was the only GS-13 level branch chief I thought it was because I was new to the position.

Sometime shortly after I had been in the position at the GS-13 level one of the branch chiefs in the GS-14 level was reassigned to the newly created Laguna Niguel District. Her former position of GS-14 remained in the Los Angeles District.

A white male manager from a district in another region had been assigned to the Los Angeles District on a temporary basis to work on a special project. While there he was approached and asked if he would like to work in the GS-14 position. No one asked me if I was interested.

Since I was a permanent member of the Los Angeles District the logical and right thing to do would have been to ask me to work in the GS-14 position and to assign the outsider to my position. This person wasn't even a permanent branch chief. He was a group manager, the position below the branch chief level and here I was a permanent branch chief.

People in large organizations such as IRS love to gossip and so I heard about the opportunity that had not been offered to me through the gossip rumor mill from "friends". I became very upset over this situation and I went to the person who was acting for my chief while he was away from the office for an extended period of time.

I asked this acting chief if the gossip was true and he admitted it was. I then asked him why I had not been offered the opportunity for the GS-14 assignment. He actually had the gall to say, "Well, under the circumstances I think the visiting manager is the best person for the assignment. You need to stay on your current permanent assignment where you will be able to have more impact". These comments were particularly upsetting to me because this manager was unknown in the Los Angeles district until he arrived there to work on the special project.

I decided I wouldn't get anywhere with the acting chief and so I told him I was going to talk to the director about it. He didn't have a problem with that because he wasn't an employee of the Los Angeles District. He had actually been a division chief in another district and had been taken out of his position for something wrong he had done. He had been reassigned to the Los Angeles District to ride out his last year until he qualified for retirement. Los Angeles District wasn't too anxious to take him but did so as a favor to the other district. He was used to fill in any vacant management assignments and he usually just baby sat. He never tried to actually do what was required of the position.

An appointment was made for me to see the director. When I went for the appointment the director asked me how things were going in Collection Division. I told him they were not going too well for me right then. I explained the situation to him and he asked me why I wasn't a GS-14 branch chief. I told him I didn't know why not, I only knew it wasn't right that the other person had been given the opportunity over me for the acting assignment in the higher position.

The Director was known to be somewhat eccentric, but was thought of as a straight shooter, and was liked by many employees, especially females. He looked out for females, or so it was thought, and he righted numerous perceived wrongs.

After I had explained my problem to the Director he got on the phone and called the personnel office and asked, "Is Yvonne Wiley eligible for the GS-14 Branch Chief position?" He was told I was eligible and he told the personnel chief to process the paper work promoting me to the higher grade on a permanent basis. Thus, I became a GS-14 branch chief because I stood up for myself in the face of blatant discrimination. I saw this as a good thing although as I look back on it something should have been done with the acting chief as a result of his having made such a discriminatory decision.

Having completed five years as a branch chief, I decided I wanted to move up again and so I competed and was selected for the top level management program. Competition for the top level management program consisted of two oral interviews.

The first one was conducted in the applicant's home district. Usually the division chief and/or the assistant chief, along with the district director or his representative sat on the interview panel. I passed that interview with flying colors and was then recommended for interview at the regional level. The interview panel at the regional level consisted of the assistant regional commissioner and his executive assistant. I also passed this interview and was then officially placed in the top level management program.

Applicants successful at the regional level interview were placed on a list in accordance with the districts they listed as their areas of availability. When a vacancy occurred in the district of the applicant's availability, the applicant was contacted, interviewed again, and a selection was made to fill the position, assistant chief or chief, which ever the case might be. Once you were on the list having been screened in for top level management, you were then also available for temporary assignments in those districts for which you had shown availability.

A white male branch chief and I were the only ones in the Los Angeles Collection Division top level management program at the time I was selected. I had told the new division chief I was interested in temporary assignments as assistant chief should anything become available. Shortly after announcing my interest I heard through the unofficial rumor mill, the grapevine, that the other branch chief had been given a ninety day assignment in Laguna Niguel, California as acting assistant chief.

This was a man who had been counseled by the Los Angeles assistant division chief for "fixing" his month end reports. He was accused of having changed the number of closures on his reports to ensure he met the goal. Yes, we had numeric goals. This branch chief had been rated as a distinguished performer that year even though there was a common feeling that he had "fixed" his numbers on his branch reports.

Can you believe that an organization as large and powerful as IRS had no method of being able to verify numbers shown on reports prepared by managers? The reports were prepared manually with closures, payments, etc. having been counted manually. If was very easy for anyone to doctor their reports if they chose to do so and it was alleged internally that many chose to do so.

On several occasions during so called coffee klatches in my office, another branch chief and I had spoken to the assistant chief about the branch chief being rated as a distinguished performer even though everyone knew he had changed numbers on his reports. The assistant chief would only laugh and joke about it and say that the branch chief was "alright" and that we were just jealous. He never thought it was even important enough to deny that the man had cheated.

I was the only female branch chief and the men, all white except the black assistant chief all banded together and looked out for each other. On a day to day basis I was treated well and with respect; however, I had to be very vocal and to demand equal opportunity for special assignments.

It is important that the reader understand that many special opportunities were provided as a result of knowing the right person. I have to admit I was the recipient of special assignments for that same reason on several occasions during my career, although most of the time I had to stand up and say, "Hey, look at me, I'm here and I deserve some of the assignments even though I am female and minority." Believe it or not, there were times when I actually said those very words. I found out early on in my career that I had to be my own public relations spokesperson as no one else was stepping up to the bat for me unless I expressed my concern vocally.

After finding out about the ninety day assignment for the other branch chief, I went to the division chief and asked him why I had not been considered for the assignment as I had been selected for the top level management program before the other branch chief had. The chief apologized, gave me the old song and dance routine often used when dealing with women, "I didn't think you would be interested in making the commute down there." For whatever reason he never wondered whether the male branch chief would have a problem making the commute.

He then arranged for the assignment to be split, forty-five days for each of us. In later years looking back on this situation, I realized again how important it was that I spoke up for myself. If I had not done so in this situation it is highly probable that I would have missed the opportunity of becoming the division chief in Laguna Niguel.

Those of us working in Collection Division in the Los Angeles District were very familiar with the employees in Laguna Niguel as we were all part of the Los Angeles District prior to the split. Prior to going to Laguna Niguel for my forty-five day assignment, I was aware of how the district and the division were performing. The division chief had been demoted out of her job about a year or so before my temporary assignment there. I knew this could be a difficult assignment.

According to information provided to me by the Laguna Niguel branch chiefs, they were not allowed to close cases in "uncollectible" status even when the criteria for that status was met. This made the division look bad by creating a very large inventory of overage cases. It also caused continued harassment of taxpayers for payments they could not make.

The yellow book that provided the statistical reports for the entire region was issued once a month and was anxiously received in each district office. In Los Angeles, during my time as a branch chief, each month on the morning the reports were received, several of the branch chiefs would bring their coffee to my office and we would go over the reports.

First of all we looked to see what Los Angeles had accomplished during the month. Next we looked for Laguna. We looked upon Laguna as though it was our first cousin since we had all worked together for years prior to the split. Also, we knew from the extremely negative reports showing Laguna as having the highest overage in the region that someone's head was going to roll.

While I don't know for sure the reasons why the Division Chief was demoted, I do know the programs aspect of Laguna Niguel were in very poor condition according to the monthly reports.

The IRS manual provides procedures for cases meeting certain criteria to be placed in an uncollectible status. The cases are coded so that when a taxpayer files subsequent returns showing specific increases in income the case will be regenerated back to the field into the hands of a revenue officer. The uncollectible status accomplishes several things for IRS and taxpayers. It allows IRS personnel to work on productive cases where money may be collected while setting aside those non-productive cases for a temporary period of time.

The IRS manual requires certain actions before reporting cases uncollectible. This helps to ensure cases are not closed just to increase closure numbers. Once the manual requirements have been met the cases can be temporarily placed in suspense status. A high percentage of those cases never yield any money yet they remain in active inventory being worked with futility, every rock being looked under for the taxpayers assets.

When inventories are high the most efficient and productive thing to do is to close non-productive cases as uncollectible with a sufficient code that will provide an alert to regenerate the case when there is a possibility for collection.

Laguna Niguel's inventories were extremely high, but the branch chiefs were not allowed to close the cases until every possibility for collection had been checked twice. It was my understanding that these orders came from someone other than the Division Chief.

The branch chiefs had to review the entire inventory during each quarter. This was a tremendous job as each revenue officer had 100 or more cases in their individual inventory. There were an average of seven groups in each branch with an average of 12 revenue officers in each group. This resulted in a tremendous inventory of overage cases and huge overage inventories usually cause low collections. It was easy to see that some change was going to be made in the division. Unfortunately, the chief was that change.

My forty-five day assignment in Laguna Niguel went well and considering the length of time I was there, was very productive. The new division chief was away on an assignment with his new assistant chief acting in his position. I then acted in the assistant's position. The assistant chief told me he had been disappointed with the other branch chief's performance during his forty-five day assignment. He had to counsel that branch chief on a couple of occasions and the branch chief had ended the forty-five days without completing everything that had been assigned to him. I received a very positive write up regarding my assignment.

Interestingly enough, the other branch chief was promoted to a position in another district a year or so after his assignment in Laguna Niguel. After about six months to a year in the new position he reportedly made some negative remarks about his boss's obesity in a huge public forum. His stock in that district immediately went down and the last I heard of him he was once again a branch chief.

About six months after my assignment in Laguna Niguel had ended, the assistant chief position became vacant. One day I ran into the former assistant chief who had since been promoted to the chief's position and he asked me if I was aware that the position was vacant. I told him I was not aware and he suggested I contact the personnel office as he wanted me to apply for the position.

When the vacancy was announced I applied, was interviewed, and selected. Had I not stood up for myself and been assertive in requesting the division chief to provide me the opportunity to share in the ninety day assignment in Laguna Niguel my chances for being selected for the permanent position would have been slim. The temporary assignment gave the assistant chief the opportunity to see me in action.

The world of Laguna Niguel was quite different from that of Los Angeles. As a result of the management style of the former director, who had ruled with an iron fist, few questions were asked by managers or employees. Managers were able to manage the groups which was a task virtually impossible in Los Angeles. Things changed drastically in Laguna after I had been there a few years. Some of the reasons for the changes have been spelled out in the chapter on Labor -Management Climate.

The new director in Laguna Niguel and the new Collection division chief believed in treating employees firm but fair. Management was in a delicate position trying to offset the damage that had been done by the former regime. This was fine for a few years but the union became more and more aggressive giving employees a feeling of protection whether or not they were doing the job they were hired to do. This created an unbearable situation for management and many employees. It also had a negative impact on the success of the district in many instances causing morale problems because many employees did not trust management.

I was in Laguna Niguel for eight years and by the time I retired the union and management were in an all out war that required intervention by a professional contractor from the outside. In the meantime Western Region was at the bottom of the barrel in the numbers considered critical factors, total dollars collected, dollars collected per staff year, overage percentages, and numbers of TDA's and TDI's closed.

The region conducted quarterly chief meetings that I started to attend after being in Laguna Niguel for a year. The division chief was on the move upward and was often away for extended periods on special assignment. In his absence I acted as chief. After I had been there for about a year and a half the chief was promoted out. I competed for his vacancy and was successful.

At one of the quarterly meetings in fiscal year 1995/1996 the assistant regional commissioner made no bones about it when he said, "This year is the year of the dollar!" In so many words he said you could be successful in every category and fail in dollars collected and your overall performance would be considered a failure.

At each of the quarterly meetings statistical reports were shared (See Exhibit 1). As mentioned before, the reports were generated in a "Collection Progress Report" with a yellow covering and was commonly referred to as the "yellow book". If your statistics for the quarter were low you knew you were in for public ridicule in an open setting at the next all chief's meeting.

While Laguna Niguel Collection Division had its share of ridicule, fortunately for me the division looked better than most other divisions nationwide during the last two years of my career.

The "yellow book" generated monthly by the region was anxiously awaited by everyone. It told you, and what seemed like the whole world, how your division was doing and whether you could relax for a day or so or whether you were going to be called to the director's office as a result of phone calls the director had received from the regional office.

Again, dollars must be collected, yet congress and national level management were saying the way to collect them is by voluntary payment or at least without creating any negative publicity. Levy, lien, and seizure actions always have the potential for negative publicity. The cases in revenue officers' inventories were there most of the time because taxpayers could not or would not pay. So much for voluntary payments. How can money be collected involuntarily and still keep everyone happy?

As the division chief in Laguna Niguel I periodically conducted meetings for all managers. In 1993 I conducted a meeting as I felt it was time to make changes to improve our statistics in dollars collected per staff year. Our total dollars collected were the highest in the nation; however, the dollars collected per staff year left much to be desired. The statistics for dollars collected per staff year were below our goal and I had determined we were not meeting the goal for three main reasons.

The first reason was that the formula for computing dollars collected per staff year in Collection Division was one of the most unbelievably asinine procedures required by regional and national management. To determine the results of dollars collected per staff year, every person working in Collection Division was counted in the formula whether they worked cases or not. It was not computed in that manner in Examination Division.

In Examination Division's formula for dollars assessed the only employees counted were the ones actually assessing the dollars. It is my understanding that in the past year Examination Division has been directed to use the same formula being used in Collection Division.

The second reason for the goal not being met was having too many revenue officers and managers doing too many jobs not directly related to collecting taxes. The meeting in 1993 was what I called getting back to basics meeting.

In this meeting with about forty-five group managers I addressed our third primary reason for not meeting our goal. I asked how many managers had employees in their groups who were not performing. All hands went up. I went around the room asking how many were in each group. We arrived at a general consensus that there were about three to four employees in each group who were not performing, not doing the job they were being paid to do. This meant the division had more than 100 employees being paid with taxpayers' dollars for jobs they were not doing.

We were also able to arrive at a general consensus that employees were not performing and were getting away with it because the managers felt they were wasting their time trying to make all employees productive. Managers generally felt the abuse they had to take from the union and lack of support from the director's office made anything they did a losing battle.

It was a well known fact that the union had direct access to the director's office bypassing the Collection Division chain of command. The director and his assistant dealt directly with the union's Chapter Presidents and they appeared to believe the union over management. Many times when management attempted to take action against an employee it was stopped as a direct order from the director's office. Now, this can be looked at from two viewpoints. Either the managers were correct in their assessment of the level of support they could expect from the director or the director was correct in undoing what the managers had done because he considered the mangers actions as inappropriate.

Okay, let's say the managers action may have been incorrect, so if this type of situation occurred over and over again wouldn't you think the appropriate management decision would have been to determine why? Did the managers need training? Should specific cases be discussed with the manager involved before agreeing with the union that the manager had "screwed up?" This was never done.

IRS management from first line to national level has been in desperate need of training for a long, long time. The organization does not seem to understand that just because a person may be able to collect taxes doesn't necessarily mean they can also perform effectively as a manager.

Most managers in IRS are selected from the professional working level. They are selected to manage if they show an interest and if they are performing their current job well. Many IRS managers do not have the education nor the training to manage effectively. They do work very hard at trying to do the job but they primarily learn through trial and error with no more than a couple of weeks training here and there throughout their entire careers. Is it any wonder there are so many management problems inside IRS?

Immediately after the above mentioned meeting in 1993, my assistant and I started establishing procedures and requirements that would allow us to know who was being productive and more importantly, who was not being productive. Our major objective became ensuring employees were earning the money they were being paid, that the organization and the taxpaying public received eight hours of work for eight hours of pay. Can you imagine having about one quarter of employees not working yet receiving a full salary and everyone from the director's office on down being afraid to take the union on about it?

Collection Division had seven revenue officer branches during this particular time and each branch had approximately seven groups with approximately twelve revenue officers in each group. This would total up to

500 plus revenue officers in the division. If we were correct we had about 125 revenue officers with little or no productivity.

Some of the employees wanted to do the job, but they were not in a position to be as effective as they should have been because they needed training. The reason they needed training was the result of several issues including having received ineffective training in the beginning, not being suited for the job, ineffective coaching, among many other reasons. I felt it was my responsibility and that of the organization to provide the necessary quality training so that these employees would at least have the opportunity to attempt to do the job.

Our biggest challenge was the twenty-five percent who simply were not working and nothing was being done about it. I'm not sure whether the public prefers to have public employees doing their job even if it isn't a popular one of collecting taxes or to know that twenty-five percent of employees are socializing on the job, hiding behind the union, and not being productive. At any rate I took my job seriously and working with my assistant we came up with a plan that turned the division around.

All hell broke out from the union and even somewhat from the director's office. IRS continues to operate as though it is in the dark ages. During my time, even though it was as late as 1996, the organization did not have the ability to generate computerized reports showing group statistics. Statistics has been a word to avoid in IRS even though everyone has always collected them. You can not improve in any situation unless you have enough information to know exactly how you are doing and know exactly who is working and who is not.

I personally went out to each branch and met with all employees. I advised the employees that twenty-five percent of the revenue officers were not working and that it was my expectation that all employees would immediately begin to do the job they were being paid for. I further advised that I would provide any training determined necessary, but that I would also do what was necessary to terminate employees who refused to give eight hours work for eight hours pay.

As can be seen on the bulletin from the union (Exhibit 2) my message went over like a lead balloon. The union geared up for an all out attack on Collection Division managers. The union also went directly to the director and complained about what I had said about the twenty-five percent non-performers and guess what, the director agreed with the union that I should not have made those statements.

Again, IRS may be a government agency; however, it is a business and it is a big business. I can't imagine a private business being reluctant and/or afraid to take on situations involving non-productive employees. Can this be a major reason why IRS continues to fail? I think so.

Executive level management seems to feel there has to be a separation in collecting taxes and managing effectively. During my term as chief in Laguna Niguel, the director would go to any length to prevent negative publicity, both internally with regional and national executive management and externally with Congress and the general public.

Upon hearing the complaints from the union regarding my message to the employees, the director visited me in my office to advise me that he did not think I was doing the right thing by announcing my twenty-five percent non-performance theory. He asked me how I arrived at the twenty-five percent figure. I told him my subordinate managers had advised me of that percentage and that I had verified it by reviewing reports showing our productivity level.

The director was very clear that he did not approve of my meeting. He did not give me a direct order to stop however. He would never tell me specifically what to do. He let me know he didn't like my message to the employees, so that he could say he had warned me should it blow up in my face. However, he did not give me a direct order to stop my message just in case my plan became successful. With that kind of attitude he was safe anyway it went.

Since I knew my neck was on the line if we didn't improve and because my philosophy has always been to do it my way, I decided to continue to do it my way because by that time I only had a few more offices in which I needed to deliver my message. In the meantime, from time to time a number of individual employees met me in the hallway of the building and told me they were very happy to hear my message because they were embarrassed by the reports they had seen showing how our division measured up to others and they were particularly tired of watching certain co-workers doing nothing but socializing every day.

Shortly after the director's visit to my office, the assistant director visited me the same day. It was obvious he and the director had been discussing the situation. The assistant director advised me the director did not approve of my message because it did not seem appropriate for a female to conduct such "get tough" meetings. The assistant director told me he did not think the director would feel the same way if one of the male division chiefs had done what I had done. I agreed with the assistant director and told him I planned to continue with the message until I had visited all of the employees. He told me he agreed with my message but he also told me he felt the union was not going to let up in their negative press.

He was correct in that the union did not let up and one chapter even went so far as to print some untrue statements in the chapter's newsletter about me and the message I was giving to all employees. However, with me being me, I confronted the chapter president and threatened to file a law suit if she printed any additional libelous statements regarding me. I was not mentioned directly again in any subsequent newsletters. Additional details regarding the newsletter situation are provided in the chapter on Labor -Management Climate.

My meetings had put everyone on notice so now I had to follow through and specifically identify those employees who were not working. The best way to do this was through review of the daily reports. Revenue officers are required to prepare a daily report showing their productivity for the previous day. The report shows the number of cases in the individual revenue officers inventory, identifies all closures and dollars collected, and lists field activity if any, for that day.

My assistant devised a weekly report for each branch to show how many dollars were collected per staff year by each individual group. Requiring the branches to report weekly would allow us to take immediate necessary action should we see numbers going in a downward direction rather than wait until the end of the month when it would be too late to change anything for the month.

The reports received from each group were consolidated for the entire division and copies were sent to all managers. In addition to consolidating the reports, we itemized the results from each group and showed that on the report as well. Circulation of reports of this nature let everyone in the division know which groups were meeting the objectives of collecting and which were not.

We could not identify individual revenue officers; however, once a group was identified as a group with non-performers I personally became involved and reviewed cases to determine the nature of the problem. Managers were required to review each daily report and to provide case reviews and counselling to employees not showing any dollars collected. The counselling was only required and necessary when after reviewing the actual case documentation the manager determined that the appropriate action should have been in the form of some collection action.

Collection action could be simply making a demand for payment and receiving it. On the other hand it could require enforcement action such as liens, levies, and/or seizure action. Continued deliberate failure to perform on the part of the employee was to result in progressive discipline.

Progressive discipline started with counselling, progressed to letter of warning, suspension, and ended with termination. Managers were advised they must not evaluate employees on statistics alone, but I told them we were a collection division and our job was to collect money. They were further advised that they needed to follow the rules and be sure everything done was within the rules and regulations and that nothing illegal was being done. Lo and behold - we immediately started to turn the division around with increases in dollars collected reflected on the very first report.

The director was very happy to see the statistics improve. He remained somewhat uneasy because he always anticipated bad publicity. He seemed to be continually in a state of de javu. He had been assistant district director of IRS in Los Angeles and he was aware of what happened when the Criminal Investigation Division in that district became the subject of senate hearings and was identified as being out of control. The Chief, Criminal Investigation Division's career was abruptly ended.

The Chief, Criminal Investigation Division during that time became embroiled in a highly publicized situation that resulted in significant negative publicity for IRS and the chief as an individual. The situation even resulted in the chief being ridiculed in a book written about some of the events. The book entitled Skin Tight by Christopher Byron highlighted numerous unfavorable allegations about the then chief. I was a manager in the Los Angeles District during those years.

During his career, the director was never subjected to any personal allegation of illegality, but I always believed he remained running scared until he retired, not that he had been responsible for any wrong doing, but because I'm sure he realized how fragile an IRS career can be. He was a senior IRS employee as well as being one of the few minorities that had "made it to the top" becoming a member of the executive ranks. I truly believe he allowed his fears to control many of his major decisions throughout his career. He had to bear the brunt of what happened in his district, but as far as I know he was not suspected of any wrong doings.

The director is a member of a minority group and he had to struggle, not unlike other minorities, to reach his position. I always got the impression that he was very much afraid that something would come alone and have a negative impact on his retirement. Therefore, he was never able to manage the district without first being concerned about the extra minority baggage on his back, I clearly understand those feelings, but many times they do tend to prevent some minorities from taking necessary business risks. When you have come from the lowest socio-economic level such as the director had, you do everything you can to prevent having to return to that level.

As a direct result of the reports generated to identify individual groups and branch statistics we became number one in the nation in most critical factors and remained there until a year after I retired. My sources keep me informed on what is going on in IRS, and collections in Laguna Niguel are at rock bottom once again. In addition, in light of the 1997 IRS Congressional hearings, all reports with statistics have been banned. IRS can be relied on to over react to any negative publicity. Managing and controlling are foreign subjects to IRS and cannot be intermingled.

I never understood why IRS did not expect managers to be able to operate effectively enough to control utilization of reports. Although I suppose the message was that IRS did not have confidence that management was top notch quality and could be effective in controlling utilization of reports. The answer from IRS was always to ban the report rather than make management accountable for utilizing reports appropriately and effectively.

The best thing Congress can do for IRS and the taxpaying public is to decide whether collecting taxes is a priority or not. On the one hand IRS is criticized and verbally beaten up when collections are down. On the other hand IRS managers' hands are tied when it comes down to being able to do the job the way it should be done.

IRS is prohibited from gathering statistics that identify how individual employees are performing as well as prohibited from using statistics to evaluate employees. I can't imagine private collection companies operating the way IRS is required to. It is virtually impossible to be successful not knowing who is performing and who isn't. No wonder IRS continues to experience management problems particularly in the fiscal arena.

The problem is further compounded because IRS managers down to the lowest level of management, if they are worth their pay, do gather statistical information yet when they meet with employees to discuss the employees performance, the manager has to be creative and beat around the bush avoiding any mention of actual numbers. The rationale for not evaluating employees on specific collection goals is to prevent employees from taking unnecessary enforcement action just to meet a goal. Sound, effective management should be able to ensure the job is being performed effectively without playing games.

It is my sincere belief that while changes are undoubtedly taking place in IRS as a result of the 1997 Congressional Hearings, IRS will continue to operate under the basic system. We will not see a flat tax system or any other major deviation from the current system implemented anytime soon, if ever.

The undertaking of a major overhaul such as converting to a flat tax system is so overwhelming that those who truly understand how the system currently works also understand it would take years for a flat tax or any other major change to be worked out to the extent it could operate even as efficiently as the current system. It is possible to change the system but the members of Congress do not have a clue as to how the current system is being worked on a day by day basis. The very basic questions asked by members of Congress during the 1997 Congressional Hearings were very enlightening.

Certain members of Congress see the IRS and its problems as a major opportunity for their campaign efforts. A Congress that would shut down the entire federal government as they did a few years back cannot be too concerned about the operations of one agency other than how it will impact them individually.

During the time the federal government was shut down, employees in IRS were placed in what was called a furlough status. Most employees were not allowed to even be in the building during that time. To assure some kind of coverage was provided to process payments received from the public one manager and one clerk were assigned to work. The rule was that leave, vacation time, could not be used, yet everyone got paid for being off from work. I worked during that time as the director required the chiefs to be there.

What kind of business sense is that to furlough thousands and thousands of employees for several days and pay them there full salary while Congress fought over the budget. What a waste of the taxpaying public's money.

Chapter Three

EXTRA CURRICULAR ACTIVITIES

Throughout my entire career the one theme I heard consistently was that government employees, IRS in particular, were supposedly held to higher ethical and moral standards than that of the taxpaying citizens. In other words, since we were judge and jury for taxpayers regarding their tax delinquencies, we needed to be as clean as a fresh snow fall to avoid negative aspersions being cast towards the organization.

In spite of the repeated attempts to reach higher ground, the organization operates on a double standard. Generally speaking, in practice, but not in theory, expectations for employees are much higher than those for managers, especially for executive level managers.

This double standard is often extended to employees sitting at the right hand of certain managers and/or executives. How do I know this? I know it because when I was sitting at the right hand side of management, supported by executive level managers, I was afforded every opportunity available for promotions and upward mobility. I was never in real disfavor; however, there were many times when I wasn't at the top of the current executive's list and few opportunities were made available for me during those times.

How did the favoritism come about? Many ways. Sometimes it was just a matter of having worked in the former districts with whoever was currently in charge. Sometimes it was the result of being responsible for achieving notable success for a particular program that was in the current limelight. The old adage is true, "It's not always what you know, but who you know".

Disturbing as it may seem, favors, promotions, and special assignments are frequently meted out for personal relationships. IRS does not lead with a management by example philosophy. The philosophy is more of a "Do what I say, not what I do." philosophy.

The examples of what I call extra curricular activities are from various offices throughout the nation. For obvious reasons I will not name the individuals nor the districts from which the examples are taken. However, most of the information is well known inside the organization, many employees reading the book will have instant recall.

A very interesting aspect to the favoritism theory is that during the 1998 Congressional Hearings it was made known that even though numerous complaints regarding various subjects, some of which dealt with sexual harassment, were made against executives none of them, and I do mean none of them were followed through to the extent that any executive was fired. The incoming Commissioner found that the complaints ended up at the Deputy Commissioner's desk only to remain there. On a few occasions an executive would be transferred to another district without any disciplinary action having been taken.

Sexual Harassment

The subject of sexual harassment was so significant in IRS it warrants its own section. When I joined IRS sexual harassment was an unknown topic. It was happening on an on-going basis; however, the law had not recognized the subject as one in need of concern and scrutiny; therefore, it wasn't being dealt with. Also, many women were too embarrassed to report sexual harassment situations that happened to them. IRS, as most other organizations, work hard at keeping all of its' dirty laundry inside. However, there are occasions when someone slips up and something is done that cannot be kept inside. One such situation involved a male Branch Chief in one region, consistently making passes at three female employees and inviting them to go out with him. The invitations were made separately on individual bases; however, the three females knew each other and they each found out they were being subjected to the same sexual harassment from the same manager. All three of them complained to the Branch Chief's manager yet the unwarranted sexual harassment continued. The women finally filed a sexual harassment suit against IRS and the manager. They were awarded a judgment in the amount of $500,000. The not too smart Branch Chief enhanced the case of the female employees by admitting to a news reporter that he had asked them to go out with him. He didn't seem to have a clue that unwanted solicitations were forms of sexual harassment.

No matter what anyone thinks, IRS employees are just like other people and they reflect the outside public world. Some of the employees are the best people you could ever hope to know and some unfortunately, belong in jail, in hospitals, etc. The idea of sexual harassment was a hard sell to IRS management when the concept finally came into vogue. It actually had to be force fed to both management and rank and file employees who at the time just happened to be a majority of white males.

IRS started trying to approach the concept of sexual harassment in the late 1970's while I was a relatively new manager. I can remember classes that were conducted to introduce the idea to managers and during the entire class large numbers of white males groused and disagreed with everything being said. While the idea has finally started to be taken seriously by some managers and employees, it is still being treated as a foreign subject by many males in IRS. During my tenure I had to take numerous adverse action against managers and employees at various levels of the division. I took a hard line and made no doubts about it; however, many of the males just didn't seem to get the point or more than likely, they didn't want to get it. The most egregious situation I am aware of was a situation where I was told a female employee in an eastern district reported sexual harassment on the part of her manager, the manager was replaced by another manager who almost immediately followed in the previous manager's footsteps and sexually harassed another female member of the same group. The situation became somewhat public knowledge throughout the district because the female employees told other members of the group.

Top level management became aware of the first sexual harassment situation as the result of the first female employee telling a female manager in another division that she had been sexually harassed by her manager. That manager then went to the employee's second level manager and told her what had happened. The employee's second level manager took the information to the division level management. Supposedly the division chief called the accused manager and the branch level manager to the division office and advised the manager of the accusation.

The accused manager panicked when questioned by the chief and admitted to the allegation. He was surprised at the subject of his meeting with the chief as he thought he was being summoned for something procedurally work related. He was ultimately removed from management and he subsequently retired. The replacement manager, selected from another district, went to the group and almost immediately started propositioning another one of the female employees. He also told X-rated jokes to females including managers. He was ultimately fired after putting up a vigorous but futile fight to keep his job. One of the primary reasons why both managers were dealt with swiftly and were fired was because most of the managers involved were strong conscientious female managers.

As an aside, after retiring, the replacement manager moved to California and found employment in the same place I worked in after I retired. He left just before I was hired and after I arrived there I was told by a female employee that he had sexually harassed her on numerous occasions. I guess it is true you can't teach some old dogs new tricks.

In the first example of sexual harassment, I was told that the division chief scheduled a meeting with the employee and her branch chief to get details regarding the allegation. The employee said the manager had asked her to meet him after work as he needed someone to talk to about his marital problems. They met at a hotel and it went as the manager had said, they had a drink and discussed his problems. He then asked the employee to meet with him on several other occasions and she reluctantly complied. She told the division chief she had been afraid to say no to her manager.

Finally on one of the trips to the hotel, the manager told the employee he thought it would be more private if they went to a room to continue the discussion. They went to a room and as could be anticipated, they ended up in the bed having sex. Again, according to the employee she was afraid to say no to her manager. Later she said she regretted having gone to the room and this is when she confided in the manager. She said she did not want the situation to continue but did not know how to make it end without making her manger retaliate against her.

Now why would a man be so blatant as the replacement manager was as to follow in the exact footsteps of a manager who had been fired? Both of these acts were supposed to be kept confidential; however, the IRS grapevine is notorious and both situations became public knowledge what with both females readily validating the situations to members of the work group.

One of the reasons why the incidents happened is the result of the kind of leadership in power in IRS. As will be discussed later in this chapter, it was common knowledge among many employees and managers alike that a former regional commissioner had openly demonstrated blatant sexual harassment acts while working for IRS. The acts went unreported and I imagine some subordinate male managers thought if the regional commissioner thought it was okay to sexually harass employees they could do the same.

A district director from one of the largest districts across the country from California told me a story that is supposed to be true but is hard even for me to believe. An EEO (Equal Employment Opportunity) complaint was filed by a female employee alleging sexual harassment. She accused her manager of raping her twice.

After the first rape she didn't tell anyone and after thinking about what the manager had done to her, she went into his office one day and asked him why did he rape her. Supposedly he raped her again. She still didn't tell anyone until another manager noticed she was depressed one day and asked her what was wrong. She told the manager of the two rapes.

The accused manager was put on administrative leave, which is leave with pay while the matter was investigated but he eventually returned to work as the allegation couldn't be proven. This was one of those cases where it was one employee's word against another one's.

Sexual harassment situations rear their ugly heads during some of the most interesting and unlikely places as seen a few years ago when I attended an IRS collection division all managers meeting. As it was common practice to invite executive level management to this type of meeting, the then current regional commissioner had been invited to attend and to address the group.

The meetings usually lasted about three days with at least two nights spent in a hotel with many employees/managers having to commute long distances to get to the hotel. All managers within a certain commute distance were authorized per diem for food, hotel bill, and travel so that they could attend the meetings. During each meeting a group dinner was usually planned and most of the time the group was provided a hospitality room free of charge by the hotel. The free room was usually provided because the group guaranteed a certain number of attendees for hotel reservations.

During these times per diem was authorized to pay the hotel bill which was generally at a discounted rate for government organizations. Travel costs were reimbursed along with all meals. At this time meals were reimbursed based on the actual cost. Today a specific amount is allowed for reimbursement of meals and anything over that amount has to come out of the employee's own pocket.

During the period that reimbursement of meals was based on actual cost, IRS employees ate very well, most far above what they ate at home. Dinners would be lavish affairs with steak, lobster, wine, you name it. While liquor was not authorized for reimbursement by IRS, since it was not itemized and was included in the total cost, IRS travelers wined and dined themselves very well. I can remember seeing people make total pigs out of themselves.

Great quantities of alcohol and snacks were bought for all managers meetings. The drinks and snacks were paid for by assessments to each manager for their fair share. The hospitality room was opened after each days meeting and it remained open until the dinner hour. It was then opened after dinner and remained open until the last person left. Anyone wanting the key later could arrange to get it from the manager coordinating that particular meeting.

One evening after dinner three other managers and I went to the hotel lounge, listened to music, danced, and had a few drinks. We noticed that the much married regional commissioner came in to the lounge with one of the married female managers. They were not married to each other by the way. Those of us already in the lounge knew the two of them coming into the lounge together did not necessarily have to be something not on the up and up, but they did get our attention and curiosity, particularly when they did not join us and spent the complete time in the lounge alone, just the two of them.

We really sat up and took notice when they got up to dance. The way they danced, very suggestive, very close, rubbing each other's back showed clearly something was going on or at least about to go on. Mind you now, the regional commissioner was well aware we were in the room, but he was typical IRS management, arrogant and obviously didn't give a damn that his subordinates witnessed what was either sexual harassment or at the least a morals issue.

At any rate, around 11:00 p.m. the band stopped playing, it was a week night, and my group and I left the lounge and decided to go the hospitality room because after all we had paid for the drinks and snacks. Shortly after getting there and preparing drinks, the regional commissioner and the manager came to the hospitality room.

Although they spoke to us, it was obvious we were cramping their style. Even though we were IRS managers we didn't have to be hit over the head with a ton of bricks to know what to do. We drank up and left them to their own devices (?).

What happened when we left? Well, we never knew for sure, but what kind of example did this high level executive set for his subordinates. The least he could have done was to attempt to be discreet.

A few years later this regional commissioner and the manager each divorced their mates and married each other. In the meantime their reputations and credibility reached an all time low. Faster than you can blink an eye the gossip of the events of the night before were passed on the next morning to every manager in attendance at the meeting. Yes, I did participate in the gossip. I was young and a relatively new manager. This was exciting gossip although at the same time it was disgusting.

In between the time the all managers meeting took place and the marriage of the regional commissioner to his subordinate, another all managers meeting was held. This time it wasn't an all nighter, but once again this same regional commissioner was invited. This time there were two new female managers at the meeting. They had both relocated to the Los Angeles District from out of state. They were both young and both attractive. The Los Angeles managers did not know at the time that they were not only gay, but were each others lover, although they were out of the closet, so to speak.

The regional commissioner was not aware of this gay situation otherwise I'm sure he would not have allowed himself to become so enamored with one of them. He made a pass at the gay young woman and she ignored him. After the meeting he began calling her at her office. She was located in the east part of the Los Angeles District and he was located in the regional office in San Francisco. Since she was obviously not interested in him she tried to avoid him by not being available in the office or by having her secretary say she was not available. When she did not make herself available he went to the division chief and said he wanted her for a special assignment in the region.

Ordinarily newly selected managers are very impressed with getting assignments in the regional office; however, since this manager knew the regional commissioner had an ulterior motive she had to flat out refuse to accept the assignment.

Eventually the regional commissioner found out the manager was gay because as I said earlier, she was out of the closet. It took a while for many people to know she was gay because she did not fit the stereotypical ideas about lesbian women as she was very feminine looking.

I've often wondered how foolish the regional commissioner must have felt. However, I'm sure in his arrogance he found it appropriate to see it as the woman's loss and not his.

In spite of the manager being gay, the actions of the regional commissioner were blatant, out and out sexual harassment on the part of one of the top leaders in IRS. This is the same man who was going around talking about the stand IRS would take in situations where sexual harassment was identified on the part of any manager.

An ironic aspect of this sexual harassment environment was relayed to me since I retired. Shortly after the two gay women joined the Los Angeles District the lesbian lover of the woman sexually harassed by the Regional Commissioner made moves on two female employees in what could be considered sexual harassment.

Just recently in 1998 I was visited in my home by two female managers I had previously worked with. One was a branch chief and the other had been a group manager until she successfully competed for a branch chief position in another district. Both women were attending a convention near the city I live in and they visited with me for several hours.

During the visit we rehashed the "good old days" and to my surprise they both told me how the lesbian manager's lover, who also happened to have been a manager, made a move on both of them. In one of the situations the manager appeared to be preying on the woman while she was in a vulnerable position just coming out of a nasty divorce. According to my information, the lesbian manager approached the straight manager and offered her sympathy regarding the difficult divorce. She then proceeded to rub up and down on the manager's arm telling her over and over again how much she hated men. She then told her she wanted her to know she was there for her if she needed her. On the surface this could seem innocent; however, the straight manager advised me that she was afraid of the lesbian manager because she was an extremely aggressive personality with her actions coming across as being intimate. She gave the appearance of being a "sexual predator", the same as the commissioner.

My other visitor had worked in the same branch with the lesbian and straight manager and she said the lesbian had made a move on her and she too was afraid. I was very surprised even though it was a known fact that the lesbian was out of the closet. Since her lover had been sexually harassed by the Regional Commissioner I would have expected her to be sensitive to other women's feelings. I guess I was wrong in my thinking.

As time went on during my career in IRS I found that sexual harassers did not discriminate in selecting their victims. I personally experienced several incidents of sexual harassment shortly after joining IRS. None of the situations were damaging to my career, but each made me very uncomfortable.

The first situation occurred during my second year on the job. One of my first group managers made it his personal agenda to tell me daily how good I looked and how "fine" he thought I was. Again, the issue of sexual harassment was just coming into "vogue" and there were no rules for what a woman should do should the situation occur.

This manager took every opportunity while doing his daily duties to see that I was sexually harassed as often as possible. Managers were required to make field visitations at least once a year with each employee to observe the employees field performance. While the requirement was once a year, the managers had the authority to accompany the employees as often as they wanted to. My manager decided to accompany me at least once a month. His ritual while on these field visitations was to start out telling me how good he thought I looked and then to start talking about sex including the sharing of details of his sexual experiences with his wife. He would then ask me to go out with him on a date, an invitation I always turned down.

Since I was a mature woman in my early thirties when I started working for IRS I did not find the situation intimidating, but did find it embarrassing and tiresome hearing the same thing over and over again. I treated the situation and the manager as though he were making a pass at me and I told him I wasn't interested.

I do have to say that I took an easy way out by telling him I would never go out with a married man. I somehow intuitively knew he could accept that reason better than if I were to attack his ego and make him think I thought he was unattractive or that I was going to complain to someone about him.

To give him some credit, he never touched me and he never retaliated against me in my performance appraisals for refusing him. As a matter of fact he recommended me for a performance award and he provided significant support for me in preparation for applying for the management program. All of this after I had turned down his requests for "dates".

Had I been younger, easily intimidated, or desperate to keep my job I would have been in a serious predicament. Since I wasn't either of those, I tolerated the harassment until I was able to leave it all behind me a few years later by being accepted into the management program and given a managerial assignment in another office.

The other incidents of sexual harassment I experienced were being hit on the behind with a pencil by a co-worker during my training year and being patted on the behind by a branch chief co-worker when I became a branch chief.

In the case of the trainee co-worker, again my level of maturity and nerve enabled me to advise the co-worker that he was traveling in dangerous waters and that if he ever touched me again he would be sorry. He heard me loud and clear and he never touched me again.

In the case of the branch chief patting me on the behind I became so furious I almost created some thing equivalent to an international incident and I even frightened some of my employees. The situation occurred at one of the now infamous managers meeting. I suppose I should consider writing a book about IRS all managers meetings as a significant number of my examples for this book occurred at IRS all managers meetings.

This particular meeting was conducted in the Los Angeles District. The division chief, branch chiefs, and all first line managers were in attendance at the meeting. Meetings and workshops were conducted all day on this particular day and a group dinner was planned for the evening as we were off-site at a hotel.

Upon arrival at the restaurant I was standing at the entrance with a group of my employees waiting to be seated when my co-worker, the branch chief, came up and told us where everyone else had been seated. It was obvious he had been drinking and as he walked away from us he patted me on the behind.

I am known to have a short fuse and to be very vocal regardless of how embarrassing or intimidating the situation might be; therefore, several of my employees who witnessed this situation became alarmed not knowing how I might handle it. Not only was the pat on the behind demeaning, it was embarrassing.

The branch chief walked away before I could really make myself believe he had had the nerve to put his hands on me. I did not fraternize with the branch chiefs except in work type situations. At that time they were all male and all white.

They shared personal situations on the weekend such as golf and ball games. I did not want to participate in those things with them, but I knew that I needed to go to lunch and coffee with them on occasions so that I wouldn't be left in the dark about things that were happening in the division, the district and IRS in general. I always tried to conduct myself in a way that demanded respect from them and except in this situation I had always received respect from all of them. We were all friendly to a certain degree what with going to lunch on occasions and visiting each other's office to have a cup of coffee and/or to discuss business.

Once I realized what this man had done I became incensed. My employees told me later I appeared to be on the verge of ranting and raving I was so angry.

I could hardly eat my dinner and I did rant and rave about the situation throughout the entire dinner. Because of their concern for me, after dinner when we returned to the hotel, my employees, who also happened to be managers, and another concerned branch chief approached the branch chief and read him the riot act about his actions.

I was told they literally demanded he apologize to me and they practically dragged him to the hospitality room where they knew I was. I listened to his apology, but in all honesty I never really accepted it, partially because I never felt he meant it. I knew he had apologized because it just happened to be the politically correct thing to do. I was held in high regard in the division and he realized even in his drunken stupor that he had over stepped his bounds.

I am a very private, proud person and having something like that happen to me was incomprehensible. To make matters worse both the division chief a white male, and the assistant division chief, a black male, knew about the incident and neither did what they were supposed to do. Both of them appeared to be hoping the matter would go away if they pretended it had never happened.

The Equal Employment Opportunity (EEO) rules in IRS require immediate action on the part of management to prevent sexual harassment, to make the workplace environment safe and comfortable, free from sexual harassment situations, and to investigate situations that have taken place.

The assistant division chief even found the situation amusing as he considered himself to be one of the "boys". The "boys" included the branch chiefs. On one occasion the assistant chief came close to sounding as though he wanted to say it was my fault the situation had happened. Before he made what would have been a serious blunder he changed the subject. If he had gone down that road I would have filed an EEO complaint against him and the branch chief.

I decided to try to let it go and not to take any action against the co-worker branch chief as I felt I had handled the situation by telling him in no uncertain terms how I felt about him and his despicable act. However, I never really was able to fully let it go in my mind and I lost respect for both the chief and his assistant for their negligence and uncaring attitude. In their worlds they were considered to be nice, friendly people generally well thought of. I don't think they intentionally wished me harm. They were both from the dinosaur age and they did not have a clue as to how demeaning something like that is to a woman. There is also the possibility they wouldn't have cared even if they had known.

Both of those "gentlemen" are still in the IRS hierarchy, one is a division chief and one is a district director. I often wonder how they handle sexual harassment situations they are confronted with today.

Having experienced sexual harassment first hand and knowing how humiliating it is, I was always very sensitive to the subject during my career. I also felt very strong about providing a work environment free from that type of situation. On many occasions I spoke to all of my managers about their EEO responsibilities regarding sexual harassment. I also advised them of the serious consequences should they err. I even went so far as to invite the regional EEO Officer to attend one of my all managers meetings and to speak to the group regarding IRS policy on sexual harassment.

Did this stop them? No, but at least they were forewarned. Did I follow up on what I said I would do? Yes, and I took disciplinary action against managers on several occasions when they were found guilty of sexual harassment.

During my third year in IRS I had the occasion to work in an office with a known sexual harassment offender, a manager. He was unaffectionally known to employees as "Hands Louie". It was a known fact that any female sitting next to "Hands Louie" would find him rubbing his leg against theirs.

Sure enough, while I was still new to the office, before I had heard about ole "Hands" himself, I sat next to him at the little café across from the office where everyone convened for coffee breaks and lunch. He sat next to me with his leg up against mine. I moved my leg over because I just thought he did not have enough room. I moved over and he moved over next to me again. I then made a big deal of it and asked the person sitting on my other side to move over so that we could have more room.

Everyone at the table knew why I needed more room. "Hands Louie" did not display any visible emotion on his face but appeared to have taken it in his stride. Later, I was advised that this manager was called "Hands Louie" and that he had just given me his official welcome to the office.

"Hands Louie" evidently had a well-known reputation long before I worked in the same office where he was located. A women who is currently a manager in the Laguna Niguel District told me that when she worked in the office with "Hands" she was just out of high school and really wanted to be able to keep her job. Even though she tried to avoid "Hands" it appears she found herself locked in a closet/supply room with him one day. Finding herself locked in the room with him she became terrified. She said he advanced towards her and fortunately she was able to go out through another door. She then went and told her manager, a male manager who even though he was a manager was not as high on the hierarchy as "Hands".

This lower level manager advised her to not tell anyone about the incident. Interestingly enough the woman was also given the same advice by several older women in the office. Of course this was pre-sexual harassment days.

It is amazing when I look back on this situation because it was laughed and joked about by employees and managers. Since "Hands Louie" was not my manager I avoided him in the future. Just recently I spoke to another one of the managers in the office I retired from and in our reminiscing she told me when she was about eighteen and right out of high school she worked in that same office during "Hands Louie's" time. She said she and the other women in the office were afraid of him and did every thing they could to never be alone with him.

How could this have been allowed to go on for so many years? Who knows whether any young woman was intimidated into doing something she did not want to do. I have to confess I did not try to stop it either although I don't know what I would have done if I had wanted to try to stop it. There were no procedures for that type of situation.

BROWSING

In an effort to depict both management and employees in a fair manner it is only right that the public is aware of the browsing that takes place in IRS. By browsing I mean employees accessing taxpayers' accounts when they do not have a need to know anything about that particular taxpayer.

Accounts are assigned to revenue officers based on an assignment grid prepared by the manager of each group in accordance with Internal Revenue Manual procedures. Each IRS district covers certain parts of a state(s) territory. The territory is then divided up among the various branches of a district. Subsequent divisions are then made among groups and among each revenue officer in a particular group.

The revenue officers are then assigned taxpayers' accounts within the group's assignment grid. The cases assigned to a revenue officer make up his/her inventory. Those are the only cases in which each individual revenue officer has a right to investigate and to seek information leading to those taxpayers' assets or whereabouts.

As long as I can remember IRS has had rules that prohibit employee access to information that is not necessary to work and close a case assigned to a specific employee. However, rules without means of follow up and detection are meaningless. Remember, IRS has more personal information regarding more citizens than any other government or private organization in the United States and probably the world. This information is very tempting to some employees, particularly when it deals with celebrities.

IRS even stresses the necessity and importance of employees not sharing taxpayer information with co-workers in the same group unless there is a need to know. This rule doesn't seem too important unless you recognize how significant it can be. Cases are frequently discussed within the group. Sometimes on a need to know basis, but most of the time just as discussion items. Taxpayers who give employees problems are known throughout the entire group with discussions held on informal bases.

During my second year working for IRS I had a neighbor who had a friend that worked for the Post Office Department. I only knew the neighbor well enough to say hello and how are you although he seemed to be a respectable upstanding citizen. I knew his friend worked for the Post Office because I saw him there in his postal uniform.

I started to notice that the neighbor and his friend were in his garage late at night on many occasions and I wondered what they were doing. However, I was too busy to worry about neighbors. Time passed and the neighbor disappeared for a time. Still, while I noticed I had not seen him for some time I still tried to mind my business.

Finally one day in the office I passed a co-workers desk and lo and behold I saw a TDA with my neighbors name on it. It was what was called a termination assessment.

A termination assessment is a signal that the taxpayer has been involved in something illegal. When a taxpayer is arrested and has large sums of unaccountable, untaxed money in their possession the police confiscate the money and at some point they call IRS. This is done as a means of government agencies cooperating with each other and also as a means of "getting" the taxpayer one way if the other way (the arrest) fails.

IRS then terminates the tax year for that taxpayer. While individual tax returns are due April 15th of each year, the IRS has the right to end the tax year at any time large sums of unaccountable, untaxed money is discovered in the possession of the taxpayer.

IRS then assesses a tax liability based on that large amount of money. At that time the taxpayer is not allowed any deductions thereby resulting in a large tax delinquency and the possibility of tax evasion charges depending upon the circumstances. IRS and the police share in the funds as they are definitely not returned to the taxpayer unless the taxpayer can produce a legitimate reason for having the money. Because the money has been confiscated during alleged illegal actions most taxpayers in this situation will not claim the money. They will usually allege that they have no idea where the money came from. Of course IRS does not buy this; however, the various police departments are happy to hear it because they can then keep the money.

When the following April 15th comes around the taxpayer has the opportunity to file a corrected return if it is appropriate. However, by that time most people involved in this type of situation probably have more important things to deal with as they may be looking at jail time for drug dealing, prostitution, gambling, etc.

This example shows why it is important that tax information is only accessed on a need to know basis. I definitely did not need to know about this situation. By being able to access my neighbor's tax information I could have gossiped about it and shared it with other neighbors. I didn't do that because I was sensitive to the importance of confidentiality although I have to admit it would have been considered to be some very hot gossip for my quiet, respectable neighborhood.

Many times information has been accessed unintentionally, or simply out of curiosity, but unfortunately information has also been accessed as a result of an employee's personal agenda. Following the Nixon years in the White House, as a result of the information that came out about Watergate, IRS clamped down significantly on employees ability to access information.

Of course IRS being IRS it was seriously overdone. Most IRS employees did not have access to computers and of course computers had not come into common access for the average citizen nor employee. The inability to access information through a computer certainly limited any access by unauthorized employees.

Again, IRS being IRS, implemented rules whereby managers were required to conduct unannounced searches of employees' desks to determine if the employees had any information regarding any taxpayer that was not assigned to them. If any of this type of information was discovered the employee paid the price by receiving some type of adverse action usually by way of a Letter of Warning or Admonishment.

Again, IRS being IRS, after a few years that kind of search was abandoned and some time later computers became available. Surely you would think that with the advent of the computer generation one of the priorities of IRS would have been to implement procedures to detect unauthorized access of taxpayers' accounts. For years and years and years IRS did not have any means of detecting unauthorized use of the system. IRS only started to become able to detect unauthorized access in the early 1990's. After seeing what was detected in the late 90's one can only imagine what went undetected.

I was told that during President Reagan's term an employee accessed his account, supposedly just to see how much income the president had. In addition, employees accessed movie celebrities information and sold it to newspapers, tabloids and such.

Again, while accessing unauthorized information appeared to have been done out of curiosity most of the time, it was also done for illegal monetary gain by employees and in many instances to avenge a wrong done to a relative or to seek incriminating evidence for civil suits.

In another California District an employee illegally accessed thousands and thousands of taxpayers' accounts. That situation was believed to be the record at that time. This employee accessed accounts in what appeared to have been based on curiosity as well as in an effort to discredit a person with whom the employee's relative had some negative business dealings.

Many times employees' accessed accounts of ex-husbands and ex-wives in an attempt to discover assets that had not been disclosed in divorce cases. Also, estranged and /or ex-wives accessed accounts of husbands in an effort to try to locate assets of the person and/or assets for delinquent child support.

To give IRS its' just dues I do have to say that I was told the employee holding the unauthorized access record was dealt with severely. He was a senior employee and he and the union fought tooth and nail to keep his job, but he was terminated. Part of the reason he was terminated was because by then national office was receiving some direct heat from Congress and the public on the subject of unauthorized accesses.

As a result of that heat, procedures were implemented so that national level management was informed of all cases regarding unauthorized access and the districts were required to advise national office management of the outcome of the cases including the action that was taken against the browsers. Naturally with national office looking over the shoulder of the district, the district began to hand down serious adverse actions for each infraction.

The most amazing thing about all of this is that IRS, the largest accounting agency in the world, did not have the computer capability nor knowledge to detect and to prevent these unauthorized accesses. The next most amazing thing about all of this is that once an unauthorized access was discovered Congress would scream about the inadequacy and ineffectiveness of IRS, yet that same screaming body of people would cut the IRS budget at every opportunity. With the little money allocated to IRS the organization has always had inferior equipment, purchasing it from the cheapest bidder.

IRS was just being introduced to the world of computers at the time I joined the organization and the computer equipment initially used was second hand equipment. How can an organization be expected to perform in a top notch manner without top notch equipment?

After all these years and many unauthorized accesses Congress finally worked on an anti-browsing bill. On April 9, 1998, the House Ways and Means Committee passed a bill H.R. 1226 that proposed unauthorized access to taxpayer records by IRS personnel a criminal offense. The committee approved the bill after adding an amendment sponsored by Representative Jennifer Dunn stipulating that the Treasury Secretary notify affected taxpayers when a criminal indictment or charge is brought against an IRS employee.

The bill also provides taxpayers with civil remedies similar to the unlawful disclosure rules in the IRS Code. All of this came about as the result of a case in Boston in which an IRS employee associated with the Ku Klux Klan was convicted of unauthorized access of a taxpayer's records. The conviction was subsequently overturned as a result of insufficient proof that the employee disseminated the information or used it in a criminal way.

On August 5, 1998 President Clinton signed the Taxpayer Browsing Protection Act. H.R. 1226, criminalizing the unauthorized access of taxpayer information by Internal Revenue Service employees. This law allows fines of up to $1000 and/or a sentence of a year in jail, requires the IRS to notify any taxpayer of a criminal indictment of a government employee or contractor involving their confidential tax records, and permits the taxpayer to seek civil reparations.

Even with the criminalization of unauthorized access of taxpayer information by Internal Revenue employees, as late as July 1998 according to the article IRS Reform received on the Internet, certain IRS employees were testifying at the 1998 Hearings of "Institutional Misuse" on the part of IRS employees.

One employee testified to having personally witnessed tax data being accessed on prospective boyfriends, being checked on ex-husbands for increasing child support payments, information being accessed on people with whom IRS employees were having some kind of personal disagreement, and access of tax data on prominent or newsworthy individuals, friends, relatives, neighbors and just about anyone else that comes to certain employees' minds. As I said before, the testimonies are true.

GAY RIGHTS

The IRS population reflects the general population so therefore the workforce has its share of gay employees. While most employees appear to take the gay employees working in the organization in their stride, management has failed many times to demonstrate that it is the position of IRS that gay employees are entitled to their rights.

The first situation I experienced on a large scale regarding gay employees started at the time the Los Angeles District split. In a meeting I attended with other branch chiefs and division level management the "inside position" on treatment of gay employees became apparent shortly after the meeting started.

The main agenda was to reorganize the district in preparation for the splitting of the district. Unknown to most of the attendees at the meeting, one of the branch chief's was a close friend to a group of gay IRS women employees. Over the years some employees had expressed their opinion that even though she was married, this branch chief who will be known as Sue, had latent gay sexual tendencies.

At any rate, during the course of the meeting the discussion centered around the placement of some of the managers in the new district. The split caused a significant re-organization within what remained as part of the Los Angeles District. Therefore, managers in several branches had to be reassigned.

Branch chiefs expressed their desires and opinions as to which manager should be placed in which branch. It turned out that it was recommended that three gay women were to be assigned to one branch. The receiving branch chief for that branch immediately spoke up and said "Don't put all of them in my branch".

Now, mind you there wasn't ever any open discussion regarding the sexual preferences of these women. It was just somewhat of an unspoken acknowledgment that they were gay. Even though no one said the words gay nor lesbian, everyone knew what the discussion was all about.

The friend of the gay women, the branch chief, never changed facial expressions during the conversation regarding placement of the three women, she simply sat there and looked straight ahead. After a much heated discussion, the three women were placed in separate branches.

This particular situation had considerable significance in the not too distant future from the date of that meeting. Sue the branch chief ultimately divorced her husband, became a division chief, came out of the closet, and started a long term live in relationship with her lover.

However, it was apparent Sue never forgot the discussion regarding placement of the three gay female managers. Several years later in her position as division chief, Sue refused to accept several requests for reassignment from the branch chief who did not want "all of them" in his branch.

Several of this branch chief's buddies were unsuccessful in their requests for reassignment. One of them had been assigned to Sue's division during the district split. After working in that district for several years and failing to gain Sue's support for upward mobility positions, he finally had to request a lateral assignment back to the Los Angeles District so that he could gain support for promotions.

Around the time the district was splitting, another now infamous all managers meeting was held. This was said to have been a "coming out" meeting as several women let it be known they were gay over the course of the time the meeting was going on. These were women who were thought to be straight by everyone in the division.

One evening during the time of the all managers meeting, the gay group had a private party. Prior to the start of the private party, the group of known gay women had grown from two to four. After the all managers meeting there was an additional four for a total of eight.

In addition to Sue having been married, another one of the women had been married for over thirty years, she had several children, grandchildren, and was a devout member of the Catholic religion. Not only did she go to mass on Sundays she also attended daily mass before going to work most days. After the all managers meeting she divorced her husband and took up housekeeping with another middle aged woman, her new lover.

Prior to these changes this woman had let it be known her husband was impotent and had been for years. During those years she had made a few attempts to establish relationships with a few men. She had shared this information with me on a one on one level. None of these situations worked out for her. Did this have anything to do with her decision to start living a gay life? I'll let you be the judge of that. Loneliness is a terrible thing. She did appear to be happier after getting involved in her new relationship.

There are probably numerous stories about gay women in IRS; however, one of the most interesting and unfair one is about a gay woman working in Atlanta and her career after she competed for a division chief position. Supposedly, the district director in the district where the woman was assigned at the time she was competing for the chief's position suggested to her that she should dress more feminine for her interview and that should the opportunity arise she should mention her husband. This information was shared with me by a supposed friend of the woman, someone in whom she confided. The suggestion regarding dress was certainly appropriate whether the woman was gay or not. She always wore pants and they were not top notch material nor did they match or coordinate with her jackets. In other words the woman needed a make-over, gay or not.

The Director provided those suggestions to the woman, June, because her sexuality was becoming questioned by her co-workers in their daily gossip. She was a very plain woman, she wore pants most of the time and never wore makeup. She had married a long time friend who was labeled by the gossips to be someone whose sexuality was also being questioned. After their divorce she remained friends with him and he visited her and her female lover.

It is important not to get ahead of the story because the "dirt" on June's current Director at the time of her interview for the new position was that he "hated" the director in the district June was competing for. This director in the new district was an upstanding, middle aged white male from the old, old, old school. He lived a life full of double standards. He had a wife and a girl friend and was totally unprepared and even more unwilling to promote a gay person.

Well, June was successful in her interview and she was selected for the position. Now June wasn't a very strong person and she was not prepared to come out of the closet without sufficient backup. She would have never been able to stand up under the pressure of coming out of the closet without strong support.

Several known gay women applied for reassignment in June's new district and she took six of them with her along with one male that was very close to the group of women. This group of seven were all assigned to the same building in the same office, with one becoming June's right hand person. This person ultimately became June's live-in lover.

Within a few months of June's selection and the reassignment of all of the women, a regional analyst called the director and asked him what was going on in the district and why did he select an office full of gay women. Word has it the director became unglued. He immediately conducted his own internal investigation and found the analyst's words to be accurate.

He also found out from the branch chiefs who worked for June that they were having extreme difficulty getting in to see her on business because her gay subordinates were always in her office. June's former director had achieved his objective. He had made a fool of June's new director. He obviously did not care about June or what the future held for her.

The new director immediately set about reassigning all of June's gay subordinates, getting them all out from under her immediate control. He then set up obstacle after obstacle to make June's job difficult.

He succeeded in helping her to fail while also making the division fail. Failure of the division had a significant negative impact on the district. There wasn't any doubt in anyone's mind who happened to know the people and circumstances involved, that June had not been the strongest branch chief around and it was always quite interesting to the spectators that she was selected to be responsible for a large division.

June was a very smart person when it came to books, but she gave the appearance of being very insecure which stood in the way of her decision making. She was an introvert and only friendly to those included in her inner circle. However, it was believed that she probably could have achieved a modicum of success if she had had support from the director. It would have been an uphill battle, but she was a hard worker.

Once the director decided to go after her and her job she no longer had a chance. June was taken out of her position and demoted. She filed a complaint and rumor has it she won although what she won was never known as she did not get her job back.

The district was in such turmoil that the region became closely involved to the extent a replacement was put in June's position, one who was told to deal directly with the region, bypassing the director. The Director was out of favor in the eyes of the region because they had inside information on what was going on in his district. He was destroying the Division because of his personal feelings.

Many of the branch chiefs had once worked in the region with the analysts and they remained in close communication with them. The analysts were always great sources for gossip and information because they always knew how each district was performing as well as any problems that were occurring there. They were also known to have big mouths because they all worked in the district offices before being selected as analysts. Since they wanted to be promoted back to the district when their stint in the region was over they maintained close relationships with employees and managers in the districts.

The chief's replacement was told he was not obligated to take orders from the director. Having been one of the good ole boys, and because he was eligible for retirement, the director was allowed to retire without any action being taken against him and without any major negative publicity being generated although the entire district as well as neighboring districts, were sitting back looking at the scenario just the way people observe soap operas.

Everyone was anxiously waiting for the next chapter to end. The double standard was very much apparent with June being demoted in disgrace while the "disgraced director" was being celebrated with retirement parties after almost destroying the district.

As I said before the IRS workplace reflects the public population. However, in the districts I worked in it appeared that the known gay population percentage may have exceeded that of the public. This seemed to be even more so in the last district I worked in. This may have been because Orange County had been and still is to some extent, one of the most conservative counties in the nation, yet right inside IRS, a very conservative agency, many ultra liberal lifestyles were being observed daily.

One of my subordinates, a branch chief we will call Jack, started his career in the Los Angeles District, was promoted upwards in several other districts, and eventually came home to Orange County to die. He was gay and was working in Denver, Colorado when he received word one of his friends was dying of Aids. He told me he went to San Francisco, California to bury his friend and the night he returned home from the funeral he received a phone call from his doctor advising him he had AIDS.

He continued to work in Denver for a while until it became apparent he was on the downside of the disease. He requested a hardship transfer to southern California so that he could be with his relatives when he could no longer care for himself.

We accepted him in the Laguna Niguel District. We just happened to have a vacancy in the same position he had held in Denver. Accepting him in the district was a difficult issue because AIDS was just becoming well known and many people were known to panic when faced with the possibility of working with someone diagnosed with the illness. However, it was never officially known what his illness was. It was never discussed although it was obvious. My boss never told me about the nature of the illness.

The illness and death of this man was a tragedy, yet for me it provided a great opportunity to reflect on my many blessings. It also provided me with a great opportunity to learn many things from this man.

He was very small in stature but he had a giant's heart. I will never forget how hard he tried to live as normal a life as possible. He was one of the most committed, hardest working people I have ever known. He maintained a positive attitude until the end and never complained even when it was obvious he was in pain.

I had great admiration for him and will always remember him in a very positive light. He came to work on days when it was very obvious he could barely function. Near the end when he wasn't able to contribute as much as he wanted to, he still managed to gave it his all. He always had a smile and when asked how he was doing he always said "I'm making it okay."

I also had great admiration for his assistant because even though she had been in line for the branch chief's job and would have been a top contender she graciously stepped back and accepted him as her immediate manager. In addition, she, Jack and I were put in a position of having to work very closely together and to share the information that he had AIDS. Initially no one but top executive level management was supposed to have access to that information. I decided to tell the assistant because she was going to have to work very closely with him and being the bright young woman she was I knew she would soon realize how sick he was. I knew what the illness was because I had several other employees who died from it.

In addition to being very bright she also has a very kind, generous heart and the time she spent with Jack was very heart rendering for her. She grew to care for Jack as though he had become her very good friend. We had many discussions about him and his illness because we could not talk about it to anyone else. As a result of Jack, she and I had the opportunity to share very close confidences and even though I was her boss, to become good friends.

Jack worked up until about a month before he died and one of the last work related conversations he had that I was aware of was when he said to his assistant, "Please let the chief and the director know how sorry I am that I have not been able to finish the assignment she gave me." He was apologizing for some task I didn't even remember assigning to him.

Government employees are given so much negative press it's too bad that Jack's story has never been told. While I personally have criticism for IRS in some areas, I do attempt to have a balanced picture. This situation provided one of the best opportunities I knew of to see a human side of IRS, the compassion rarely seen by insiders or outsiders.

When I realized Jack was not going to be able to continue to do his assigned duties, I had a heart to heart discussion with him to tell him I had to assign his priority, time related duties to his assistant. Jack was devastated and his initial reaction was to say I was trying to take him out of his position and that he would not voluntarily step down. Jack and I had had a very good relationship up until that time and so I explained to him that while I was concerned about him I was also concerned about the overall completion of duties in a timely manner and that it appeared he was not able to meet the necessary deadlines.

After several lengthy conversations with Jack about this matter he finally admitted he understood my position and he finally even said he knew he would feel the same way if he were in my position. He said he would voluntarily step aside if I would allow him to keep his title and his desk. I agreed to that request and I went to my boss, the director, and requested that I be allowed to double encumber Jack's position.

I knew double encumbering of a position could be done but I also knew it was rarely approved. The few times I knew it had been approved was when a person in a particular position went off on some important special assignment, yet the regularly assigned duties had to be done also. This was almost always only done when it would benefit the government. Another person would then be temporarily assigned the job at the same pay as the person permanently assigned to the position.

My Director agreed with my request, but he had to go to the regional commissioner because of the level of the position involved. I was very pleased but somewhat surprised when the regional commissioner approved the request. Approval meant I could allow Jack to retain his dignity while having some one else perform the priority, time related duties.

I then assigned Jack to duties that were important, but not time related. Jack was still able to contribute to the organization, it just took him a little longer sometimes than I could afford to wait on certain things. That was a time I felt proud to work for IRS. It made me feel the way I had when I first joined the organization when I still had stars in my eyes.

Even though I could not see them, dark clouds were looming on the horizon for Jack. He hung in there far longer than anyone expected. I have to give credit to the 200 or more employees who worked for Jack. As I said earlier, little was known about AIDS during this time other than that it ultimately took your life. This was during the time when the public believed you could catch AIDS through basic human contact. However, even so, once this confidential matter got out in the rumor mill none of the employees panicked nor refused to work with him. They had to have known he was terminally ill and since it was a known fact that he was gay, it was easy to put two and two together. To my knowledge everyone gave him the respect expected for someone in his position.

Dark clouds appeared overhead the day Jack died. I was grateful he was out of his pain. I had visited him in the hospital near the end and even though he maintained his positive attitude I knew he was suffering. I was very disappointed when the Director did not attend his funeral.

Ordinarily the Director would be expected to attend funerals for employees at branch level and above. Also, the director had known Jack for years when they were both in the Los Angeles District at the start of Jack's career.

With over 2000 employees the Director could not be expected to attend funerals of employees at all levels; however, he had attended funerals of managers and other branch chiefs.

None of Jack's peers attended his funeral. The true colors of IRS mentality came out. Overall I knew the most important thing was how Jack was treated during his illness and for that my hat is off even to the director.

Jack happened to have been Hispanic and one of my employees, a Hispanic person, told me they believed Hispanic co-workers did not attend the funeral because the knowledge that Jack was gay and had died of AIDS was totally unacceptable to many male Hispanics' "macho" character.

I believe this statement was somewhat true because I had discussions with several mid level and above Hispanic managers and while they never expressed negative remarks about Jack or any other gay man, the expressions on some of their faces at the time of our discussions were a dead give away. They were very cautious and careful with their words because they anticipated someday someone might discuss them and their attitude the way I am doing now. They were right in their fear and I suppose you could say their fear protected them from being singled out in this book.

If I had never worked for IRS I suppose my description of IRS employees might have been cold, uncaring, and dull. Well some of those words are valid. However, during my time in IRS it seemed as though something strange happened every day, each day stranger than the day before.

One of the strangest situations I was informed about occurred in a branch managed by a gay branch chief in the national service. This branch chief received a complaint from a gay employee regarding unwanted overtures received from a gay manger. The situation started out with the gay manger sending the gay employee so called love messages on the computer.

Then one evening the manager showed up at the employee's home with bags of groceries. Supposedly the manager was reluctantly allowed in. He and the employee had drinks and dinner and because of the lateness of the hour the manager invited himself to sleep on the employee's couch for the night. The next morning while the employee was in the shower the manager joined him and attempted to rape him according to a complaint made by the employee. The employee filed an EEO sexual harassment complaint against the manager.

In trying to determine what should be done, branch level management took a look at the employee's personnel folder and found that he had been fired from several previous jobs for "causing trouble". Management was now in a predicament because it was the employee's word against the manager's regarding the attempted rape and the manager was disputing the allegation.

The manager was relieved of his managerial duties because he had become too personally involved with his employee by going to the house, taking groceries, and spending the night. The matter of rape could not be proven. The manager then turned around and filed a complaint against branch level management for taking his job away. Now mind you all of this is going on while all of the people involved were being paid a salary with taxpayers' funds.

In the meantime, branch level management found sufficient reasons to fire the employee. He had lied on his employment application when he said he had never been fired from any previous employment. Now IRS had a complaint filed by the employee and the manager. Once the employee was fired he filed a law suit against the organization.

Neither the employee nor the manager won the complaints nor the lawsuit. However, many, many hours were spent in dealing with the situation. Many people were involved in trying to resolve the complaints including the director, several employees from the personnel office, members of the EEO staff, and several employees from the immediate staff.

One of the reasons for the problem was that the manager was selected from inside the ranks. He was the result of crisis management. The branch needed managers right away because of last minute approval of a hiring budget.

The unwritten rule was that once a budget had been approved the money must be spent immediately or it would be taken back. IRS certainly did not want to return any approved funds, therefore ready or not, the hiring was done. If qualified, experienced managers were not available, the next best thing was done. Managers drafted someone who was doing their current job well, they drafted someone they liked, or volunteers were requested. At that point education and/or experience were irrelevant.

In the above mentioned situation, the manager did not have any training and wasn't aware that he had to maintain an objective distance from his subordinate employees. IRS is well known for placing people in positions they are not prepared for. Sometimes employees are placed in managerial positions against their will. Many times they are desperately needed, but they are not interested in management and their manager will "twist their arm" and get them to take the position as a favor to management.

Some employees will stand firm with a negative response, but most finally accept the managerial assignment. Some may accept out of fear of retaliation from the manager but most probably accept because they are committed employees willing to do, although reluctantly so, whatever management ask them to do.

MORAL CHARACTER -CONDUCT UNBECOMING

The unwritten rule that IRS employees have to be held to a higher standard included their tax situations as well as moral character. Conduct must always be favorable so that negative aspersions may not be cast against the agency's "good" reputation.

Some employees do believe the agency has a "good" reputation. However many, many employees believe there is a double standard that applies favorably to management. The ones issuing the message regarding the higher standard are the ones needing to adhere to it the most. Again, maladies suffered by IRS employees are the same as those suffered by the public in general.

However, how these maladies are handled is what becomes important. Also, while others in the general public may suffer similar maladies few, if any, would have the potential for the significant personal impact that IRS employees have on the taxpaying public.

A perfect example of how the double standard works can be seen in the situation regarding the alleged failure to adhere to the rules and regulations by a top level executive of IRS. IRS has very strict rules regarding treatment of travel funds. Employees traveling on government business are able to obtain travel advance funds to cover their expenses.

The employee would generally estimate the cost of the trip, hotel, airfare, automobile rental, food, and various other miscellaneous costs. The requested advance should be as close to the actual cost as possible. The rule is that once you have obtained the advance you should then proceed to file a travel voucher every thirty days to offset the advanced amount. Within thirty days of completing the travel the travel advance should be accounted for on a travel voucher with no funds outstanding.

Since there are employees who are in travel status consistently they are often allowed to maintain a travel advance outstanding in an amount that would cover sixty to ninety days of travel costs. This is to prevent the necessary business travel from becoming a hardship on employees.

It was a known fact that an IRS national office top level executive had maintained a $7000.00 travel advance for well over a year. Admittedly he did travel a lot, however, not to the extent that he should have used the government's money for such an extensive period of time. He was one of the top bosses inside IRS so therefore no one questioned him. However, he couldn't keep it a secret because travel vouchers all go to the same central location for reimbursement regardless of whether the traveler was an employee or a manager.

IRS employees being IRS employees, the news of the amount of the outstanding travel advance traveled faster than anything you might imagine and it became common knowledge that once again the double standard was being used.

Observing all of the outrageous things going on in IRS, I knew at the beginning of the 1998 Congressional Hearings that someone in IRS had to be the fall guy. The problems that were identified during the Hearings were really the result of executive level management's incompetence; however, even if that had not been the case someone had to fall in IRS' attempt to appease Congress and the public.

What is most interesting to me about the situation is the double standard aspect that IRS continues to operate under. According to an article in the In Government Executive magazine Dick Kirschten states, "Mike Dolan paid the career bureaucrats ultimate price giving up his job in the midst of political controversy and lived to tell the tale." Most managers would not have lived to tell the tale.

Kirschten goes on to say, "In the theater of Washington, the classic Punch-and-Judy ritual of politician thwacking bureaucrat is always an audience favorite. When federal agencies come under attack, the script frequently includes howls for the scalps of highly placed executives. But the behind-the-scenes secret shared by the entire cast-is that the stoic civil servant who takes a high-visibility beating is usually simply paying the price for an unpopular policy gone awry."

I am in agreement with the following statement quoted by Kirschten, "The Washington Post identified Dolan as "the necessary whipping boy" whose departure would clear the way for a fresh start by a new IRS commissioner." It is clear that the Post was correct; however, once again a double standard was used because had a lower level manager been responsible for anything that contributed to unfavorable publicity for IRS that manager would have paid a higher price. He or she would have been taken out of the job and demoted to a lower level professional position or terminated depending upon the person in charge. At any rate that manager would not have been lauded in public and certainly would not have been presented with an award as Dolan was when he received the Government Executive Leadership Award, cosponsored by the National Capital Area Chapter of the American Society of Public Administration.

Dick Kirschten's article continued to comment on Dolan's role as a whipping boy when he said, "When the Senate held hearings last September to rail against purported abuses by federal tax collectors, Michael P. Dolan, then acting commissioner of the Internal Revenue Service, was featured on television news reports as the man in the hot seat."

While Dolan was at the helm national executive level management of IRS was alleged to also be responsible for allowing many, many executives to go unpunished for various infractions including sexual harassment and cheating, to name a few. It was alleged that complaints regarding executives were sent to Dolan's level, an allegation that came out during the Hearings and it was alleged that not a single one was processed to the extent that anyone suffered any consequence. A few executives were allowed to resign and a few were sent from one region to another. Again, employees and some lower graded managers would have been fired for the same complaints.

Kirschten's article stated that during the Senate's airing of gripes against the IRS Dolan was charged with failing to take disciplinary action against top agency officials allegedly guilty of wrong doing. He continued on to say, "The

General Accounting Office is reviewing the matter, but Dolan says he's confident he will be fully exonerated. "I took a number of disciplinary actions, including several that were severe," he says. "On the other end of the equation, I found allegations made against senior managers that turned out to be baseless."

Dolan's statement may turn out to be true; however, most IRS managers do not believe that executives and lower level managers are treated the same. I have personally seen employees and lower level managers fired for indiscretions while executives accused to the same thing are just transferred to another district for having done the same thing.

One of the best examples of the double standard was brought to my attention during the last division chiefs conferences I attended before I retired. The conference was held in Walnut Creek, California and one of the invited guests was a well known national office executive.

He was known to be a non-recovering alcoholic who had demonstrated serious conduct unbecoming to him as an individual as well as to the organization. In the late afternoon of the first day of the conference our then highly respected assistant regional commissioner went to the airport to pick up the executive who was flying in from Washington, D.C.

It was after the dinner hour when he returned with the guest and a group of division chiefs were in the hospitality suite having drinks. The assistant regional commissioner brought in what was an obviously drunk executive. The assistant regional commissioner said hello, stayed around for about ten minutes and made a hasty retreat from the room.

Before I get further into this discussion, I need to clarify a point. Many times the executives are invited not because anyone is interested in having them speak, but because schedules of conferences are shared with national office and certain executives indicate an interest in attending and participating in the conference. Therefore, they are considered invited.

Back to the story, the national office executive was obviously drunk when he had been picked up because the assistant regional commissioner had not been gone long enough to have stopped in a bar. The assistant regional commissioner was highly respected and considered to be a straight arrow kind of guy. He was also well liked. He was not the kind of person you could picture accompanying a drunk all evening. Evidently he felt the same way about himself which is probably why he left soon after delivering the executive.

The executive almost fell onto the couch after entering the hospitality room. He was talking loud and slurring his words. Even though we were all adults this was a very bad example of the leadership at the top. It was also another example of the double standard by national level management allowing a known non-recovering alcoholic to continue to function in his position while embarrassing everyone with whom he came in contact.

If he had been a rank and file employee he would have been fired a long time ago or at the very least made to participate in the Employee Assistance Program (EAP) as a condition of his employment. The EAP was a program for employees with problems that interfered with successful performance on the job. Had he been required to get involved in EAP he would have had the opportunity for whatever treatment determined appropriate, physical, mental, or emotional.

It was a well known fact that this executive drank too much and that a lot of his drinking was done during his lunch hour on work days. The unwritten rule of the loyal employees in his office was that he must always have an employee accompany him when he left the office in an effort to prevent or at least minimize the number of drinks he had. This didn't stop him from drinking, but I suppose it may have prevented him from driving as subordinates always drove when accompanying the boss. Don't they in every organization?

A couple of nationally known stories circulate about this sad man. Once on a dance floor at an organization gathering, while drunk, he made a nasty pass at an employee's wife in front of the employee. The employee "decked" him and knocked him out. The employee was given a letter of warning for conduct unbecoming. Nothing was done to the executive. After all he was an executive.

At another gathering the executive urinated all over himself and he didn't even know it. Ultimately this man was transferred to a small district in a position of less needed authority and involvement. He was able to maintain his pay level and the last I heard of him he continues to drink and continues to humiliate everyone around him.

Setting a good example is clearly not on the list of priorities for a lot of IRS executives. Misusing leave, vacation and/or sick leave is an offense for which one can be fired in the federal government. This rule clearly is not applied to IRS executives.

IRS employees earn a specific number of hours a month for sick leave and annual (vacation) leave purposes. Sick leave does not have a cap. In otherwords an unlimited amount may be accumulated and carried over from year to year. Thousands of hours can be earned and at the time of retirement it can be converted into time to be added to the actual years of service worked.

While employees cannot receive actual dollars for unused sick leave it ultimately becomes a monetary reward because it increases the length of time worked on which retirement pay is based.

All employees below the executive level are able to accumulate a maximum of 240 hours of annual leave. This leave can be carried over from year to year. Any annual leave over 240 hours must be used before the year-ends or it will be lost. Until a few years ago executives were allowed to earn and retain an unlimited amount of annual leave.

Upon retiring, employees receive a lump sum for unused annual leave. Obviously this rule provides an incentive for employees to hold on to as much annual leave as possible. Annual Leave accrued over a period of thirty years of employment increases in value from what the employees were paid when they were hired to what they were paid at the time of their retirement. For executives this amount increases significantly as they may have been making $25,000 a year at the time they were hired and most have retired making over a $100,000.

Employees start earning annual leave as soon as they are hired. Those who eventually become executives have been making what would be about $20 an hour and end up making $80 an hour or more. This means the annual leave that was worth the equivalent of $20 is now worth $80 or more an hour. One director I worked for told me he was going to receive a lump sum in excess of $60,000 for his unused annual leave when he retired.

Somewhere along the line someone in IRS discovered executives were misusing leave privileges. Executives were carrying all of their leave over each year and not using it for vacations, yet they were taking off from the job for extended periods of time. They just didn't call it a vacation. A cap was then established to limit the amount of leave that could be carried over.

An executive in one of the eastern districts had established a record for not having used leave for a significant number of years. However, everyone in management knew he actually did take vacations. He tied most of his vacations into business trips, therefore he did not have to use personal leave. He simply tacked on additional days when traveling on business and neglected to use his accumulated leave. With this kind of situation being common knowledge in the organization, what kind of example did he set for subordinate managers. Again, "Do what I say, not what I do." was the main theme in this situation.

The integrity among executive level managers has been reduced to a very low level. Part of this is due to a general feeling that if you are high enough in the organization the "good ole boys" will circle the wagons to protect the image of the executive level. There are some women executives now and it will be interesting to see whether the "good ole boys" will allow the women to join the club.

If you are a manager but not executive level, heaven help you. A perfect example of the level of integrity among executives was demonstrated in a conversation with one of the assistant district director's assigned to Laguna during my tenure. On a trip to a division chiefs conference while waiting for a shuttle bus outside the airport in northern California along with the assistant director and several of my peer division chiefs, the assistant director told us before he retired he would be sure to use all of his sick leave.

Now, you have to be an insider to fully appreciate and understand what he meant by that statement. First of all, it is a fact known by every manager, and I do mean every manager and most employees, that using your sick leave provides better monetary return than saving the leave to be added on to years worked at the time of retirement. If you use eight hours of sick leave you get paid at the current rate of your salary. If you save the leave you get a partial benefit in that there is a formula used to add the leave on to your total years of service which increases the time paid for retirement purposes. You do not get paid hour for hour therefore you lose from a monetary standpoint.

Many, many employees, executives included, take off on sick leave just prior to retiring in an effort to use up their sick leave. I have known employees and managers to take off for more than three months on sick leave only to retire before coming back and they were not sick.

Just about everyone knows this and everyone looks the other way and allows it. The major problem I have with this kind of a thing is that IRS and other government agencies pick and choose which actions they consider illegal and/or immoral.

The same executive that made the statement regarding usage of his sick leave was involved in a rather unpleasant situation early on in his stint as Assistant Director. The details of the situation have been kept under wraps.

However, I do know that the Director in the district in which he was selected did not want this person as his assistant and he told me so. He told me he favored someone else who was in the running, but he refused to tell me why.

The unwelcome status of the Assistant Director became apparent during an offsite meeting with the director's staff, which included all of the division chiefs. This meeting happened to be the very first one the Assistant Director had the "pleasure" of attending in his new district".

During this particular meeting, as one of his first tasks, the new Assistant Director advised the staff of his expectations for us. Being an arrogant group of people this did not go over well as some voiced loudly at one point when the Assistant Director left the room. He was so new to the district he was still dealing with his move from another district and had to leave the meeting to make a phone call to his former district.

It seemed as though several of the chiefs felt the Assistant had talked down to them in laying out his expectations. The Director being his usual charming sensitive self immediately upon his return told his Assistant, "The division chiefs are concerned about your previous statements regarding your expectations. They feel you were talking down to them." He told him this in front of all of us.

To better understand this you need to keep in mind that the Director had not wanted this particular person assigned as his Assistant. In addition to the unknown reason for not wanting this person as his assistant, I was told it was believed that the Director who was from the old, old school did not think much of the morals of the Assistant.

It was said that in a former district the Assistant Director had become involved with his subordinate and even though he ended up marrying her certain executives seemed to hold that against him. Unwanted sexual encounters are a definite no, no in IRS on paper although in practice it is probably done everyday somewhere in the organization and it is called sexual harassment. However, this situation did not seem to fit in that category as the two people got married.

What is so humorous about the high morality the executives tried to demonstrate is that many of them were guilty of their own transgressions, they just happened to chose to point fingers at ones they wanted everyone to believe they were not guilty of.

At any rate, the Director chose to embarrass his new Assistant and all of the division chiefs by telling the Assistant to his face in front of the chiefs what the chiefs had said. Of course the Assistant immediately apologized for how the chiefs had taken his statements and insisted that he had not intended them as put downs.

Well, you can be sure this meeting set the tone for future relationships in the district. Even though everyone smiled at each other the Director had pitted the chiefs against his Assistant. It didn't seem like a smart thing to do from my viewpoint. However, no one ever said this Director was the smartest person when it came to social graces.

The Assistant Director had come up through the ranks in Collection Division which generally would provide an affinity to those of us in Collection Division. To ensure a good working relationship with the Assistant Director, after the meeting the chief collection and his assistant sucked up to the Assistant Director by telling him, "We think you received a dirty deal during the meeting and we want to let you know that we were not part of it. We did not have a problem with your expectations." This went over well with the Assistant Director and from that time on the Collection Division did have a better relationship with him than the other divisions. On the surface he got along well with the others however, they each took every opportunity to snipe at each other.

A manager in the region told me about an allegation regarding an executive misuse of a government car. On one occasion an executive's secretary found it necessary to report the executive to his boss. While technically speaking she was right to report him, ordinarily you would not immediately report your boss to Inspection until you were sure you had something to report.

It appears that the executive took a government car home over the weekend and unless you were specifically authorized to take a government automobile home you were required to return it to the building at the end of each work day. The executive used the automobile on a Friday and even though he only lived about one-half mile away from the building he worked in he took the car home and kept it all weekend. He subsequently used the car to go to a meeting in another district the following Monday. The impropriety was taking the car home and keeping it over the weekend.

The impropriety was discovered by his secretary, as she was the control point for all government cars. On of the most serious infractions one can commit inside IRS is misuse of government cars. Many employees have been suspended and some fired for misuse. The rules are so strict many employees will not drive a government car unless they have to. Government employees are reimbursed for mileage of their personally owned automobiles; however, to save on the wear and tear of their automobiles the government maintains a pool of cars that may be assigned to employees.

The biggest problem with using a government car is that you are not allowed to stop anywhere that is not totally job related. If the car is used during the day you may stop for lunch but after work even if you have errands that are on your direct route home you may not use the government car to run those errands. In addition, you may not have anyone riding with you unless it is job related and the passenger is absolutely necessary to the job you are doing.

As I previously said the secretary was responsible for the cars assigned to the office and when the executive did not return the car keys to her that Friday afternoon she advised his boss of the situation first thing that Monday morning. She took personal pride in being conscientious in doing her job.

The Resources Management Division had ultimate responsibility for all district government cars and the secretary informed that office about the status of the situation and an employee advised the Resources Management Chief. Now this Chief took great delight in having "something" on the executive.

The executive's boss happened to be out of the district during this time and so the Chief; Resources Management sent him a voice mail by phone advising of the situation. Since the executive was supposed to be attending a meeting in another city that Monday, the Chief, Resources Management took it upon herself to call that office and to verify that he in deed was there.

She had exceeded her bounds, as it was not her job to check up on the executive. She had a responsibility to report something if she felt there was a potential integrity problem, but not to actually do the investigating herself. The Chief, Resources Management knew the executive's wife worked in another city and since he said he drove there she felt he probably let his wife ride with him. That certainly sounds logical to me; however, executive denied it.

Well as luck would have it the executive's assistant happened to be acting for the executive's boss Jim as both the executive and his boss were out of the district on that Monday. After being informed of this situation Jim called the acting assistant and told him he wanted him to talk to the executive about this situation first thing that Tuesday morning when he returned to the office.

Now remember, the executive was the assistant's boss, and yet Jim wanted him to discuss this embarrassing situation with him on his behalf. He told the Jim he didn't think it would be appropriate for him to do that but Jim said it was what he wanted him to do.

Even though he didn't like the idea of having to more or less counsel his own boss he had enough nerve to do so. Early the following Tuesday morning he went in to talk to the executive, his boss and he did feel really silly and embarrassed. The entire scene was totally inappropriate.

He told the executive he was very uncomfortable having to discuss the situation with him, but that he had been given marching orders by Jim, the big boss. I think by then Jim had treated him so shabbily on so many occasions he wasn't surprised that he would use the embarrassing tactics he had placed them in. However, he was visibly upset with his hands shaking and he said he had kept the car over the weekend because he had returned very late on Friday from a visit to one of the outlying offices. He also said he had not used the car that weekend for any reason. He said he did take his wife to the train station, but that he had done so in his personally owned car and that he had also taken the train to his meeting.

The executive was greatly disturbed with the Chief, Resources Management for her having contacted the Director. He then proceeded to criticize his boss Jim by saying, "I use the government car to save the organization money unlike others like Jim, who use their own cars to ensure the receipt of large travel reimbursement checks." He also stated, "I think the Chief, Resources Management is a double dealing, dangerous, treacherous person."

Nothing happened to the executive regarding the alleged misuse of the car. I believe Jim and the Chief, Resources Management had gotten their satisfaction in humiliating him by accusing him of problems with his integrity. I do believe the executive failed to utilize good common sense with the government car. He should have at least returned it over the weekend since he lived so close to the office. By holding it through Monday evening he prevented someone else from being able to use it in their daily duties.

Most IRS districts have experienced situations that were an embarrassment to the Director and to the entire organization. Many of these embarrassments occurred at all managers meetings. Many of those all managers meetings, division chiefs conferences, and meetings in general have been bad news for IRS. One well known situation in an eastern district occurred at the time of an executive level meeting.

The director in the district where the meeting was held required employees to pick up executives at the airport and required them to prepare the food for the guests. They were also required to wait on the visitors by serving food and providing bar service. All of this was done during work hours and was done by unwilling employees.

The director probably didn't recognize how unwilling the employees were and then again he probably did not care. The employees were so unwilling they complained to their union representatives and caused a big furor over the so called "slave labor". Most of the employees involved were in low grade clerical positions and were primarily females and minorities.

The employees were said to complain partly because the director didn't even speak to them on a daily basis when he passed them in the hallway yet he had them provide their services to the "elite" group. This executive was encouraged to retire and being a wise man he did because the public had been made aware of the situation. If it could have been kept under wraps the man would never have been encouraged to leave because after all he was a member in good standing in the good ole boys club.

Many IRS employees are terminated or given progressive discipline as a result of what is commonly called conduct unbecoming. One of the worse cases in this area occurred during an in office audit conducted by an office auditor.

The auditor was conducting the audit of a female taxpayer's income tax return. The taxpayer was sitting at a table across from the auditor. The auditor committed what has to take the prize for the most filthy, despicable act I have ever heard of.

Well into the audit the taxpayer felt something wet on her skirt. She then began to realize it was coming from the auditor from under the table. Horrors upon horrors, the taxpayer realized the auditor had masturbated and what appeared to be semen had landed on her skirt.

She immediately reported the incident to the auditor's manager who immediately called in Inspection Division. The situation was investigated, the taxpayer's skirt was professionally examined and it was determined that semen was actually on her skirt. The employee was put on administrative leave and was ultimately terminated. I was informed that this wasn't the first time the employee had masturbated while in the office, it was however, the first time a taxpayer was involved.

MANAGEMENT DECISIONS

At least once a year the regional executive schedules reviews of the various districts. They are to review certain work procedures for quality, legality, adherence to rules, regulations, and for numerous other items. Many hours are used in the districts preparing for these reviews. The district and/or division's year end appraisal depends on the success of the reviews.

Many times national office joined in the review process with the region, but only in the winter time if the review was going to be conducted in such places as southern California or Hawaii. On occasions it was obvious in Laguna Niguel, California that the review was not important to the national office, but was just something someone decided to do to get away from the cold winter weather in the east.

When the reviews were being scheduled, the district in which the review was going to be conducted generally advised the analysts of the hotels within the prescribed commute area. In an effort to be economical the reviewers/analysts were suppose to stay as close to the site of the review as possible, in the most economical hotels possible.

However, southern California was so popular in the winter time and so well known that the analysts made their own decisions and many times stayed in hotels thirty miles or more away from the site, in ocean side hotels.

A most popular site was Dana Point an area near the ocean. These hotels cost more and required long commutes in the southern California traffic. To be sure they did not work overtime the analysts arrived late and left early only working about six hours a day. Many times they arrived a day or two earlier than they needed to and extended the review longer than necessary. It was a long standing joke in some of the offices as to what deadbeats the analysts were, particularly the national office analysts.

Even the first line managers recognized how the analysts were ripping off the government. Did this happen all of the time? Absolutely not, but it happened often enough to be noticed by managers in the district. I suppose this kind of situation should not have been surprising as the reputation of some of the analysts in the national office was atrocious. Employees working in national office had extremely difficult times getting promoted out of that office unless they knew someone very well in the districts.

Although common sense told us all analysts were not deadbeats we were very cautious in selecting anyone from national office. The overall national office was ridiculed and laughed at. It was said there were so many people working in national office that no one knew the exact number.

Once when I attended a meeting in national office I asked several managers how many employees worked there and they told me that no one really knew for sure but that it was suspected that there were somewhere around 12,000. Now that's a perfect example of how IRS the largest accounting agency in the world operates.

The national office management and IRS in general suffers from lack of effective controls, particularly in the financial area. The fiascoes of the national office analysts being able to defraud the government in the way they misused travel funds is a perfect example. My knowledge of the misuse of travel funds is not special information available only to a few, this information is well known throughout the service in the management ranks. This is one of the many reasons why IRS is always running out of money. The organization really does not know what the money is being used for many times.

I personally attended several meetings in national office that required me to travel the day before because of the time difference, stay overnight at a hotel, rent a car, and leave about noon the next day on the return trip for home. The agendas at the meetings were questionable many times and a definite waste of money. I once attended a meeting where a group was supposed to be formed to plan training for managers. I made two trips to national office and then I never heard anything else about the group. It was never formed.

In 1994 I was selected along with a large group of people from around the country to participate in a task force to redesign IRS. This group had been going on for several years. Many, many managers and union officials participated in this study. Millions of dollars were spent.

One of the group's primary objectives was to establish positions that would combine the duties of both collection and examination division employees. I personally spent two months, January and February of 1994 in Washington, D.C. working on this project. I was given approval to travel home every few weeks at government expense. My hotel, travel, and food were paid for on a per diem basis for the entire two months.

Many employees were there when I arrived and many were there when I left, some remained many more months than I did. Many of the employees involved in this project were managers, division level and above. Several executives came and went for days and weeks at a time. Two executives were assigned full time on-site responsibility for everyone involved in the project.

After years of work and millions of dollars the plan was determined to be too faulty to be workable. During my assignment many discussions with other division level managers centered around how ridiculous and unworkable the entire project was.

The deputy commissioner and his staff were believed to have blinders on because they seemed to believe they were on the verge of something big for IRS. Even the union thought the project was ridiculous and they fought it tooth and nail and refused to accept any part of it. Once again the deputy commissioner and national level management had thrown away millions and millions of dollars.

Several years ago IRS started to place special emphasis on OIC (Offer in Compromise) procedures in an effort to collect more money as well as supposedly, to allow taxpayers a way of getting straight with the tax system and resolving their tax problems. OIC procedures provide for taxpayers to make the IRS an offer to pay a lesser amount on their tax liability when it has been determined the total amount is uncollectible. Many taxpayers want to get the matter of their tax liability resolved in a final manner and this is the only way it can be done other than paying the full amount.

The procedure for placing liabilities in a suspense status, a temporary uncollectible status, is just that, a temporary status which means the account may be reactivated at some period in time. The OIC program has been available since at least before I joined the service. However, it was never popular and many IRS employees did not like the program and did not make it available to the public unless they had to.

Most individuals did not even know about the program. Finally, IRS wised up and looked at the many hundreds of thousand delinquent accounts in the queue inventory. Many of these cases had been in the field and IRS had not been able to collect any money because the taxpayers financial situation did not show funds available.

IRS began to realize that many delinquent taxpayers might be able to find a way to come up with the money if they had the opportunity to pay a lesser amount. Therefore, special emphasis was placed on the OIC program.

The basic idea was for a taxpayer to request an OIC and for the revenue officer to collect financial information from the taxpayer to determine if the taxpayer could pay the full amount or whether the revenue officer could collect the full amount if the taxpayer didn't voluntarily pay.

Once it was determined the full amount was not available, if the taxpayer met certain criteria used in a formula, and if the taxpayer felt that he/she could beg or borrow the money from a relative or friend the revenue officer would approve an OIC. The taxpayer would pay the lesser amount and the account would be closed for all eternity. Liens would be released if any had been filed and the taxpayer could breathe easier.

Word came down from national office that the district collection divisions were expected to make OIC's a priority. As usual in IRS some districts adhered to that direction, but most didn't. In Laguna the program was elevated to a higher status than it had been in most districts. The director in Laguna Niguel, being the good trooper he was told me we needed to get moving on the program right away.

With me being the good trooper I was, I immediately got my subordinate managers involved. My director was very much into outreach programs where employees went out in the public to "help" the taxpaying public. He had all divisions going out to meet with taxpayer representative groups pushing the OIC program.

Well, we were so successful we received thousands and thousands of requests for OIC's. We received far more than we had the staff to handle. In addition, the staff assigned to work most of the OIC's did not get the kind of managerial direction they should have from their branch chief and so our efforts suffered.

We received what seemed like daily beatings from the taxpayer representatives and from the press in our failure to process the OIC's in a timely manner. It took at least six months to really get adjusted to the turn around in IRS attitude and to get the program set up. Eventually we got a handle on the situation and got it under control. The main problem here was that we were told to start marching in one direction without anyone taking the time to look into what lay ahead.

IRS has never been an agency that planned ahead. The agency is now trying to make a turn around on the OIC program. Of course the public has not been made aware that offers are no longer a priority with IRS.

After the high profile marketing strategy IRS used to sell the OIC program the organization cannot afford to let the public know what a fiasco it turned out to be. In the final analysis it was found that most of the offers were made on liabilities below $10,000 while the division cutoff score for working cases at that time was $75,000.

The division in Laguna Niguel as well as Los Angeles and many other west coast districts had to establish dollar cutoff scores for the cases they could not afford to work due to limited human resources. The inventories were so large the Laguna Niguel division established a score that would only allow cases with liabilities of $75,000 or more to be automatically generated from the service centers.

Taxpayers liabilities are generated out to the district offices from service centers. If a district has more cases than the division can handle effectively the cutoff score will enable cases with a lesser liability to be stored in the division's queue which is maintained in the service center's computer data base. Cases at or above the cutoff score are considered priority cases and therefore they are generated immediately after the required notices are sent to the taxpayer. Other cases are culled out as needed in the district. To market a program that causes the division to work cases with an average liability of $10,000 while the queue holds thousands of cases with significantly higher liabilities is asinine. But, this is exactly what IRS did.

About a year or so after we had expended significant resources towards trying to work the OIC program effectively IRS started a project that seemed sound for all intents and purposes. The project was called CMIS (Collection Management Information System). The system was designed to cost out work projects to determine cost effectiveness. The projects were rotated to various districts and the one rotated to Laguna Niguel was the OIC project.

It just happened that as the CMIS project in Laguna was winding down a member of the IRS Commissioner's Advisory Group was visiting the district. In an effort to attempt to impress the visitor a presentation was provided of the findings of the OIC project. The director was always willing to have Laguna showcase its projects because in all honesty the district was one of the most effective in the nation in most things.

However, the director made a mistake this time. The CMIS group had found little monetary value in the OIC program, yet the collection division had been required to become tremendously involved and as a result had the largest inventory in the nation.

The member of the Commissioner's Advisory Group asked a very pertinent but embarrassing question that made the district and IRS look very foolish. He questioned, "Was cost management done prior to emphasizing and publicizing the OIC Program?" The answer was a very quiet no.

The Academy of Sciences, an organization that often evaluates IRS, has been quoted as saying, "IRS always moves on to new programs before old ones are validated." A cost effectiveness evaluation should have been done before emphasizing OIC's. We could then have worked OIC's in a more routine manner and while we probably would have still experienced an increase in inventory we could have held it at a workable level. Once again IRS had squandered thousands and thousands of dollars on a failure.

At some point someone just has to hold the Deputy Commissioners accountable and responsible for all of the failures that happen during their watch. I say the deputy commissioners because the past couple of commissioners were obviously just figure heads and left the managing of IRS to the unqualified actions of some of the deputies.

Examples of bad management decisions are readily available throughout IRS and most of them just needed common sense decisions made. A perfect example of a not only bad but a stupid example was seen in one of the Service Centers. It was found out that an executive level manager there was living with an internal auditor who was conducting a review of the service center.

It is the duty of Internal Audit to review districts and service centers to ensure all requirements are being met and to identify and/or prevent illegal actions. It was unconscionable for this executive to have allowed the audit to go on with his live in lover participating. I can't believe no one knew about his living status. In IRS the saying is that there are no secrets, that everyone knows everyone else's business. The executive was subsequently reassigned to a higher position in a district. The auditor, his live in lover, quit her job and moved with him to the new district.

Chapter Four

IRS HIERARCHY

Most Americans are required to pay income taxes and many, in terms of numbers, end up having to deal with IRS either because they did not file required income tax returns, did not pay taxes due, through a mistake made by the taxpayer or, as a result of an IRS error. Most Americans do not have any idea how IRS works and most don't care as long as it docs not impact them negatively from a personal standpoint; however, in order for a taxpayer to be able to have his/her rights protected and to have any advantage in the system it is necessary to have some knowledge of how the system works. Having some general knowledge of the IRS hierarchy enables taxpayers to know who is in charge and what path they need to take when problems arise, particularly when the problems appear to be irreconcilable.

To some intent the IRS is like any other bureaucracy with so much red tape it is near impossible for an average citizen to be able to penetrate the management hierarchy sufficiently enough to be heard. However, IRS management will do almost anything to prevent being tarnished in the public. In the position of being one of and maybe the world's most visible government agency, IRS responds to what is called "controlled correspondence" much more readily and timely than many other agencies.

Correspondence that fits into the "controlled correspondence" category include complaints from taxpayers that have been sent to political representatives, IRS national or regional executive level management or, to the President of the United States. Routine complaint letters that are received direct from taxpayers to the employee working their case will not receive as much attention as those sent to the taxpayer's congressional representative.

Complaints sent to the taxpayer's congressional representative or to members of Congress and/or the President, according to IRS rules, will be responded to within prescribed time frames and for the most part mangers attempt to meet those time frames. In addition, those complaints sent to IRS executive level management will be responded to promptly because IRS recognizes that anyone sending a letter through the hierarchy will also send it to others such as elected officials.

Letters received from the executive level of management in IRS are considered to be of topmost importance and are given short time frames for responses. These letters are monitored all the way down the line from national level to the district field offices. The responses are expected to address each issue listed in the complaint. Admission of guilt on the part of IRS employees is not necessarily expected and in all honesty it is frowned upon.

Apologies are expected if IRS has erred; however, the apologies are expected to be written in what is known to IRS managers as "a round about way". These apologies are easily identified because they are generally phrases with certain words such as, "If you were offended --------, we are truly sorry", or something such as "It is not our intention to create an unnecessary hardship".

One of the obvious reasons why complaints that have been sent through political representatives become a priority with IRS is because IRS does not want the ire of congress to descend upon the agency. The urgency and importance of these complaints then create a method for taxpayers to ensure IRS takes the complaints seriously.

As a U. S. citizen and having had to contact a few other government agencies regarding personal issues that impacted my life, I realized that regardless of the reason why, IRS is much more committed to addressing written issues. I remember once having written the Social Security Administration registering a complaint and requesting a written reply. I did not receive a response and so I decided to write my congressional representative and request assistance. I did receive assistance, but even then it took about four months before I received a response from Social Security.

IRS guidelines require a written response from the local District Director within fifteen days from receipt of the complaint. Of course an extension may be granted if it is absolutely necessary.

The IRS maintains and controls a somewhat elaborate system on complaints received through political representatives. The complaints are logged in and copies sent down to the next level of management all the way down to the manager of the alleged taxpayer abuser. The alleged abuser is required to provide a written response to the immediate manager who responds to the next level, who responds to the next level and so on and so on.

The final, or what is hoped to be the final level response, is prepared by the Division Chief for the District Director's response. Changes are made all along the way with letters sent back many times because either they do not address all issues outlined in the complaint or the issues are not addressed adequately.

The IRS is currently in the process of overhauling its entire hierarchical system with various positions being eliminated. The purpose of the changes is to enhance IRS' ability to be more accountable and to provide better treatment to taxpayers, treatment that is more technically accurate and courteous at the same time.

The basic hierarchy in operation during my career included what is shown on Exhibit 4. The IRS regions, districts, and service centers underwent a drastic change just at the time I started preparing to retire. Exhibit 4 shows IRS during my tenure. Since then regions were restructured into four operations explained in detail below.

As a result of the 1997 IRS Hearings great debate was initiated towards restructuring the Internal Revenue Service. A National Commission on Restructuring was implemented and this body issued a report released June 25, 1997. According to the report the commission recommended drastic changes for IRS management and oversight of IRS.

The commission saw these changes as critical based on the interaction of IRS with more citizens than any other government agency and the fact that IRS collects 95% of the revenue needed to fund the federal government. The report further stated that "The current structure, which includes Congress, the President, the Department of the Treasury and the IRS itself, does not allow the IRS to set and maintain consistent long-term strategy and priorities, nor to develop and execute focused plans for improvement."

The commission recommended nine key changes including congressional oversight of the IRS becoming restructured, a new board of directors, five year term for IRS Commissioner, stable funding additional training, updating its technology, development of a strategic marketing plan for electronic filing, improving taxpayers' ability to recover damages for wrongful actions by IRS, and simplification of tax law.

What with commissions being commissions and consisting of some members of Congress, in the great debate on what is needed to restructure IRS, there were five dissenting members with twelve others signing the report Included as members of the commission were Fred Goldberg, former IRS Commissioner, two senators, one representative and Bob Tobias national president of NTEU (National Treasury Employees Union).

The commission's report recommended the establishment of an independent seven-member board of directors to oversee the IRS within the Department of the Treasury. It was further recommended that the board consist of the Treasury Secretary, a representative from NTEU and five individuals from private industry. Board members would be appointed by the President with confirmation required by the Senate to serve staggered five-year terms. The board would have responsibility for overall governance of IRS with no involvement in areas of interpretation or enforcement of tax laws.

One of the most significant and most needed aspects of the board of directors would be to appoint and remove IRS senior leadership and to hold IRS management accountable. It was recommended that the members of the board have experience particularly relevant to a 100,000 employee organization. The board members were recommended to receive "appropriate compensation" for their responsibilities.

Holding IRS management accountable for their actions is something definitely needed and long past due, particularly at the executive level. The executives have operated as a good ole boys club for many, many, many years with the Deputy Commissioner being a member in good standing. That is one of the reasons why no action has been taken against many executives for transgressions including fraud, sexual harassment, and conduct unbecoming, to name a few.

It was recommended that the board members not have access to taxpayer information. In my opinion this is a wise decision as the fewer people with access to taxpayer's personal information the better the entire system is.

It was recommended that the board would appoint the commissioner to a five-year term with flexibility to pay the commissioner a more competitive salary. It was very interesting to read that the report stated that only five of the current 73 most senior executives have been at IRS for less than fifteen years.

This is one of the most serious problems IRS is faced with, starting with the Commissioner's position.

It is very apparent that many commissioners have little or no knowledge of what goes on in IRS. While most of them have some kind of tax experience and tax background they are shielded from daily goings on. The Deputy Commissioner actually runs the organization and while this should be acceptable to some degree if there is an ineffective Deputy Commissioner such as has been seen in the past, then the Commissioner is left in the dark.

Having attended meetings where the last three former Commissioner's spoke to management it was very apparent who knew what. Commissioner Shirley Peterson, the first female commissioner was definitely a figure head. She gave a goodwill kind of message and then turned everything else over to the Deputy Dolan. Dolan is a very large, overweight man and she is a very small feminine person and at every meeting Dolan towered over her and she gave the appearance of acquiescing to him on issues that were important to the organization.

The next Commissioner, Margaret Milner Richardson, another female, gave the appearance of being in charge and let it be known that Dolan answered to her; however, she was unable to answer questions that were important to the organization and to management. She had to look to Dolan to answer questions he should have briefed her on before the meeting.

As mentioned above, three members of the commission dissented regarding the restructuring of IRS. The primary reasons for the dissent involved concerns regarding inadequate oversight of the IRS, delays and uncertainty in the process of reform, potential conflicts of interest, and a lack of accountability of the proposed board of directors.

A major concern expressed dealt with the idea that a part-time board of directors may not be able to give IRS the type of oversight it needs. The dissenters felt IRS needs full-time oversight and attention from a group who would make IRS their priority and not just their part-time interest.

The dissenters also expressed a concern that the recommendations as written would make the commissioner exempt from accountability and they felt that would be unconstitutional. The recommendation would have the commissioner appointed by the board and would not be directly accountable to the President or any other elected official.

Regarding the area of constitutionality the dissenting report stated, "The courts have held that any limitation on the President's power to remove officials performing core executive functions, such as the IRS Commissioner or members of the proposed board, impedes the President's ability to satisfy his constitutional obligation to take care that the laws can be faithfully executed."

In 1998 IRS underwent a Restructuring and Reform Act designed to reorganize into four separate operations divided by service to taxpayer groups. As a result of the many complaints from the public regarding the allegations of taxpayer abuse and the U. S, Senate hearings in 1998, congress actually came together in bipartisanship to enact tax reform measures in an effort to provide relief for taxpayers.

The restructuring part of the Act established organizational units that are intended to serve taxpayers with similar needs. The four operations are intended to serve individuals, small businesses, large corporations, and tax-exempt organizations. The establishment of the four operations eliminated the IRS's three-tiered geographic organizational structure of national, regional, and district offices.

In an attempt to better serve the public the Restructuring and Reform Act expanded the authority and independence of the Taxpayer Advocate by taking it out of the local districts and establishing a National Taxpayer Advocate. This position actually assumed responsibility for local Taxpayer Advocates, the replacements for the IRS's problem resolution functions that were under local District Directors authority.

The removal of the District Director authority from the taxpayer advocates is one of the best actions taken by IRS. It is extremely difficult to be objective when complaints to an advocate about the district in which the advocate is working. Through the years directors become close to subordinates and I have witnessed the inability to be objective. IRS employees and management bond closer than many non-governmental agencies because it often becomes part of an us and them attitude when dealing with hostile public complaints.

Much of the relief was intended for small business taxpayers who had provided tales of taxpayer abuse in the worse kind of nightmare forms. While on one hand this is good news for small business taxpayers, on the other hand the auditors examining small business tax returns will have more expertise in their particular field. The IRS is specializing in certain business segments.

A few years before I retired IRS had started to create MSSP's, market segment specialization programs. Special teams are formed to focus on certain industries. Some of the industries currently included in the MSSP are entertainment, auto body and repair, car washes, commercial printing, manufacturing, pizza restaurants and used car-dealers. By the time this chapter is being read by the public IRS is expected to have implemented more than one hundred specialization teams.

This market specialization is likened to a double edged sword. If all goes as planned by IRS, in the future small business owners will be audited by an employee who is expected to be customer oriented and efficient with much more effectiveness than in the past. This kind of specialization certainly changes the hierarchy line, but with so much emphasis on customer service the key to being heard when complaining about treatment from IRS employees is to request a meeting with whoever is the person in charge. It is important that the taxpayer making the complaint take steps to be sure that the person hearing the complaint is indeed a manager and not just someone sitting in for the manager.

Chapter Five

REVENUE OFFICER TRAINING

The future of any organization is significantly dependent upon the quality of recruitment and training of new employees. The IRS' track record in both areas leaves much to be desired. Revenue officer training is extensive with a combination of classroom and on the job training provided for newly selected revenue officers. The entire first year is considered the training year.

Since nothing is perfect you can rest assured that IRS training has many shortfalls. The most positive thing that can be said about the training is that an effective time frame is provided. Ordinarily, a full year of training should be sufficient to prepare a trainee to do the job well. Unfortunately, aside from the time frame, IRS training resources are limited and deficient many times.

Problems in IRS revenue officer training begin with the recruitment process followed closely by the selection process. As a result of the official Agreement between IRS and the union, IRS is required to select a percentage of new hires from the inside. Ordinarily, I do not see this as a problem because I do believe employees should be provided with a potential means of being able to progress upward within the system, to better paying jobs with more responsibility. They also need to have incentives to do the best job possible in their current position. It becomes a problem when IRS management starts the hiring process and the anticipated mistakes are made.

I say anticipated mistakes because no matter what is done to avoid them, some of the same mistakes continue to be made. If a procedural mistake is made in the paperwork or in working the hiring lists received from the resources management personnel, many times the resolution to the problem becomes a requirement for IRS to select someone for the job whether they are qualified or not.

Another problem that may not be isolated to IRS is one that results from the appraisal system. Employees rated high for the current job they are doing will be placed high on a hiring list for a potential job whether they actually deserve it or not.

IRS managers are required to provide employees with periodic documentation of the kind of work they are doing. Each employee must be evaluated on a mandated appraisal form on which a number of critical factors are listed.

These critical factors are job related and the documentation provided periodically is supposed to be compiled at the end of the employee's rating period (generally a year) at which time an appraisal has to be prepared. The appraisal is to be completed using numerical factors. The factors are changed from time to time depending upon the agreement with management and the union; however, for numerous years up until I retired, the numeric rating was 5, 4, 3, 2, 1 with 5 being the highest and meaning excellent. It is mandatory that any bargaining union employee rated with a certain number of 4's and above is given a work performance award.

Work performance awards are fine, and again this provides an incentive for some employees. However, in many instances employees are rated 4 and above without any documentation in their folder to back up the numbers. For years this has been a serious problem in IRS, one that management seems unable to resolve.

It is easy to rate someone high if you don't have to provide documentation to back it up. For years many employees were rated so high most of then were starting to get awards when nothing substantial in the quality or quantity of their work had changed. While all divisions in IRS Laguna Niguel became embroiled in this awards situation, the two major divisions, Collection and Examination, were the ones with the most serious impact.

When one of the major divisions started to receive the bulk of the awards the other divisions' managers started to increase the numerical rating of their employees, thus the start of a so called ratings war. After all you could not have most of the awards going to one division. With so many awards being given and the district still being in need of improvement in some areas, management began a push to rate employees in accordance with what they truly deserved.

In Collection Division this became a battle cry to the union. To provide the majority of employees with the rating they truly deserved meant the numerics given on the appraisal for work done the previous year had to be lowered. This did not necessarily mean that the employee's performance had changed. Nor did it necessarily mean that the employee was not performing satisfactorily, but this was the impact the lowered appraisal had on the union and the employees.

In actuality anyone rated an overall 3 was being rated satisfactory. However, since a work performance award was not given for an overall 3 rating it became an accepted fact in the minds of the employees that a rating of overall 3 was unacceptable. Since the rating of 3 was in the middle of the numerical system available to be given to employees on appraisals the employees viewed it as comparable to the grade of c given in California colleges and universities. With the grades a and b being at the top, the grade c is frowned upon many times.

Any change in any appraisal almost always caused a grievance to be filed by the union on behalf of the employee. The over inflated appraisals made anything other than an overall rating of 4 with a sprinkling of 5's unacceptable to most employees. This over inflated rating of employees caused significant budget problems as it became very costly to provide monetary awards from a budget that was being cut annually at the whim of congress depending on which way the wind was blowing at any particular time.

In addition, the over inflated appraisals caused significant problems in the hiring process. Employees applying for revenue officer jobs, the plum job sought after by lower graded clerical type employees, in the Collection Division, ranked high for the job based on an appraisal they did not deserve. This made it very difficult to not select many of them even when it was apparent during the interview process that they were not suitable for the job. It got to the point every non-selection was grieved by the union.

During the grievance process the union always requested the interview papers and they went over them with a fine tooth comb. If a procedural error was made, in accordance with the national Agreement, we had to select the employee.

Unfortunately, as mentioned before, we had many inexperienced managers who were all called on to interview during large hires. Because budgets were frozen almost every year, by the time we got approval to hire so much attrition had occurred we always had to hire large numbers of fifty or more. The newly selected inexperienced managers made many, many mistakes on the paper documents used to document the interviews and to rank the applicants prior to interview. The whole system became a nightmare and was just one more example of an organization out of control.

Several years prior to my retirement, at a time when we had numerous managerial vacancies, I had the opportunity to attempt to do things the way they should have been done all the time and I selected a group of ten potential managers. Since we were in a frozen budget situation and I could not permanently promote the employees to the rank of managers, I established a cadre of managers in an effort to prepare them for the time in which they could be reassigned on a permanent basis.

This cadre of managers was used to provide a temporary selection in a vacant position or when managers were out for any reason for periods of two weeks or more. If a manager was only going to be gone for less than two weeks they generally asked a senior revenue officer to fill in for them.

I decided this was an excellent time for the division to train these future managers and get them prepared for the time when they would become permanent managers. I provided classroom training for them, provided opportunities for them to gain experience by using them to fill in behind managers, and on a periodic basis I had meetings/seminars conducted for them at which time they were able to interact with me and other managers in the division. This was an excellent opportunity to attempt to avoid past problems of having too many inexperienced managers trying to do the job.

I had the Labor Relations staff provide training regarding many personnel situations such as how to deal with grievances, hiring, firing, and many other personnel actions. I was able to keep the cadre managers in place for at least a year when the unfortunate long awaited interference of the district director and the region started.

The regional office issued a mandate that all revenue officers caseloads should be at the maximum level and that the group size of each revenue officer group should be increased from 12 to 15. I did not have a problem with either of these mandates; however, it also included taking the cadre managers and putting them back into groups as revenue officers and assigning them caseloads.

The major problem with all of this is that IRS management goes out of its way to prevent any efforts to forecast or to plan for the future. Some of the major problems in the IRS organization results from not having sufficiently experienced managers as well as not having enough managers with training and or education in the field of managing.

The answer to many of IRS top management problems is to operate on a crisis management basis and to select managers exactly at the moment it is determined they are needed and not in advance when it really counts so that they can be prepared with training and experience.

With the region pressuring the district director, he started to pressure me into placing the cadre managers back in the field. Being the kind of person I am, I ignored his subtle attempts. As I have said previously, the director was the kind of person who did not tell his division chiefs specifically what to do. He just expressed his opinion, his likes and dislikes and expected us to operate in accordance. Well, once again, since the success of the division was my responsibility I decided to hold on to the cadre managers as long as possible. This wasn't easy as I met with the director and the assistant director on a monthly basis at what was considered to be an operations briefing session to discuss the overall operation of the division.

Each month the director asked me for an update on the status of the cadre managers. I never lied outright; however, I did stall and hem and haw around the subject with the bottom line being I held the cadre managers in status quo.

Well as luck would have it I had made the best decision possible for the division, the district and the region because true to form we were given a mandate to hire a large number of revenue officers and for the first time in my entire career the division was better prepared to handle the managing of the new employees. I was able to place all of the cadre managers in a position previously vacant. Even then with the employee turnover being what it was I still had several positions vacant. However, this put the division in the best position possible under the circumstances although I was only able to do this one time. I never again had the luxury of having on hand the staffing standing in the wings waiting to be placed.

A few years later we were once again faced with the problem of where were we going to get the necessary staffing to fill management positions upon hiring new employees. To add to the problem, a few years before I retired we phased out the ACS (Automated Call Sites) located in Fountain Valley and Kearney Mesa, California.

The ACS site was one where most of the collection division clerical and para-professional employees worked. These employees primarily worked on telephones calling taxpayers regarding their delinquent taxes. The ACS sites were located throughout the nation with Laguna Niguel being responsible for the largest one in the organization. Several hundreds of permanent employees were on board in Laguna Niguel at any given time with a hundred or more temporary employees working there during times when we were unable to hire the additional permanent employees we needed.

The ACS sites were some of the most effective and efficient workplaces in IRS during their time. The ACS employees collected more money than the field offices and were excellent at closing small dollar cases. They were a means of freeing the professional revenue officer employees from working small dollar cases. Revenue officers were needed on the many large dollar delinquent cases we had in inventory.

At any rate ACS operated well for about 15 years or so. It then became less cost effective to maintain the sites in high rent districts when the work could be done in the Service Centers. Most IRS Service Centers were located in low cost of living areas away from busy cities. The location of the ACS sites in low cost of living areas made it easier to recruit and hire as the citizens were more willing to work for IRS in those lower paying jobs than citizens in larger cities. Therefore, the Laguna Niguel ACS sites became a thing of the past. However, even though we were closing ACS we had to find jobs for all of the employees as we were required to keep them on the payroll.

IRS had a history of never terminating permanent employees when work was phased out. Actually this was one of the most attractive elements of working for the IRS as many people prefer security of having a government job over a job that might pay more, because along with more pay in private industry came the risk of potential layoffs. The Service always found jobs for all of the employees and fortunately for the employees it almost always turned out to be jobs that led to higher pay and/or career paths.

At the time the ACS sites were being phased out it was decided by management at the regional level to retain and assimilate all of the permanent employees into the other divisions. Of course this meant Collection and Examination would be selecting most of the employees. Since Collection Division could not absorb all of the employees it became mandatory that Examination Division select its share. While I thought this was a good idea, I did realize many of the collection employees were not going to be able to make it in Examination Division.

To be able to land a job leading to a career path in Examination Division employees needed to have an accounting background. Some of the Collection

Division employees were qualified for the Examination Division positions, however, the training for Examination Division employees was more difficult and foreign to Collection Division employees.

Some of the phase one training slots for the revenue officer position in Collection Division were the same for the clerical employees; therefore, it was much easier for them to make it through the initial training. Of course as the training progressed they would also encounter more difficult training in the revenue officer position, but initially they had a better shot of succeeding in Collection.

Well, as I suspected, after the selections were made for both Collection and Examination Division a significant number of employees demonstrated an inability to meet the training requirements. Some had to be let go and some who were represented by the union fought to keep the new positions, winning sometimes and losing sometimes.

On the surface, IRS training, particularly that for the revenue officer job which was considered to be at the professional level, appears to be top notch with on-the-job training interspersed throughout the year between phases of classroom training. Revenue officers are provided with approximately two months of class room training and the balance of the year is on the job training.

The classroom training is usually provided in increments of one week of pre-unit one orientation, four weeks of unit one, and two weeks each for unit II and III. Instructors are primarily from within the division. If a revenue officer is doing a "good job" as a revenue officer his or her manager may ask him or her to be an instructor for the trainees.

Instructors are supposed to be chosen from a list of employees who have been provided with what is called Basic Instructor training. If the organization could operate according to plan it would stand a much better chance of succeeding; however, as said before, the budget, or lack thereof, causes serious problems, repercussions of which are felt for many, many years afterwards. During so called good budgetary times the organization provides Basic Instructor training and maintains a list of those employees who are considered qualified to instruct. This list is supposed to be used when ever the need arises for instructors.

The problem comes about when money has not been available for instructor training or when as a result of a last minute budget approval, a large number of employees have to be hired. When this happens the only approved fall back for additional instructors is to select from the senior revenue officer ranks.

A grade 12 revenue officer is a senior employee and should be relatively good at the job. Even so, this does not mean that all of these employees will be successful at instructing and it certainly doesn't mean they all want to teach. Many, many of them have only done it to please management when they have received friendly coercion. As you can see the training starts out with built in reasons to fail.

During my last experience with hiring and training in March 1994, the regional office advised the collection divisions that hiring would take place at the beginning of the fiscal year which starts in September. Plans were made, a roster was established and because of inactivity the roster expired after six months. We then started all over again and then congress caused a hiring freeze by cutting the budget. Within a few months we were told once again we would be hiring. Again, it was called off as a result of insufficient funds.

Prior to hiring we were required by civil service procedures to establish a roster of qualified applicants to be used in the selection process. Vacant positions were announced and interested employees filed applications for the positions. The Human Resources Division would conduct the necessary research to determine whether or not the applicants met the basic qualifications for the positions. Those employees meeting the basic qualifications would subsequently be interviewed and selections would be made. The rosters were only good for six months. If they were not used within the six months they would expire and we would have to start all over from scratch.

After the September 1994 roster was allowed to expire without having been used we were told that we were to hire 66 revenue officers and that they had to be redeployables. This meant they all had to come from the ACS sites and had to be employees whose jobs were being done away with as a result of the closure of both of the ACS sites.

Once again we announced the vacant positions and this time we even reached the point of conducting interviews. Then we were given an increased number of 71 and we were told to bring them on board June 28, 1995. The increase did not create a problem because we always interviewed a sufficient number of employees if possible so that we often had excess applicants after the selections had been made. Before we could bring these employees into the revenue offer position we were told we could and actually were expected to hire 112 for fiscal year 1995.

Lo and behold, I was advised by the Assistant Director that at a meeting he had attended in the region he had received a memo changing the number from 112 to 48 with additional authorization to hire 26 additional clerical positions. The additional clerical positions made sense because any substantial increase in revenue officer hiring usually meant the number of groups would need to be increased as there is a rule outlining the number of employees that should be assigned to each group. This rule is called the span of control rule. However, the reduction of hires from 112 to 48 was totally unexpected and meant we had wasted a lot of time preparing to hire more than we could.

The above fiasco is an excellent example of the gross mismanagement that goes on in IRS. Ultimately, we did hire 112 but in the meantime we played numerous numbers games. When I speak of "hires" I am speaking of hiring from the outside and the inside as well. The example included inside hiring because employees selected from inside are considered to be new hires when they are selected for other positions.

Finally we were able to hire but it had to be done in thirty days or we would lose the money. The numbers we were told to hire were mandatory numbers and had to be accomplished. This mandate presented many problems.

First of all we did not have sufficient space and so we had to seek additional space in several of our currently occupied buildings as well as space in two new buildings. Groups had to be restructured, new managers selected, instructors and on the job training coaches selected as well as case inventories requested from the Service Center or taken from excess inventories of current employees. The severe time constraints caused managers to be selected who did not have managerial training nor experience.

Managers are recommended from the revenue officer groups based again on their performance as revenue officers. Therein lies the problem. Revenue officers are considered to be performing effectively if they are closing cases timely and collecting money.

Cases are closed by collecting full payment and securing delinquent returns with full payment of tax due. Upon contact by a revenue officer, full payments are made by some taxpayers but most are unable to full pay. Therefore, those who are attempting to comply may be granted an installment agreement. Mind you, taxpayers are not entitled to installment agreements and most of the time it is left up to the discretion of the revenue officer working the case. Those taxpayers unable to pay, those who refuse to pay, as well as those who are afraid and try to avoid the entire situation can rest assured any assets they own will be pursued and seized if possible.

Now, if you are looking to be successful and you know the road to success is paved with closed cases you need to look towards immediate enforcement action upon failure to receive full payment. This kind of leadership selection perpetuates little or no concern for taxpayers and their rights. These are the kind of employees selected to instruct new employees. I believe you might agree with me in that many of the kind of characteristics you might look for in an instructor will be different from those you might look for in a revenue officer.

This scenario might sound as though it is an indictment against the revenue officers. It is not. Many of them did admirable jobs in instructing and most of them deserve commendation for taking on a job that is vital to the success of the organization and I am sure they did the best they could.

In my opinion the fault lies with congress and the IRS organization. While congress deserves a major portion of the fault for creating the budgetary problems when they could have been avoided, IRS certainly deserves a large portion of the blame. It is still unbelievable to me how IRS, the largest accounting agency in the world, could screw up internal budgeting the way it did.

During my last years in IRS as a division chief I had the opportunity to be greatly involved in the budgetary process as I was responsible for the division's budget. On numerous occasions the regional office would advise the district that funds were available only to find out they were not. Many years we were in freeze statuses only to find out at the end of the year we had surplus funds that had to be spent at the last minute. It was a known fact that if funds were not spent the budget would be cut in a like amount the following year as it would be determined the money had not been needed. Heaven forbid that was allowed to happen.

In those situations each division was given marching orders to order supplies, equipment, furniture, etc. just as long as the money was all used. You were considered a failure if you ended up with a surplus. In addition, if one division had a surplus it was taken and passed on to another division if we could get away with it without the regional office finding out. That was difficult to do but like anything there were ways it could be accomplished.

One division might be called upon to order furniture needed by another division. The regional and national office tried to build in controls to prevent this from happening, but as you know for every control implemented there are numerous ways to defeat its purpose. The divisions were very selfish and did not want to give up any money. We paid lip service to the director by seeming willing to hand over funds to another division and then we would go back to our offices and attempt to find ways to use the money therefore making in unavailable for another division's use.

Rather than praise a division for being able to operate and save money at the same time, division chiefs were severely criticized for ending up with a surplus. If you were smart you simply did not allow it to happen. If you were smart you monitored the budget and found ways to spend the money as the year progressed so that you did not end up in the doghouse with a fat purse at the end of the year.

With the budget being in shambles there wasn't a lot of hope for top notch training. One could only hope it would be the best possible under the circumstances. The Collection and Basic Training Instructor Guide (Exhibit 5) contains the Mission statement of IRS and it outlines the purpose and the goals of the training program. This document is provided by the Treasury Department, Internal Revenue Service and is used throughout Collection Divisions nationwide. One of the most interesting and important issues with the purpose and the goal is the omission of the necessity to be sensitive to the rights of the taxpayers and to provide positive customer service.

The main objective of Collection Division is apparent in its name. It is necessary to collect delinquent taxes; however, all emphasis is on collecting with none placed on collecting in the right manner. Through the years, instructors have shared war stories with trainees based on their experiences. All of these war stories revolve around difficulties and/or problems in collecting money. Some of the stories outline how the revenue officer outsmarted the taxpayer. Some of the stories are about threats made by the taxpayers and how the taxpayers were restrained and even arrested for attempting to halt a seizure. Trainees should leave the training well prepared to face potential obstacles presented by taxpayers.

During my classroom training we were told that all trainees were expected to have conducted a seizure between unit I and unit II classroom training while receiving on-the-job training. I am aware that this expectation is still being shared with the trainees. This presents a dilemma because revenue officers do need to know how to conduct a seizure, yet instead of the attention being placed on closing cases in the most expeditious way possible, the emphasis is on finding enough seizures in the group for all trainees.

Problems can also be seen in the reverse of the above. An example was seen in the area of seizures in the Los Angeles District during my branch chief days. An employee who did not believe in taking enforcement action (seizures in particular) even in the most egregious situations was chosen to instruct in the revenue officer unit I and II training.

During the course of the training the instructor let it be known that if a revenue officer had to take seizure action the revenue officer had failed in his or her job. While seizure action should be the last resort, according to procedures, particularly those regarding trust fund taxes, there are times when seizure action is required. This instructor caused innumerable problems for the entire branch and particularly for the group in which he was assigned.

One of the students in this seizure class later became a staunch union steward and he assumed a leadership role in his group. He let it be known to employees he personally felt a revenue officer had failed at his or her job if seizure action became necessary. He even told me. "Revenue officers should be able to collect the taxes through voluntary payment, installment agreement and as a last resort, levy action. They should not be required to conduct seizures." I was also told that this statement was shared with many employees in the branch.

This caused most people in the group to consult with him when the manager advised that the next step must be seizure action. When this union steward said seizure action was not appropriate the employees agreed with him. Most people really do not want to have to take seizure action regardless of the circumstances and this was the method these employees chose to try and avoid it. This caused cases to remain open in the group for long periods of time with no action taken. This group was managed by Cherry who has been discussed in Chapter Nine, Labor Relations Climate.

How did I know what was taking place in this group? There are always employees willing to "spill the beans" and tell on their co-workers. Many of them would do it voluntarily without being asked to and they would ask to remain anonymous, as they did not want to be thought of as a "friend" of management.

On the surface, the readers will probably agree with the tactics of the union steward because after all most people sympathize with taxpayers experiencing problems with IRS. However, failure on the part of IRS to work cases timely and appropriately can cause insurmountable problems for taxpayers.

Generally speaking, employment tax liability accounts are generated once a quarter. Taxpayers with liabilities meeting certain dollar criteria are required to make federal tax deposits to a bank during each quarter so that at the end of the quarter when the return is due all taxes will have been paid. It is basically the same theory as the withholding and estimated tax procedures for income taxes.

Let's use the example of a taxpayer who owes $5000 and because the revenue officer can't find a levy source the case remains open. The following quarter if the same scenario occurs the taxpayer now owes an additional $5,000 plus interest, failure to deposit penalty, and failure to pay penalty. Carry this through at least two more quarters and now you have a taxpayer who could not afford to pay $5000 now owing $20,000 plus. This almost ensures the seizing of the business somewhere down the line once management discovers the failure of the revenue officer to move timely.

If the revenue officer had moved faster perhaps the taxpayer could have borrowed the money or maybe requested an installment agreement. While installment agreements for trust fund taxes on businesses that are currently operating are frowned upon, many times taxpayers are able to convince a revenue officer to obtain group managerial approval for an installment agreement for a few months. However the taxpayer must remain current with all subsequent filing of tax returns and payment of required tax deposits.

While the public may or may not agree with the seizing of a business, I'm sure most reasonable people can see that by the revenue officer procrastinating in letting the taxpayer know the seriousness of the situation, irreparable harm can come to the taxpayer. As stated earlier trust fund taxes are a priority and IRS requires that they be treated as such. Remember, the words trust fund means the funds are being held in trust for the taxpayer's employees after being withheld from their wages. Funds are supposed to be turned over to the Social Security Administration for the employees' retirement years.

To be eligible to receive funds from the Social Security Administration an employee must have contributed to the system for a total of 40 quarters which is ten years if an employee has worked consistently with no interruption and funds have been withheld from his/her wages. There isn't a requirement that the 40 quarters must be consistent however, an employee will not meet the requirements if an employer has failed to pay the withheld funds to Social Security.

I truly believe the public would feel less sympathy for a business owner whose business has been seized by IRS if they realize what has actually taken place and how much harm the taxpayer, the employer/business owner has created for a non-suspecting employee.

While liens, levies, and seizure actions create significant problems for taxpayers, on the other side failure to timely file liens, serve levies, and conduct seizures also create significant problems for another set of taxpayers. In addition, the training inefficiencies of IRS also creates problems for taxpayers in general as well as for IRS. Obvious inefficiencies are easily recognized even during my training days in IRS.

The basic kinds of cases revenue officers work on are TDI's (Taxpayer Delinquent Investigations) and TDA's (Taxpayer Delinquent Accounts). TDA's are generated as a result of taxes due on returns that have been filed. TDI's are generated as a result of tax returns not filed as required.

During my training year we spent weeks on the TDI slot only to have the entire slot thrown out at the end of the classroom training because most of the trainees, including me (somewhere in the range of 60 people) failed the slot. It was obvious the training was deficient. The instructor had not been able to satisfactorily explain the procedures necessary to close a TDI.

The training was never done over so therefore approximately 60 revenue officers left the training center to go out and work with taxpayers on something many of them were not quite sure of. The students in this particular class were from all throughout the United States including two students from Guam. Some of these revenue officers later became managers, including me, and/or instructors teaching something they still may not have understood.

The primary problem identified in the classroom training had to do with the appropriate and correct way to close out a TDI. This subject, the closure of TDI's remains in very poor quality throughout IRS and continues to create problems for taxpayers. A primary reason for the necessity of quality closures of the TDI should be to prevent having to repeatedly contact taxpayers unnecessarily.

If a TDI is not closed correctly it will eventually be rejected from the Service Center where all closures end up. Three of the major objectives for TDI investigations are to correct the delinquency by having the taxpayer file any and all delinquencies; to secure full payment of all taxes due on any delinquent returns; and to insure future voluntary compliance which is the single most important issue in the IRS.

One of the biggest problems demonstrated by IRS employees in working TDI's has to do with conducting and documenting complete compliance before closing a TDI. While working a TDI, an employee is required to investigate and verify that a taxpayer has filed all tax returns for which they may be responsible. This is what is called conducting compliance. It also includes what is called cross compliance if a taxpayer is responsible for income and business tax returns.

Many times an employee will be assigned a TDI for a taxpayer's income taxes and if during the course of the investigation the revenue officer finds out the taxpayer has a business it then becomes necessary for the revenue officer to also conduct compliance on the business tax returns.

One of the major complaints voiced by taxpayers is that they are often contacted by more than one IRS employee regarding their tax return requirements. This is definitely a valid complaint. Tax cases are generally assigned by zip codes. Therefore, if a taxpayer has a business in a zip code different that the one he lives in there is a good chance two revenue officers will have assignments on this taxpayer. If the revenue officers are on the ball they will find this out and will then agree that one will work both cases. You would not believe how often this kind of situation arises and how often each individual revenue officer is unaware that someone else is working with this taxpayer. In spite of all of today's technology IRS remains in the dark and more often than not a revenue officer finds out information from a taxpayer rather than from its own system of assigning cases.

There are numerous reasons why cases continue to be worked by more than one revenue officer in addition to the lack of sophistication of IRS computers. The reasons include neglect and/or indifference on the part of the revenue officer as well as simply a matter of lack of concern for harassing the taxpayer. The IRS computer system and IRS procedures play a major part in this fiasco. The system should be geared towards generating all tax accounts to one revenue officer. However the system is faulty and this does not happen.

An article, "IRS Chief Names New Management Team" found on the Internet written by Curt Anderson, AP Tax Writer, dated August 11, 1998, announced that "Paul J. Cosgrave becomes the new chief information officer. Formerly a partner at Andersen Consulting and most recently top officer at Claremont Technology Group, Cosgrave has 24 years experience in information technology. He has been consulting for the IRS since earlier this summer."

In addition, Curt Anderson goes on to say, "The IRS spent $3.3 billion earlier this decade on a failed computer modernization and desperately needs better systems to make the reforms work, Rosotti said." Rosotti is the newly appointed IRS Commissioner.

I was part of IRS during the failed computer modernization attempt and the entire fiasco was joked and laughed about by employees, particularly those in management. This gives you an idea why IRS computer systems continue to fail.

In addition to cases being assigned to revenue officers based on zip codes they are also assigned based on the dollar amounts of the taxpayers tax returns. Revenue officers start out as trainees at GS-7 or 9 (GS =grade) depending upon their level of experience and or education at the time they are hired. After performing successfully for at least a year they are then eligible to be promoted to the next grade.

The grades available for promotion are 7, 9, 11 and 12. The GS 12 revenue officers are the seniors and they are supposed to be assigned the most difficult cases and cases with large dollar amounts. Therefore if a taxpayer has an income tax return with a small dollar amount and a business tax return with a large dollar amount unless the business is located in the same zip code as the taxpayer's residence, the cases will undoubtedly be assigned to two different revenue officers.

It is possible for a taxpayer to have a TDI generated with a small liability outstanding on an income tax return, yet have a TDI generated with a large liability outstanding on a business tax return, particularly if the business has several outstanding delinquent returns on which federal tax deposits have not been made. At the risk of repeating myself I do have to say that it is still unbelievable to me that the largest accounting firm (IRS) in the world is so far behind in technology that they cannot fix this problem.

This is a problem not only for TDI's but for TDA's as well as seen in the 1997 Congressional Hearings on IRS practices. One taxpayer, who had been continuously harassed by IRS while being told her case was closed through full payment only to then to be told that she still owed the money was the victim of one hand not knowing what the other hand was doing. IRS employees for the most part are not malicious, evil people. They are simply people trying to make a living doing the best job possible with the equipment, information, and technology available to them.

In the case of the taxpayer mentioned above, liens were filed, released, only to be filed again. Levies were served attaching money belonging to the taxpayer which was then applied to the tax liability. Then to add insult to injury the money was refunded. These incidents are examples of mismanagement, inferior quality of work and ill-trained employees and as sad as it is to say this kind of situation happens every single day in IRS and I would venture to guess it happens all over the nation.

At the backbone of the inefficiencies of IRS is lack of stability, and lack of appropriate oversight as well as sub standard computer equipment relied on by IRS employees to do the job. Congress stands at the forefront of the line in terms of responsibility for both lack of stability and lack of oversight. Budgets that are consistently subjected to freezes leaves the organization unprepared to train and manage appropriately and effectively.

To better understand the problems associated with the faulty TDI training some background information is necessary. A TDI is generated by the IRS Service Center if a taxpayer fails to file a required return. When this happens, the Service Center sends a series of notices to the taxpayer requesting the return. If the taxpayer does not respond to these notices, then a TDI is issued and eventually worked by a revenue officer.

The instructional objectives for teaching how to work TDI's include enabling new employees to be able to explain the TDI investigation process; interpret the coded information on a TDI; determine TDI closing codes to report the results of the investigation; and to fill in and complete the necessary sections of a TDI to close the investigation (See Exhibit 6).

According to Exhibit 7 the TDI instructions are so important because 'TDI's can represent a significant portion of a revenue officer's inventory. TDI's are potential accounts receivable and have the potential of producing large amounts of revenue. The quality of work that a revenue officer puts into the TDI area has a direct bearing on increasing the potential revenue yield."

Many, many TDI's are rejected from Service Center because they have not been closed properly. This not only causes the problem of work having to be done over, it creates a problem with taxpayers having to be contacted again and again because the revenue officer did not get all of the necessary information to close the case. Technically speaking, when a revenue officer works a case he/she is supposed to conduct compliance on all filing requirements of the taxpayer for all periods of time starting from the date of the last shown tax return.

An example could be a revenue officer receiving a TDI for an income tax return that was due in 1995. This revenue officer is required to ask the taxpayer to produce copies of income tax returns for 1995, 1996, and 1997. If the taxpayer is required to pay estimated taxes the revenue officer needs to ask for proof of the payments for the estimated taxes as well as for proof of any liabilities shown on the copies of tax returns for 1995, 1996, and 1997.

In addition, if the taxpayer has his/her own business the revenue officer is required to check the records in Service Center to see if the taxpayer has filed all required business tax returns. If the business tax returns and full payments do not show up on the computer the revenue officer is required to ask the taxpayer to produce copies of all tax returns in question and copies of canceled checks showing payments for all of these returns which may include proof of federal tax deposits.

If a revenue officer is operating effectively and efficiently all of this research should be done before going to the field to contact a taxpayer. To go one step further all of the research should have been done by Service Center before sending out the TDI. In most cases the research has not been done because Service Center has consistent problems in quality of work.

Most of the employees at Service Center are what is called seasonal employees. They work there when needed and are furloughed when not needed or when the budget is cut or frozen. This means the Service Center should be in a consistent training mode with new employees always coming in. This lack of experience as well as lack of enough employee resources causes significant problems for IRS and for the taxpayers.

To add to the problem, if Service Center has not done the research, many revenue officers fail to do it once they receive the case either out of negligence or inability to understand what is needed or inability to receive the kind of support they need from the clerical staffing assigned to each group.

Generally there has been only one computer assigned to each revenue officer group. The secretary and or the clerical person, if there was one, had to provide all research to a group of 12 to 15 revenue officers and a group manager. If the budget was tight or if IRS was in a freeze status most likely there would not have been a clerical employee assigned to the group.

IRS is attempting to resolve the problem of not having sufficient computers available for all employees. However, once again the budget is part of the problem. IRS is making an effort to provide all revenue officers with computers and computer training. However, they are only able to do this on a district by district bases. A decision is made as to which district should be next and the funding and equipment is then provided. A better managerial decision would be to provide the equipment and training to all districts at the same time; however, as said before the funds are only available incrementally.

Once the research is done for the revenue officer the level of quality training the revenue officer has received then comes in to play. Many, many revenue officers do not know how to read TDI's and TDA's because the research information attached to the case is written in codes that have to be deciphered. Material is supposed to be available to enable one to decipher the codes, but again budgetary problems cause many groups to not have all necessary information and tools readily available. If the training was not of the quality it should have been the revenue officers will not know how to read the information nor how to interpret it even if they could read it.

If this were fiction it would be a horror story. With it being real life it is more horrible than fiction. Many, many revenue officers are totally unprepared to fully discuss a taxpayer's overall situation once they have been able to locate the taxpayer. Information obtained at the initial contact many times is generally incomplete which means the taxpayer has to be contacted again. Many times the revenue officer believes, out of ignorance resulting from poor or lack of training, that they have conducted complete compliance on the taxpayer's tax history only to close out a TDI, send it to the Service Center and have it regenerated once it is determined that it is incomplete.

In my reviews of case work done by revenue officers I consistently found serious problems with revenue officers not obtaining all information during the initial field contact. The taxpayers had to be contacted again and again before a case could be closed accurately. Time and again I wrote managers up regarding this area and time and again it continued to be observed as a problem. Perhaps now that everyone is getting a computer if the system is perfected enough the revenue officer will be able to get the information off the system, thereby eliminating the necessity to obtain the information from the taxpayer.

Sure, it is the taxpayer's responsibility to meet filing and paying requirements and their failure to do so results in large amounts of interest and penalties being assessed. However, IRS aids and abets the taxpayer in their neglect. The longer it takes the revenue officer to secure a delinquent return, the more money it is going to cost the taxpayer. There are many penalties assessed by IRS; however, the biggest penalty and one of the easiest to avoid is the penalty for failure to timely file returns with taxes due. The penalty is 5% per month of the tax due up to 25%. Just by filing a return when it is due a taxpayer can save a lot of money.

Realizing that most people do not want to have to pay taxes makes it even sadder when one realizes that ignorance on the part of the revenue officer or negligence from allowing the cases to sit for long periods of time can be the financial ruin of a taxpayer, especially if the taxpayer happens to own a business. The size of overage inventories assigned to revenue officers is unbelievable. Based on my extensive experience, cases become overage for a few basic reasons.

Primarily cases become overage because managerial oversight is faulty and revenue officers are allowed to operate however they want. Many revenue officers will work cases to a point until the case becomes difficult and it then goes to the back of the drawer while the revenue officer then starts working on another new assignment.

These cases can sit for years unless a manager is competent enough to review the listings that show when cases become overage. Many times the cases sit until they show up on the list for cases with statutes that are about to expire. Adverse action can and often will be taken against managers and employees if a statute is allowed to expire as a result of negligence. The severity of this adverse action causes managers to pay more attention to cases highlighted with statutes soon to expire.

Income tax cases have ten years before the statute expires and believe it or not I have seen cases that have been around for five or more years without any action whatsoever being taken on them. Up until a few years before I retired the statute was six years and many employees and managers were written up for proposed or actual adverse action for not protecting the statute.

Once a case has been identified as nearing statute expiration the revenue officer hurries out to see the taxpayer and attempts to get the taxpayer to sign a waiver to increase the time for the statute. If a taxpayer refuses to sign the waiver the revenue officer will take immediate action to close the case through levy, lien, and/or seizure action if he/she is able to locate any assets. Many taxpayers don't realize they do not have to sign the waiver. If the revenue officer can't locate assets before the statute expires the case has to be written off and cannot legally be collected unless the taxpayer voluntarily agrees to pay.

Cases are allowed to become overage in some instances because inventories are actually far too high for a revenue officer to be able to work them effectively and efficiently. This problem has many causes, among them congressional mandated hiring freezes and budget cuts.

The worse and probably most easy to resolve problem in the overage situation is the poor quality of training. During my time as group manager, branch chief, assistant division chief, and division chief I conducted many, many randomly selected caseload reviews. As a manager I reviewed the work of the revenue officers assigned to my group. As a mid-level and top level manager I would often require my subordinate managers to select certain cases assigned to revenue officers for my review. I was almost always appalled by what I saw and I wrote some scathing review results for both revenue officers and managers.

The quality of the work I saw was totally unacceptable. It was almost always obvious that many, many revenue officers did not know how to work the cases appropriately. It was also quite obvious that many mangers did not know how to work the cases appropriately. My reviews also found that what I had expected was true that a troublesome number of managers were apparently in the wrong job. Some because they no longer liked working the field and sought management for what they thought was an easier job. Some fell in the category mentioned previously, they were effective revenue officers who had become managers out of necessity to please management, but they were not committed to doing the job as required.

Okay, by now I'm sure the reader wonders what did I do in the midst of such enormous problems. As a manager I provided training in the group to attempt to rectify the problems. I also assigned one of the best revenue officers to review TDI cases as they were closed by individual revenue officers before they were given to me as a final level of approval. This training, attention, and several levels of reviews enabled the quality to improve significantly within the group; however, we paid a high price for the improvement. Many hours were spent re-doing things that should have been done the right way the first time around.

As a branch chief and as a top level manager, I implemented some of the same efforts to improve quality, but again even though results were positive, again, we paid a significant price in re-doing work. Even though I consistently expressed my concern regarding the level of inadequate, inferior training I wasn't ever able to establish an impact that could improve the budget and operation by crisis management situations. Everyone agreed with me, but no one was able to circumvent the major obstacle of congressional involvement in the budget process.

For the most part the same revenue officers I am speaking of here are still there working cases. The same revenue officers who did not know how to work cases themselves turned around and became managers. It stands to reason that if you don't know how to work a case yourself, you will certainly not know when a case closure should be rejected back to a revenue officer. This means many cases get through the group managers and go on to Service Center only to be rejected and reissued back to the field.

I have received much information and read many news articles about the plans the new IRS Commissioner has for re-inventing IRS; however, I have not seen any mention of providing re-training for employees who have been on board for many years. The problems within IRS are deep seated and will be very difficult to turn around.

To get started in the right direction, the organization needs to start at the beginning ensuring that quality training is provided for all employees. Even if it is costly it will be worth it as it will save significant time, money and human resources in the future. It will also go a long way in enabling a reduction in the harassment of taxpayers in IRS' quest for information and tax collections.

The internet Tax News & Views report on "Drastic Changes in IRS" dated June 25, 1997, stated that the National Commission on Restructuring the Internal Revenue Service recommended, "The IRS must address culture, operations, taxpayer education, technology, and training so it can operate more efficiently, with more customer focus." The report also stated that the commission recommended that the IRS receive stable funding for the next three years."

Stable funding is a must because without it IRS always ends up with crisis management. Decisions to cut certain things have to be made when there isn't enough money to fund everything. Unfortunately the first things to go in IRS when cuts have to be made is training and customer service. When these areas are cut the public suffers. Without quality training employees are not able to work the cases the way they should which then prompts deserved complaints from the public. When cuts are made in customer service the counters IRS set up to service the public on a walk-in basis are generally terminated. This signals to some employees as well as the public that IRS is no longer concerned about public opinion.

Although the commission found that IRS currently has a strong plan for training, they felt it is not receiving the institutional support necessary to ensure success. The commission stated, "The functional units within the IRS are resistant to giving up resources to assist training personnel due to the IRS culture which relates power to control over recourse. As a result, tax law and administrative policies are not taught consistently across the country."

The commission is right on target with the statement regarding units within IRS being resistant to giving up resources to assist training personnel. In my management roles both as Branch Chief and as Division Chief I had to literally make managers give up their personnel even when the training was going to be for their own employees.

IRS continues to operate in the dark ages; however, efforts are being made to update technology which will enhance training, ability and knowledge. So far IRS has been unable to integrate its plan for updating technology with its business objectives. Millions of dollars have been spent in IRS' efforts to tie technology objectives directly to business objectives; however, so far they have not been able to conquer this field. This failure is the major cause of the Tax System Modernization project failure.

A major reorganization effort was tied in directly with IRS being able to modernize its tax systems. The project was supposed to enhance many operations within IRS including such services to the public including faster and more effective telephone responses. Tax systems were supposed to be updated sufficiently enough that an employee anywhere in the organization could access a taxpayer's account and provide accurate information and answers to questions. Interestingly enough IRS has not been able to achieve this objective.

At the time I performed as Division Chief in the largest district, largest division, in the Service, we had to prepare statistical reports manually because we could not utilize our systems to gather the data. When we were on a major improvement project in Collection Division we needed reports to show productivity of all employees in the division individually The only way we could obtain this information was to have the mangers prepare consolidated group reports from the reports individual employees prepared. Now of course IRS really didn't want us to be able to gather individual reports because of the paranoia of what management would do with them.

IRS was completely paranoid about receiving negative publicity from the Congress via the public that quotas were being used. Rather than holding management accountable for its actions executive level management made it almost impossible to gather necessary information to determine training needs.

Where does IRS stand today regarding training? Nothing has changed substantially although many plans are being generated for a better and more productive IRS. The entire organization is in the midst of an overhaul which generally means it will be years before the kind of stability that generates positive change will be available.

Chapter Six

IRS - A VIEW FROM OUTSIDE

In early fall of 1995 I began thinking about retiring from IRS. After all I had worked for the federal government for almost thirty three years. I had been rated outstanding for my performance in the fiscal year that ended in September 1995.

The Laguna Niguel Collection Division was in great shape having achieved all objectives and exceeded most. Even though I wasn't consciously thinking along these lines, I knew that success in achieving objectives in the IRS is very tenuous at best, as objectives changed from year to year and on some occasions, from quarter to quarter.

If I had been thinking along those lines I would have known that I should leave while the leaving was good. Pressure to collect money, if successful, is always followed by an outcry of outrage from the public followed by an outcry of outrage from Congress.

In early October 1995 I received a phone call from the collection division chief of IRS in Los Angeles. He was calling to inquire if I was going to retire anytime soon. IRS was offering an early retirement option to employees who met certain qualifications. The early out offer did not provide any incentives other than to be able to quit working for IRS. The offer required a 2% penalty for each year that did not meet the number of years required for regular retirement.

General requirements for voluntary retirement include five years of civilian service at age sixty-two, twenty years of service at age sixty, or thirty years of service at age fifty five. General retirement requirements for law enforcement employees such as the special agents in Criminal Investigation Division differ somewhat in that they may retire if they have at least twenty years in law enforcement at age fifty and meet certain other requirements.

To qualify for the early retirement you had to be age fifty with twenty-five years of service, however, you were penalized with a loss of 2% of your pension for each year under the age requirement. I met all requirements for regular retirement without having to take a penalty.

Anyway, the Los Angeles chief had been contacted by a former IRS executive who inquired if he was gong to take the early out offer. This executive was on a board of directors for a company whose responsibility was to represent taxpayers with IRS collection problems. The company was seeking someone with IRS experience to work for them. Since the Los Angeles chief wasn't gong to retire that year he thought of me.

I had not given any thought to seeking employment after IRS and my main objective in my retirement years was going to be writing, therefore the phone call caught me off guard. After giving it some thought, the idea of sitting across the table from IRS employees became intriguing for several reasons, one because it was work I would be immediately prepared for. Secondly, and perhaps most importantly, it was an excellent opportunity to observe IRS from the outside and to gain information for my first book. Thirdly, the pay was good.

Little did I realize at the time what an incredible experience it would be. After receiving some information from the Los Angeles chief, I contacted the president of the company and made an appointment for an interview. For purposes of this book I will call the company Shylock Corporation. The interview took place and it was obvious Mr. Shylock, the president, was interested in hiring me. He made me an offer I couldn't refuse after a few financial negotiations took place.

Shylock had several offices located in southern California including Los Angeles, Orange, and Riverside. In addition, there were offices in northern California located in Fresno, Oakland, and Sacramento and one in Baltimore, Maryland.

I was initially hired as the regional director of operations for the California offices. This title and the responsibilities changed several times within a few weeks and finally I became the Vice President of Operations. The many changes should have been a clue to me that this company had problems.

However, this was my first foray into private industry and I wasn't sure of what to expect so I went along with the program.

One of the branch chiefs who had been my subordinate in IRS had taken an early retirement along with a 10% penalty, therefore, I knew she would be looking for employment and so I contacted her to see if she would be interested in working with me at Shylock as the company was in need of additional managers. She was immediately interested and was hired as regional director for southern California. Another retired IRS branch chief in Oakland, California was hired as the regional director for northern California.

As the vice president of Operations I was the immediate manager of both of the regional directors. The company was primarily made up of three departments, sales, operations, and accounting. At the top was the president, Mr. Shylock. Immediately following Mr. Shylock were the vice presidents of the three departments.

The regional directors reported directly to me and they were responsible for group managers and their subordinates, the client services employees. There were various other lower level managers in the other departments, but suffice it to say that the sales department and client services department were the most important as they were the money makers.

In addition to the California offices, a little over six months after I was hired, Mr. Shylock opened an office in Dallas, Texas. He hired a retired IRS Regional Commissioner to operate as Vice President of the Dallas office. The office was small with one manager under the vice president position and initially one salesman. Both of these positions were filled by retired IRS employees.

Meanwhile in California, the regional directors and I were in place. We were now ready for what we all thought would be employment for a substantial period of time. Little did we know that before long we would be asking each other how did we end up in a place like Shylock's.

On the surface Shylock was doing very well financially. It was the largest company of its kind in the nation in terms of numbers of clients and numbers of employees. It was also better staffed with more experienced managers what with the three of us in California being fresh out of IRS and having excellent reputations. Unfortunately for us and for the clients/taxpayers all was not as it seemed.

During my orientation in the company I noted a very high refund request inventory. I also found that a significant number of former IRS employees had been employed at this company. They were not the people I would have hired had I been in the company at the time they came on board. Some of them had worked for me while I was at the IRS and I knew them all too well. However, they were almost all gone by the time I got there or were encouraged to leave shortly thereafter.

They had been there just long enough to have created problems in the casework. In addition to the former IRS employees having left after brief periods of employment, I soon found out that the overall turnover rate among employees was unbelievable. All of these signs were caution signs to me and I took mental note of them.

Background information is necessary to understand the entire situation and to understand why it turned out the way that it did. The company originally had two owners and one died an untimely and unexpected death prior to my employment.

Evidently he was the one with the practical common sense I was never able to see in those in charge while I was there. He was also apparently the one who held the company together, seeing to it that the collection cases were worked timely. By the time I arrived the company had been operating about six years and with this man having been dead several years, unbeknownst to me the company was nearing an early decline and demise.

Some of the worse managerial practices I have ever seen were being practiced at Shylock. The high employee turnover caused the cases to be transferred from one employee to anther three or more times during the period of a year. Each time a case was transferred to a new employee the work had to be started all over again because the employees did not document the actions they had taken while working the cases.

This was horrendous for the client/taxpayer as IRS interest and penalty continued to accrue. In addition, IRS continued its investigation looking for assets to seize. The most amazing aspect of this situation was that it had been going on for years and everyone seemed oblivious of it with nothing being done to rectify it nor to even try to find out what was causing the tremendous turnover.

The primary responsibility of the company was to represent clients with IRS collection problems. The employees actually working the cases were required by IRS regulations to be enrolled agents. The Treasury Department Circular No. 230 (Exhibits 8 & 9) outlines regulations governing the practice of people allowed to practice before IRS as enrolled agents.

Anyone seeking enrolled agent status must be approved by the Director of Practices of the Office of the Secretary of the Treasury. Enrollment is granted to those who demonstrate special competence in tax matters. The level of competence is determined by a written examination. However, certain retired IRS employees are granted enrollment based on their experience as IRS employees without having to take a written examination.

Enrolled agents working for Shylock had the responsibility of attempting to obtain approval of an OIC (offer in compromise) or an installment agreement for taxpayers owing delinquent taxes. The company advertised in local newspapers advising taxpayers with IRS collection problems to phone in and make an appointment.

The first person the client/taxpayer came in contact with was a salesman who listened to the client's problem and supposedly made a determination as to whether the company could resolve the problem, although no one was ever turned down because the salesmen received a commission based on the number of clients they brought into the company. None, and I mean none of the salesman, were going to allow a client to get away simply because they did not have a case Shylock could not resolve.

If the client accepted the terms and signed a contract, an appointment was made for the client to consult with one of Shylock's enrolled agents. During the appointment the Shylock enrolled agent, commonly known in the company as a tax manager, obtained financial information from the client and determined whether the client met the criteria for an OIC or an installment agreement.

My major responsibilities at Shylock included performing as top level manager of those employees hired to manage the enrolled agents/tax managers. I was responsible for the entire operations department throughout the company in all of the offices except Texas.

The former IRS executive hired to run the Texas office had the same title I had. He was still there when I left and I believe it was because he was too far away from the headquarters' office to see how things really were. Since then I have heard that he left so maybe he wised up.

All refund requests and complaints came into the headquarters office and were responded to by my employees. Once I left, the former IRS executive in Texas had to become more involved in the refund requests and complaints and I assume he began to see what was really going on because he resigned less than a year after I did.

See Exhibit 33 for a copy of the revenue officer training guide regarding offers in compromise. Basically an offer in compromise is authorized in the Internal Revenue Code section 7122. This section of the code states that IRS can compromise any tax, including penalties and interest. The code allows IRS to accept a lesser amount than the amount actually owed if in fact it has been determined there is doubt as to liability or doubt as to collectibility.

Exhibit 6 provides information regarding IRS installment agreements as well as copies of the most generally used collection information statement Form 433-A and B. Revenue officers are taught to analyze collection information statements and to determine whether the taxpayer can immediately pay the full amount of the tax due. If immediate full payment is not possible in the eyes of the revenue officer, an installment agreement may be considered; however, according to IRS rules and regulations, taxpayers don't have a right to obtain an installment agreement, it is left up to the discretion of the revenue officer.

Once the financial information was obtained the Shylock employee would then contact the revenue officer to whom the case was assigned. The objective was for the Shylock employee to work with the revenue officer in attempting to reach a resolution favorable for the Shylock client, preferably, an OIC.

Once the Shylock employee completed the paperwork on a case it was sent to the revenue officer for review and hopefully, approval of an OIC or at the very least, an installment agreement. All f the clients wanted an OIC because that meant they did not have to pay the total amount of the taxes. In many cases neither an OIC nor an installment agreement were approved by IRS as it was felt the taxpayer was able to pay the full amount immediately.

It was very difficult for me to completely understand why clients/taxpayers came to Shylock as they were not guaranteed an OIC and if one was not approved they ended up paying significantly more than they owed IRS in the beginning. Not only did they still owe IRS, with penalty and interest continuing to accrue, they also now owed Shylock and believe me the fees were substantial. (See Exhibit 11 for a copy of Shylock's fee schedule and contract.)

While Shylock's contract clearly stated that the client was not being guaranteed the resolution of an OIC many of my employees believed that the salesmen were telling the clients it would be done. We were never able to prove this because of course the salesmen vehemently denied it and of course

Shylock always took the salesmen's side as they were the ones who brought in the money.

To provide the best service to the client, the cases should have been worked to resolution within three to six months at the longest. Neither IRS nor Shylock worked towards the best interest of the client/taxpayer. At the time of my employment Shylock had an inventory of 1000 plus cases with 50% or more of them considered overaged. Overage cases were those having been in inventory longer than a year.

IRS, particularly IRS in Los Angeles, had cases in their inventory from Shylock having been received over a year with no IRS work having been done during that time. Again, this was at the expense of the client/taxpayer.

If the OIC was approved the age of the case was not important, however, if the OIC was not approved and it came down to the only options available to the client/taxpayer being an installment agreement or full payment, the taxpayer was penalized by the additional interest and penalty that had been allowed to accrue while both IRS and Shylock sat on the cases with nothing having been done.

I started working with Shylock the first week in February 1996 and near the end of the month the corporate president, Mr. Shylock himself, received $5 million dollars from the initial public offering of the company on the NASDAQ stock market. The company now had stock on the NASDAQ and was flying high.

In the summer of 1997 the company filed bankruptcy and closed all offices except headquarters in Los Angeles and the office in Texas that had just been opened in 1996.

In the meantime, on the morning of April 15, 1996, I received a phone call at my office advising me that IRS had "raided" the headquarters office of Shylock. It appeared one of the salesmen at Shylock had been "shopped" by an undercover special agent and the salesman was being accused of advising the undercover agent of ways to hide assets from IRS. The salesman had been arrested in his home prior to the agents raiding Shylock's office.

"Shopping" is a term used when IRS Criminal Investigation Division special agents operating undercover visit offices of taxpayer representatives pretending to have a delinquent tax account and to be in need of representation.

The undercover agent usually finds a way to let the salesman know that he/she would like to hide their assets from IRS. This is to bait the salesman into trying to assist the agent by providing ways to hide assets.

At the time of the raid the special agents took every file they could find in the office, those previously worked by the salesman they had arrested as well as those having been worked by anyone else. In addition, they took the file cabinets, the property of Shylock Corporation.

They did make the files available to the company for photocopying in the IRS office. However, over a year after the raid IRS still had not returned any of the files nor any of the file cabinets. The salesman pleaded guilty and was fined and given probation, yet IRS still had the files and the cabinets. The taxpayers paid a price for IRS refusing to return the files and either the special agents didn't realize this or they didn't give a damn, with the latter probably being closer to the truth.

The company did not have the monetary nor human resources to photocopy hundreds of files, some containing two or more folders, five or six inches thick in some instances. The employees could not be spared to spend all of the time needed to photocopy an entire file; therefore, they photocopied only what they thought they needed.

Many times they needed additional items once they started working the file again. This caused the problem of Shylock employees not being able to work the cases as expeditiously as they should have and they had to repeatedly go back to the clients for duplicate documents that had been previously provided.

IRS did not demonstrate any concern for the taxpayer and was always evasive when questioned about returning the files and file cabinets. It is a well known fact inside IRS that IRS employees do not like taxpayers' representatives. They also do not particularly like taxpayers who employ representatives. Taxpayers' representatives, accountants, and attorneys consistently make complaints to IRS management about the treatment they receive from IRS employees.

It seems as though IRS employees totally disregard the fact that taxpayers have the right to representation. Many IRS employees seem to take it as a personal slight on the part of the taxpayer. It appears to be a signal that the taxpayer is either too intimidated to handle their own problem or in some instances a signal that the taxpayer does not trust the IRS employee.

While working at Shylock I had the occasion to get involved in cases that had been there over two years. The cases had been submitted to the Los Angeles district two years or more ago, yet IRS had not completed the processing of the cases. Cases requesting approval of OIC's were initially assigned to a unit to determine if the cases met processibility requirements.

This unit reviewed the paperwork to see if the cases met the basic requirements for OIC consideration. If the cases met processibility requirements they were then assigned to a revenue officer. The cases in the processibility unit are the ones I am speaking of that had been at IRS two years or more.

Unfortunately, cases assigned to revenue officers are not worked timely either, however, for cases to remain in the processiblity unit for years is unthinkable. When we had the audacity to question the processibility unit, we were told the cases would be worked as soon as possible. In the meantime, interest and penalty continued to accrue on the taxpayers' delinquent accounts.

As required to maintain my status of enrolled agent I attended various continuous professional education (CPE) seminars. At the last one I attended as an employee of Shylock I ran into one of my former peers from IRS Los Angeles. He had been the branch chief responsible for the collection division Special Procedures Function and was just being transferred to a different assignment.

The Special Procedures Function in IRS is the function that reviews documents for legal issues. They are basically the collection division's liaison with IRS legal counsel. Depending upon the particular district involved, Special Procedures employees are responsible for determining processiblity of the cases. It just happens in Los Angeles the cases were processed in a separate unit; however, Special Procedures worked closely with this unit.

Since I knew this branch chief had his ear to the ground regarding what was going on in IRS Los Angeles I advised him of the problems Shylock was experiencing with processibility of OIC cases. That was my first mistake, and I have to admit it was stupid on my part as I knew this branch chief was one of the "kick them in the ass" types. He gives the appearance of being a straight-laced, up right person, but in reality he is a very narrow minded, cold individual when dealing with subordinate employees and taxpayers. He is the branch chief I will be mentioning later in the chapter who is taking a hard, unrelenting attitude regarding approval of OIC's.

At any rate, I mentioned to the branch chief about our problems and that I was going to complain to the district director if I couldn't get the situation resolved soon. He advised me that complaining would not make any difference because IRS was now no longer interested in the OIC program and that any complaints would just cause the cases to take even longer to be processed.

Now I have known this man for a long time and our relationship on the surface has always been pleasant enough; however, being on the other side, I could see that he was basically threatening me, warning me not to complain.

As I mentioned earlier, IRS employees do not like taxpayer representatives and now that I was one of them I was considered to be the enemy. The branch chief did not have the nerve to come out and challenge me face to face because he knew from past experience that I wouldn't take it, but he gave me a friendly veiled threat.

This may seem rather extreme, but I am an expert on IRS collection division attitudes having been on the inside for years observing from a vantage point and consistently having to deal with employees and managers' attitudinal problems. While these attitudinal problems were not generally sanctioned by Los Angeles IRS executive management, management knew of the problems, yet nothing significant was ever done to change them.

The Los Angeles collection division has always had a reputation for playing hard ball and for taking no prisoners. This statement includes employees, managers, taxpayers, and taxpayers representatives.

In one particular office during my time there, three white male managers were notorious for their collection tactics. They were very successful in achieving IRS objectives, but were known to have a "kick ass" attitude and they were often described as "steel toe boot wearing renegades". I mentioned that they were white male managers because they experienced many discrimination complaints from women and minorities for their so called managerial actions.

One white female lesbian manager, one of their peers, told me on several occasions how insensitive and rude they were to her. They simply did not have any room in their lives for anyone who deviated from what they considered to be the norm. The various division chiefs, all male, some white and some black, were aware of these men, but they either bragged about them or remained silent because they collected lots of money and closed lots of cases and that was the name of the game during those times.

It was a known fact that few if any OIC's would be approved in this branch in which the "renegades" were managing. Those "good ole boys" were seriously looking for immediate full pays and were willing to kick ass to get them. By kick ass I mean levy, levy, levy, and seize, seize, seize with total disregard for unreasonable hardships caused to the taxpayers. Most taxpayers were too intimidated to complain to upper management, therefore, the unreasonable actions were allowed to stand.

Many, many people including taxpayers' representatives are too intimidated to complain about how IRS employees treat them. On several occasions I had taxpayers' representatives complain to me about how my employees in IRS were treating them and their clients. When I asked for the employees names they would not give them to me because they said they feared retaliation against the taxpayer if the revenue officers found out they had complained about them.

Meanwhile at Shylock I prepared a listing of all cases two years or older and sent a letter and two follow up letters to the chief of the division in Los Angeles requesting status reports on the overage cases. Months went by and at the time I left the company a reply had not been received. To the credit of the division chief I have to say that I did find out that he had reassigned the manager responsible for the processibility unit. However, I don't know if it had anything to do with their backlog or any complaints received.

Once the raid took place at Shylock, the IRS Los Angeles collection division virtually came to a stand still in working cases submitted by Shylock. I could understand the need to be sure cases were being worked properly, but the problems caused by neglect on the part of IRS were incredible.

One of the managers in Los Angeles, a person who had worked for me when I was a branch chief in IRS Los Angeles, told me they were simply not working Shylock's clients cases. This was a person held in high regard by me as well as by the management in Los Angeles.

Allowing cases submitted by the Shylock company to sit without anyone working them was neglect of the worse kind and a blatant disregard for taxpayers rights and it was the taxpayer who would be harmed the most. While the cases sat penalty and interest continued to accrue increasing the liabilities for taxpayers.

Many of the taxpayers had gone to Shylock's in an effort to get an OIC approved because they could not pay the amount of taxes they owed. Their liabilities became larger and larger while their cases sat in IRS offices not being worked. IRS was after Shylock and heaven help anyone who got in the way, including the innocent taxpayers. Seeing IRS treating taxpayers the way there were treated finally tore down many of the positive images I had tried to hold on to regarding the organization.

In addition to neglecting cases, very poor managerial procedures were practiced by Los Angeles. They repeatedly requested copies of documents previously sent. On many occasions entire files were lost. The same thing happened at Shylock and I do have to admit the same thing happened in some of the units I was responsible for while working for IRS.

Clients were consistently being requested to re-submit documents over and over again. Files were lost, some never to be found again. The clients/taxpayers were in a no win situation, being shafted first by IRS and then by their representatives at Shylock.

The big question is why the above situations were allowed to continue to occur. There are numerous reasons and not surprisingly they seem to be the same for IRS and Shylock.

The one major difference with IRS and Shylock was the size of each organization. IRS, in some instances is too large to be manageable while Shylock on the other hand was small enough to have been managed efficiently without a supreme effort.

Both IRS and Shylock were similar in that both worked with inferior computer systems. IRS then and now continues to work with outdated systems. Shylock's equipment was cheap and the company did not have anyone to train employees on a full time basis. Very limited raining was provided and employees were working on the system without knowing what they were doing. Not only did the Shylock employees not have experience in operating computers, none of them knew anything about how IRS worked the OIC cases. Many, many mistakes were made with all being to the detriment of the taxpayer.

IRS management, in many offices, is not trained to do the job they are thrust into. The selection of managers is discussed more in detail in Chapter Five.

Shylock's mangers were selected based on need and availability. If the company needed a manager, the president, Mr. Shylock, would hire anyone who had worked for IRS. He never knew whether they had been fired from IRS or not and he didn't seem to care. He didn't even know whether they had managerial ability or not and again, he didn't seem to care. As long as they had worked for IRS he brought them into the company.

For some reason or other Mr. Shylock seemed to have a fetish towards IRS employees. Unfortunately for him and the Shylock organization I believe the incompetent IRS employees he hired contributed significantly to the demise of Shylock. I often felt he thought he might have been an IRS employee in another life. It wasn't easy to do, but I was able to get him to change his mind abut hiring former IRS employees on several occasions because I knew the people he was interested in had been fired or encouraged to resign from IRS.

He didn't even seem to wonder why someone who had worked for IRS for many years would all of a sudden quit and lose their pension close to reaching retirement age. As I had inside information I was able to tell him we should not be hiring certain people.

Actually the information I had was usually provided by someone who should not have given it to me, therefore, I did not tell Mr. Shylock why we should not hire the individual in question. I just told him based on my knowledge that particular person would not fit in. I always tried to be careful to not disclose information that should have remained private.

A part of my responsibility at Shylock was to ensure that all client correspondence was responded to. At lease 99% of the correspondence were refund requests and we received anywhere from five to ten pieces of correspondence daily. The clients were requesting refunds as soon as they realized they were not guaranteed an OIC and indeed probably would not be getting one approved.

As I mentioned at the beginning of this chapter, one of my first observances at Shylock was the enormous refund request inventory; therefore, at one of the first staff meeting I attended I asked Mr. Shylock if anyone had looked into the reasons for the numerous refund requests. He looked at one of the other vice presidents and repeated my question to her. She had been with the company since the beginning. The bottom line was that no one had bothered to be concerned about the refund requests. In addition, no one was concerned about the high employee turnover. Mr. Shylock did not demonstrate any observable concern about ether situation until it was too late.

Once the company began its speedy decline all of a sudden Mr. Shylock became concerned and started to blame everyone but himself. The vice president previously mentioned was a very smart woman; however, she had been an executive secretary with no managerial experience or training and she had been given significant responsibility for running the entire operations part of the company for several years before I arrived.

Not only was she inexperienced, she was virtually an introvert and liked to remain in her office with the door closed most of the time. When describing her personality once Mr. Shylock said she was a wallflower at parties and sat in a corner with her face to the wall. Knowing all of this, Mr. Shylock still left her in charge while he was away on his many trips to the other offices and to New York in his quest to have the company go public.

In addition, Mr. Shylock's right hand man Nick who was operating as Vice President in charge of the salesman at the time I was hired had cancer. He was in very bad condition as this was his third bout with cancer and while he tried very hard to help run the company he was obviously unable to do so, yet he and the woman mentioned above, were in complete charge for long periods of time.

Nick was a very nice person and it broke my heart to see him trying to do the job. He came into the office even on days in which he received chemotherapy treatment. Many times he could barely walk yet he drove eighty miles one way to Sherman Oaks, California most days. Sometimes Shylock did allow him to spend the night at the hotel across the street from the office.

Salesmen at Shylock were hired based on their personality and ability to sell. Most of them knew nothing about the tax system and I do mean nothing. Also because they were paid commissions based strictly on sales, they sold services we would never have been able to get IRS to approve.

Numerous clients told me the salesmen were guaranteeing we could get an OIC for them. The contract explicitly said we did not guarantee an OIC; however, people being people, most of them did not read the contract they signed. In their hour of desperation the clients believed Shylock was the answer to all of their problems. After all why would Shylock charge such large fees if we could not get an OIC approved?

As I previously mentioned, the salesmen's' incentive to sell was the commission and the rules for the commissions changed daily or so it seemed. At one time the commission situation was changed so that the salesmen received fifty dollars for each client they interviewed. Does that make any sense? If you are going to be paid just to interview someone you do not have any particular incentive to sell them anything. This was one of Mr. Shylock's brilliant ideas. He was a great idea man, but was one who never gave any thought as to how or even whether his ideas could be implemented.

He refused to listen to any naysayers whether we made sense or not. Once the salesman had made the sale, the case was then turned over to my employees, the client services employees, the ones authorized to represent the clients before IRS. Mr. Shylock was directly responsible for the salesmen. The client services employees, enrolled agents, were salaried employees. They received their salary regardless of what happened to the case.

This payroll situation put the client services employees at cross purposes with the salesmen. I called this to the attention of Mr. Shylock and even though he paid me lip service, he never took the necessary action to assure only good sales were made.

The Shylock company was doomed to failure from the beginning. Even though, as mentioned earlier, Mr. Shylock was a very smart man and a great idea man, his follow through left much to be desired. It was as though his objective was to crash and burn as soon as possible. He failed to see or to do anything about the obvious problem right before his eyes.

When I or one of the other vice presidents advised him of problems or obstacles in some of his plans, again, he paid lip service by agreeing to what was said and then he continued along the road to self destruction for himself, the company, and many clients/taxpayers. Only a fool would allow extremely high turnover to consistently occur without doing something about it, particularly as it caused the work on cases to come to a grinding halt when a case had to be transferred because an employee resigned.

The company ended up working on cases for which no money was being paid. Clients had to pay their accounts in full within a few months unless they provided post dated checks. With the submission of post dated checks they were allowed monthly payments, with full payment due before the completed case was submitted to IRS.

Many, many times, on many, many, many cases the client had full paid over a year or more and the case was still being worked at Shylock's and had not been submitted to IRS for resolution. Mr. Shylock was oblivious to the problems his company was causing the clients in their pursuit of a resolution to their tax problems. He operated with blinders on seeing only what he wanted to see. He was arrogant and pompous to the extent that about nine months before he filed the first bankruptcy, Chapter 11, he was writing letters to smaller companies offering to buy them out, yet he had an overage inventory of at least 50%.

The cases were considered overage if they had been open over a year. In addition to the overage problem, many cases were returned from IRS for re-work after having been held there for a year or more. With the employee turnover being what it was at Shylock's, by the time many of the cases were returned for corrections the employee who had submitted the case was no longer working there.

On one particular occasion while an employee was working on a case to be submitted as an OIC case, I had to become involved as the client services employee advised me he had been informed by the revenue officer that there was no way the client was going to get an OIC approved.

Even though the client provided financial information that showed inability to pay, the revenue officer refused to accept it as the taxpayer's true financial worth. The revenue officer had conducted an extensive investigation and had not been able to discover any assets belonging to the client that could be seized. This taxpayer receives considerable disability funds monthly as a result of having attempted suicide and being considered emotionally troubled. In addition, his wife was terminally ill.

Prior to his illness he had had a very lucrative career and had paid into an insurance for his disability payments and as he had been a professional person making high money, he paid enough to ensure he could maintain his living standards should he become incapacitated. His disability funds were high, but they were just enough to pay his bills and he did not own any assets the revenue officer could go after. He did have a partnership that troubled the revenue officer as the revenue officer consistently tried to find some funds coming through the partnership to the taxpayer. He couldn't find anything.

The revenue officer told me his branch chief would not allow him to close the case as an approved OIC. He told me his branch chief's name and I understood why. This branch chief is the one I mentioned earlier in the chapter. He is the one who was formerly over the Special Procedures function in Los Angeles.

The merits of the case dictated an OIC was possible, but if not approved, then certainly an installment agreement would be in line. But no, this revenue officer had orders to continue to pursue immediate full payment. Continuing to pursue immediate full payment was okay, but in the meantime the humane thing to do would have been to give the client a temporary installment agreement. How do I know this is possible? Remember, I was a revenue officer and progressed up to and past this branch chief's position. I know what IRS can and cannot do.

A temporary installment agreement would have allowed the taxpayer to reduce some of the future interest and penalty that was continuing to accrue. After granting the temporary installment agreement, if the revenue officer located assets he could then rescind the installment agreement and seize the assets.

But no, rather than work with the Shylock employee or the taxpayer, the revenue officer, at the bidding of his branch chief, would not allow the taxpayer any leeway. He continued to contact the taxpayer and on several occasions levied on his disability check in the bank only to have to release the levy. Certain income is exempt from levy and certain income requires the division chief or the district director's approval before it can be attached by levy. This taxpayer's income met both criteria and the revenue officer was in err when he served the levy. My subordinate manager, the manager of the client services employee working on the case made numerous attempts to contact the revenue officer's manager to discuss the case, but to no avail as the manager did not return any phone calls.

It is important for IRS collection employees to be firm and to do the job they have been hired to do, but the foregoing is an example of taxpayer abuse. The division chief in Los Angeles and all of the management are aware of this branch chief and his tactics and I have personally seen them laugh at it rather than take action to correct it.

I left Shylock while this case was being worked otherwise it was one I would have definitely referred to the district director. Now that the IRS is experiencing negative media publicity, this would be the best time for this taxpayer to get in touch with the district director. Rather than receive additional negative publicity I am sure this taxpayer's case would be resolved right away.

Shylock did not have any system set up to assure case integrity. No system was in place to protect the privacy of the clients or to ensure employees did not destroy casework. Cases were filed in unlocked drawers and cabinets and were left out overnight while the cleaning crew did their job. Case files contained social security numbers, location of assets including bank accounts as well as many other items I am sure the clients would not want shared with anyone not having a need to know. Also, copies of checks were left laying around on desks in the accounts receivable section.

As a result of the above deficiencies, cases were always being lost. As offices were closed cases were transferred to other offices without any system set up to ensure all cases were accounted for. Closed cases were put in boxes and were literally dumped in the basement of the headquarters building.

When employees found it necessary to look for closed cases they evidently emptied the boxes and left the cases out on the floor. Consequently, the basement ended up with cases from all offices mixed up and scattered on the floor.

While I worked for Shylock the Orange, Bakersfield, and Sacramento offices closed. When those offices closed the cases assigned to that office were shipped to the headquarters office in Sherman Oaks. The offices had been closed because the company was heading at breakneck speed towards bankruptcy and so obviously there were no employees available to work the cases. The cases were either placed in the basement of headquarters or they went to the Riverside office and those employees worked the cases if a client found their phone number and complained. Otherwise, the cases sat unworked even though the client had paid the full fee.

Interestingly enough during my last years in the IRS Los Angeles district it was a known fact that the IRS closed cases were kept in the basement until they met the time limit for transferring to the archives. There had been a fire in the federal building at one point and the fire originated in the basement of the building. The water used to put out the fire had destroyed and or damaged some of the closed files. The entire section was in total disarray.

Many, many times IRS employees were looking for closed files they could not find because of the mess in the basement. The more I think about it the more similarities I find in IRS and Shylock Corporation. Cases fitting into the closed case category at Shylock included cases not having been resolved, but all work stopped as a result of not being paid in full to Shylock and cases closed for failure to receive necessary information from the taxpayer even though Shylock had been paid in full.

It sometimes became necessary to look for a closed case because a full paid client finally got around to responding to Shylock's request for information. It also became necessary on a few occasions because the client threatened to sue the company for misrepresentation. It was virtually impossible to find many closed cases.

One of the last searches for a closed case I became involved in was the result of a client requesting a refund and threatening to sue for misrepresentation if the refund was not granted. The client also threatened to go to IRS with the misrepresentation theory. She said she had been promised a concrete resolution otherwise she would not have paid the large sum of $7000.00. (See Exhibit 11 for Shylock's fee schedule.) Mr. Shylock was besides himself at the idea of someone threatening to go to IRS.

I had my assistant spend several days and many hours in the basement looking futilely for the case. He never found it.

About two to three months after I started working at Shylock a new person was hired as the manager of the accounts receivable department. He worked hard to bring Shylock into a positive financial situation, but based on numerous discussions I had with him it was actually a losing proposition even before he or I joined the company. He even told me how amazed he was that the company was approved to go public on the stock market.

Evidently, from the bits and pieces I picked up in discussions with this manager and one of the other vice presidents, the books would have to have been doctored to reflect an untrue financial situation. Otherwise, the company would never have been approved to make the public offering. That is one of the reasons why in less than a year after receiving five million dollars the company started to downsize and eventually go out of business in California.

Another unproved theory discussed by Shylock employees was that the downsizing was part of a grand plan for Mr. Shylock to siphon money out of the company and deposit it out of the country. The ultimate plan was supposedly to close the California offices and to expand Texas.

Whether or not it was part of a grand plan, some of the scenario gossiped about has taken place. Bankruptcy has been filed twice. Chapter 11, reorganization, was filed first. Chapter 11 provides the debtor an opportunity to reorganize financially and operationally. This chapter was filed in early summer. After several months, Chapter 7 was filed and the employees were scaled down to a skeleton crew. The employees were laid off without any advance notice. They went to work on a Monday and were told that was their last day there.

Chapter 7, liquidation bankruptcy was filed in early fall. This chapter provides that the debtor turn all assets over to a trustee who will liquidate the assets for the benefit of creditors. This seems to be too coincidental to not be part of a plan.

I phoned the Shylock headquarters office in early January 1998 only to find out the phone number was no longer working. I am in touch with former employees who know what is going on there and I have found out that Shylock changed the name and continued to operate as a different company once the bankruptcy had been approved.

At the time of the first downsizing I was offered the opportunity to be transferred to an office closer to home, but I had decided to leave Shylock. Clients were calling every day at an average of three to four a day screaming and demanding better service. Better service meant getting an OIC approved whether they qualified for it or not. They all said they had been promised an OIC would be approved.

I believed some of the clients because I knew the salesmen were hustlers and were not concerned about anything but their commission. Most of the stress was coming from clients that were brought into the company before I started working there and many were there as the result of sales made by the salesman that had been arrested and from Mr. Shylock himself. This made it hard to believe Mr. Shylock when he said he was demanding good and honest service from the salesmen. After all Mr. Shylock was the salesman on many of the questionable cases.

Over a period of time I realized the stress from so many unhappy clients was more than what I had bargained for. I also figured I had more than enough examples of how things look sitting across the table from IRS. By then the downsizing had begun.

I hated to leave the taxpayers in the situation they were in, but I am a very practical, realistic person and I realized I could not even begin to resolve the clients problems and the stress from dealing with so many unhappy people was not going to do me any good. I could appreciate the fact that while I was there I did everything I could to see to it that all clients were treated fairly and honestly. While I never saw anything illegal going on I didn't feel right working there.

I resigned fourteen months after joining the company. In addition to receiving too much stress at Shylock I was also concerned about the lack of concern of Mr. Shylock. I had seen him promise many things he knew up front he could not deliver such as stock options and 401-K's for the employees. I also became concerned Shylock might be raided again by IRS and I didn't plan to be there should that happen. My last day there was April 4, 1997.

After I left the company Shylock found out that he had breast cancer. He is currently receiving chemotherapy. He also had to get a job outside of the Shylock company as an accountant because the company wasn't making enough money to allow him to take care of his large family in the manner in which they had become accustomed.

The skeleton crew continued to operate with a manager remaining from the original company. The company was doing okay financially considering it was very small with small caseloads. And then one day Mr. Shylock decided he needed more money than what he was receiving from the company and his outside job. He increased his take of the funds being received in Shylock which cut the pay of the remaining employees significantly and they all walked out and formed their own business taking the clients with them.

Once again the clients/taxpayers are coming out on the short end of the deal. The cases are being worked by a small crew of employees who do not have much experience. In addition, with the cases being transferred from office to office they have to sit once more until someone has time to get to them.

In my opinion Shylock and IRS have treated the taxpayers the same. It is unconscionable that the taxpayers have to pay such a high price as a result of deliberate neglect from both their government and their paid for representative.

Chapter Seven

ADDRESSING CONCERNS EXPRESSED DURING 1997 IRS HEARINGS

Through the years IRS has experienced significant negative publicity based on individual cases as well as based on serious situations resulting in congressional hearings. Most of the time the hearings have resulted in some minor changes in the way IRS has operated. In the early 1970's the IRS Los Angeles Chief of Criminal Investigation received very serious negative publicity as the result of allegations investigated by a congressional subcommittee.

Those allegations combined with very negative comments made about the chief in the book Skintight written by Christopher Byron significantly lowered the esteem of what may have been that of the most glamorous division chief IRS has ever had. He retired shortly after the turmoil, much sooner than anyone had expected, but he was taken down several pegs by IRS before he left.

I can remember being in the Director's office in Los Angeles when this Chief of CID was called in and asked about a trivial matter that needed some action. The director told him he wanted him to take a particular action regarding some situation and the Chief said he would have someone get on it right away. Even though I was just a lowly branch chief at the time, the Director took the Chief down a peg right in front of me and told him that when he was told to do something he needed to move faster and that he was expected to handle the matter himself and that he was not to delegate it down to one of his subordinates.

The 1970 hearings resulted in the Chief CID being thoroughly humiliated in the book Skin Tight by Christopher Byron. IRS Hearings also resulted in major changes eventually taken place in IRS procedures for seizures. Prior to some of those hearings IRS employees had carte blanche to seize and sell a taxpayers property, real and personal, without any authority other than that of the revenue officer and the revenue officer's manager. The negative publicity that came out of the hearings as well as several seizures that resulted in negative publicity caused IRS to have to obtain a court order before seizing a taxpayer's business.

The 1997 IRS Congressional Hearings by and large will go down in history as bringing about some of the largest changes ever in the organization. With a new Commissioner coming in at just the time of the hearings it provided a great opportunity to implement changes. Some of the most significant changes are those involving interest rates, burden of proof, and suits against the IRS.

The change in interest rates is a big one because the IRS is now required to pay taxpayers interest on delayed refunds at the same rate they charge taxpayers for outstanding liabilities. This change is long overdue as IRS has been able to get away with murder in this area.

The changes in burden of proof is also one that is long overdue with IRS now being required to prove that taxpayers owe taxes. That is a direct reversal of the previous rule that taxpayers were required to prove they did not owe taxes.

Changes in the ability to sue IRS includes an informal expedited hearing in Tax Court now available for cases involving up to $25000, a change from the cap of $10000.

While the hearings were going on some employees became motivated to blow the whistle on some of their managers they either believed were not operating the way they should be or in some instances to take the opportunity to take a shot at a manager they did not particularly like.

The latter instance was demonstrated in Oklahoma City, Oklahoma when some managers complained that their division chief had established a quota system and was driving them for the numbers. As a result of this complaint the division chief was taken out of his job while an investigation was conducted. I know this division chief having worked with him when he was the Executive Assistant to the Assistant Commissioner of Collections in the Western Region.

I would not doubt that the division chief was driving managers for increased numbers, but he has been around too long to do something stupid that would provide the employees the opportunity to prove he had done something illegal. During the time this was going on I spoke with numerous people who know this division chief and we all felt the same way.

The complaint from his subordinate managers came about at an opportune time for national office to show that some heads were rolling as the result of the complaint and the hearings. This particular division chief just became the scape-goat of the day.

After the so called investigation was conducted the division chief was returned to his job as nothing could be proven. To substantiate the fact that he was not liked by his employees, a white manager filed a racial suit against the division chief who happened to be black. The actual suit was filed by three former IRS mangers, one white male and two white females. The suit alleged that the division chief discriminated against them and orchestrated retaliation after they complained.

According to the Daily Oklahoman Newspaper dated August 28, 1997, the three former managers alleged they were "victims of poor job evaluations and a negative memo campaign to make them quit their jobs. Jurors ruled against each of their race and retaliation claims."

However, again according to the Daily Oklahoman Newspaper, although the race claim was lost, " the eight person jury, including one black woman, decided the agency illegally retaliated against him (the white male) for complaining about discrimination." Federal law allows employees to win retaliation damages even if the underlying discrimination claim is considered unfounded.

Many of the problems identified in the 1997 IRS Congressional Hearings are the result of what I call institutional arrogance on the part of IRS as well as blindness when it comes to eliminating unnecessary actions. During the hearing it was identified that IRS sent out tax due notices to many Alaskan citizens for cents owed. This is not surprising to me because many IRS employees get notices for taxes due for less than $20.00 and because it is a high crime for employees to be delinquent in their taxes, IRS actually initiates an adverse action investigation to determine whether disciplinary action should be taken against the employee.

The 1997 Congressional Hearings painted a very negative picture of IRS. Having been there at the forefront and also having the opportunity to sit on the opposite side of the table while working as a representative for delinquent taxpayers, I can say that it is probably similar to the way most things in life are, some of it is deserved, some of it is reported as seen through the eyes of taxpayers who do not understand the system, and unfortunately, some of it is coming from taxpayers who are trying to beat the system, those who do not intend to pay taxes unless they have to.

Many things that came out during the hearings have significant merit. Such things as the question of whether or not taxpayers should be allowed to go to court before any and every IRS seizure is made. Allowing each and every taxpayer to go to court before the seizure is made will tie up the system and prevent taxes from being paid for years and years. It will also create a tremendous burden for IRS.

It is past time for citizens to decide whether or not taxes should have to be paid. It appears that most citizens accept the reality of having to pay taxes even though many of us don't particularly like it. However, the small percentage who refuse to pay without being made to can do serious damage to the entire system unless the focus on reality is maintained by congress.

The lack of oversight on IRS was brought up during the hearings and it was said that there's no oversight because no one knows what IRS is doing. That is an absolutely correct statement. It is amazing to hear members of congress discuss IRS and its failings when it is clear most of them do not have a clue as to what actually happens inside IRS.

You have to either be inside IRS or have the opportunity for detailed briefings of the everyday rules and regulations to be able to understand. I believe if you take the average member of congress and ask him/her to describe the difference between what happens with IRS liens or levies you would get either blank looks or a lot of filibustering.

Senator Orrin Hatch made the statement during the hearings that it is not unusual for taxpayers' to pay far more in interest and penalty than the original taxes because IRS dragged its' feet. That statement is accurate; however, the question should be why does IRS drag its' feet. If the truth be known there are many reasons why IRS drags its' feet and congress is culpable for many of the problems as they are caused by budget problems.

Many, many times IRS does not have enough employees to work what could be considered a reasonable caseload. Many, many times revenue officers have hundreds of cases waiting to be assigned to them.

Ten years or so ago the revenue officers carried all of the cases assigned to them in their active inventory. Union pressure and IRS' attempts to appear to reduce the numbers created a system wherein only a certain number of cases can be assigned to any one revenue officer at a time. However, the manager holds cases in an in house queue, assigning cases each time the revenue officer closes cases. All of the revenue officers understand this process so whose fooling who.

Congress' reduction of budgets, freezing of budgets, closing down the government, all of these things makes them culpable to the IRS problem of dragging its' feet. It is very simple most of the time. IRS does not have the money to hire the numbers that are needed. In addition, training is hampered when numbers are reduced. When there are few employees available what should be done, take time out to train or keep everyone on the front-line working cases?

An idea that came out during the hearings appears to have some potential merit. It was stated that congress clearly doesn't have a clue as to how to resolve the IRS situation and they will never get substantial help from IRS current employees. It was suggested that congress get retired managers together and solicit their help.

Having been a front-line employee as well as a manager, who would be in a better position to provide suggestions and information that could ultimately help to make things better? Did congress pick up on this idea? If so, they must still be mulling it over because it hasn't been mentioned since the hearings almost a year ago. I don't believe congress cares overall. They simply want the complaints to go away so that they don't have to be bothered.

Senator Lott expressed his opinion about what he described as an IRS culture where employees start out as nice people who become nasty and he asked why? It is true that most employees start out as nice people and I like to think they remain basically nice people. However, to successfully collect taxes one has to develop somewhat of a thick skin.

You need to keep in mind that many of the delinquent taxpayers do not want to nor do they intend to pay taxes. The things tax collectors have to do to collect taxes are not nice things, but they are things that have to be done. These things can be done the right way or can be done the wrong way. No matter how you slice it when you hear that someone's wages, automobile, or home has been taken the first thing that comes to mind is what a mean nasty act.

Many revenue officers start out trying to give every taxpayer they deal with a break and very shortly they find out that the hard line delinquents lie about their ability to pay and lie about their assets. These taxpayers promise to pay and then they disappear. Once this has been done repeatedly it is very difficult to look at the delinquent taxpayer as a nice citizen willing to cooperate. Remember, most taxpayers pay their taxes as soon as they know they are owed.

A significant number of taxpayers make sure they never owe by paying estimated taxes or have sufficient withholding. The taxpayers IRS deal with are those who knew they owed taxes when they filed their return. They also receive four notices before their case is sent to the field for revenue officer involvement. Obviously, some of these taxpayers cannot pay and they have been afraid to contact IRS. The majority however, are those hard line taxpayers trying to get away with not paying anything. They make up a very small percentage of the taxpaying population, about 3%, but that equates to hundreds of thousands of delinquent taxpayers' cases in IRS.

An egregious example of an IRS problem highlighted during the 1997 Hearings was shown in the case of taxpayer Katherine Hicks. She happens to be a Laguna taxpayer and while I have no personal knowledge of her case it appeared that her case was going on while I was the Collection Chief in Laguna. Again I don't have personal knowledge of her case; however, I do know that cases similar to the situation she described during the Hearings have occurred many, many times in IRS. Those are the kinds of problems that should not happen.

It appears Ms. Hicks paid her taxes, received refunds of the amounts she had paid and still ended up in a nightmare of IRS liens, levies and seizures. Based on my experience, her situation did not come about because of some nasty, mean spirited employees. Her situation seems to be the result of one hand not knowing what the other hand is doing. It is also one of the best examples of the faulty system in which IRS employees are working. And of course a good portion of this problem could have been prevented if an employee experienced in this kind of problem had been available and had been willing to take the time necessary to get involved in the overall case rather than seeing collecting as the only way out.

During my revenue officer days before I became a manager I was assigned many cases in which taxpayers had paid their taxes only to have the money refunded. Subsequently the taxpayer was notified that the money was still due. In some cases this went on repeatedly until I or someone else became thoroughly involved and straightened the matter out. Those situations are very difficult many times and many employees do not really know exactly what to do to get the mater resolved. This includes me when I was working cases. Many times I just tried everything I could think of and finally something clicked and I could close the case,

There were and probably still are many cases where erroneous refunds have been issued to taxpayers. I personally worked many of these cases and let me tell you they are difficult. Many times the taxpayers would say they had spent the refund and could not pay the money back. This should have been a legitimate reason as most people did not understand the system and did not know whether they should have received a refund or not. Did that reason cause us to lighten up on the taxpayer? Absolutely not. We treated those taxpayers the same as those who had started out owing and refusing to voluntarily pay their taxes. We went after them with everything we had.

Those erroneous refund cases are just small examples of how IRS treats taxpayers and why taxpayers feel the way they do about IRS. Strong hostility and fear are the results of IRS actions and this is demonstrated during congressional hearings regarding IRS actions.

IRS does deserve the negative publicity received in the hearings because even if all of the taxpayers appearing at the hearings are not 100% truthful there are many, many, many more who have been dealt with unfairly and unnecessarily harsh who will never appear at a hearing.

The current Commissioner appears to be making great attempts to improve customer satisfaction; however, I see looming problems on the horizon. While many IRS problem resolution sessions are being held all over the country and numerous resources are being directed towards resolving taxpayers problems, collections are down. Those resources are being taken away from IRS employees basic jobs of collecting taxes and examining returns. It is only a matter of time before Congress starts to heat up and ask IRS why more money is not being collected and why more cases are not being closed.

What happens then? I predict the old cycle starts once more. It begins with taxpayers complaining so much congressional hearings are conducted. As a result of the hearings IRS starts to become "kinder and gentler". The "kinder and gentler" IRS' collections start to go down because the public believes they will be given more time and may not even have to pay all of their taxes.

Congress waking up from having dealt with some significant situation such as the Clinton/Lewinsky affair and finding time on their hands begin to realize IRS isn't collecting what is expected. Congress then begins to beat up on IRS and the employees get the message that in order to satisfy the mandate for more money they must lien, levy, and seize. Once again the taxpayers start to complain and so on, and so on.

In my twenty five plus years in IRS I was part of and saw this cycle repeated every few years. Believe me when I say it will go around again because while everyone is working feverishly to resolve the "IRS problem" no one seems to know exactly what it is.

Chapter Eight

INCREASING COLLECTIONS

Promoting voluntary compliance is basically what IRS is about. To do this IRS is charged with collecting taxes and securing delinquent returns. Securing delinquent returns is more of a priority with IRS than collecting taxes.

Filing tax returns for the most part is a voluntary act for taxpayers. IRS does not have sufficient resources to go after citizens should there be an overall increase in failure to file tax returns. Generally speaking, most people file their required tax returns either out of their patriotic duty or fear of IRS. If most citizens failed to file their income tax returns there isn't much IRS could do about it. In addition, the taxes cannot be collected until the return has been filed. This makes voluntary compliance the single most important aspect of the entire system.

At the beginning of revenue officer training, trainees are told of the importance of voluntary compliance demonstrated by the filing of the tax return. For some unexplainable reason, as time goes on most revenue officers prioritize TDA's before TDI's. I suppose it is because a TDA has a specific dollar amount attached while TDI's are assigned with a potential dollar amount that may or may not be valid.

A revenue officer only receives a TDA once a taxpayer has filed a tax return. Revenue officers receive a TDI after it has been determined that a return is due and has not been filed. The TDI is generally based on what was shown on the last return filed. However, many times the outstanding return is not due for various reasons including death, bankruptcy, insufficient income or no income and out of business status to name a few.

Once employed as a revenue officer, a trainee finds the collection process to be centered around how much each person can collect. As stated previously, the collection aspect of the tax business appears to be cyclical. When the pressure is on from Congress, national office, regional office, and local management, the amount of dollars collected becomes paramount. When public sentiment rises against IRS, collection activity drops.

The 1997 - 1998 congressional hearings and taxpayer complaints will ultimately lead to a reduction in the amount of dollars collected by IRS collection divisions because IRS is now concentrating once again on being a "kinder, gentler IRS". For some reason I was never able to understand during my entire career, IRS has never been able to collect taxes while treating taxpayers "right". It always seems to be an either or position. Sure, tax collectors never have been and never will be popular and well liked, but they should be able to collect taxes and still treat taxpayers courteous and with dignity.

An article entitled, "More Problems with the IRS Described at Hearing" was found on the Internet dated Wednesday, September 24, 1997, Deloitte & Touche Online, Tax News & Views. This article addresses the inconsistencies in the treatment of IRS by Congress. The article goes on to say, "When the Service cracks down on taxpayers and tries to collect all owed taxes, legislators complain that some taxpayers are unfairly or harshly treated, but when the General Accounting Office and other government watchdogs note that the IRS cannot close the gap between taxes assessed and collected, Congress charges that the Service cannot do its job."

During these times not only does Congress acclaim that IRS cannot do its job, Congress also starts to reduce the budget and to tighten up rules and regulations, demanding time consuming, lengthy responses to taxpayers' complaints.

One of the primary obstacles IRS is faced with daily in collecting taxes was identified in the article mentioned above. The article stated that "Internal Revenue Service sometimes targets lower-income taxpayers because they do not have the resources to defend themselves as do upper-income taxpayers, an IRS employee told the Senate Finance Committee September 24."

This is actually a true statement but not necessarily for the reasons stated in the article. It ties into the next statement in the article, "IRS agents also have manipulated income tax return figures to increase their office or division tax collection statistics, Jennifer Long, an IRS revenue agent, told the panel."

IRS Collection Divisions, individual managers, and individual employees do target smaller dollar accounts, not directly because the taxpayers do not have the resources to defend themselves, but because many small dollar accounts are easier to collect. Most taxpayers with small dollar accounts are wage earners and IRS can easily attach wages by serving a levy to the taxpayer's employer. Many upper-income taxpayers have their money shielded and it takes investigative efforts to locate it. With IRS being in the business of collecting money the smartest thing to do is to collect as much as possible the easiest way possible.

To add to the issue of collecting from lower-income taxpayers IRS created collection sites called ACS (automated collection sites) whose primary responsibility is to collect small dollar accounts and they do a great job of collecting. Also, IRS has a system set up wherein employees at service centers and ACS sites initiate computer generated automatic actions on small dollar cases as opposed to cases with higher dollar amounts being assigned to revenue officers for personal field contact. This automatically means it takes longer for the case to be worked as it has to be assigned to the revenue officer by the Service Center. The revenue officers then have to take the case into inventory and work it along with the many other cases that are assigned to them.

The comment in the article about manipulation of figures by IRS employees is accurate and is easily done. IRS divisions require reports to be prepared by individual employees and these are then fed up to the division to be compiled. The reports are manually prepared in many divisions as a result of lack of sophisticated computer equipment and/or computer skills. This allows anyone the opportunity to inflate their individual reports.

IRS is feverishly attempting to remedy this situation by providing equipment and training that will provide safeguards to reduce the ability for employees to inflate there productivity reports. However, IRS' inability to deal with tax systems modernization and inadequate funding keeps IRS in a very ineffective position.

The current Commissioner of IRS Charles Rosotti started his new position off with a bang. It was obvious that as a result of the 1997 Hearings someone had to pay the price. In addition to many changes being implemented and the Deputy Commissioner resigning, Commissioner Rosotti initiated action to be taken by a three-member outside review panel to take a look at IRS and its alleged use of quotas. As a result of the panels findings twelve top mangers were issued reprimands, with two others admonished and others reassigned. Rosotti plans to have 132 more IRS officials investigated according to the San Diego Union Tribune dated September 15, 1998.

The new Commissioner has established a new disciplinary office for either misuse of enforcement statistics or improper seizure of property. I can assure Rosotti that there has been misuse of enforcement statistics and improper seizure of property. The difficulty is in being able to pinpoint it. The organization is not sophisticated enough to catch a smart revenue officer or revenue agent in the act of inflating statistics and they will certainly have difficulty in identifying a manger who is setting quotas based on dollars collected.

One of the most important means of being able to monitor statistics will be updated tax systems which are still out of reach of IRS. If an employee inputs a closure on the computer and sufficient information is there for someone to be able to go back and verify that it was an appropriate closure, management will be able to ensure that the statistics are appropriate. As long as employees and managers are still preparing and working with reports prepared manually it is going to be extremely difficult to find a cheater.

According to the San Diego Union-Tribune article, "The 1988 Taxpayer Bill of Rights specifically prohibits production goals or quotas, and a 1973 IRS directive says no enforcement statistics can be used to evaluate employees. However, the review panel found both were violated in national police and field-level collections."

In line with the above it is very interesting that the newspaper article stated a major reason for the violations was, "the pressure on the IRS to collect the most taxes possible and beef up compliance, resulting in a system of ranking district offices in which "measurement of productivity was paramount" to determine effectiveness, the review panel found." This statement is amazing to me because it has long been known in IRS from top to bottom levels of management that pressure has always been on management to rank high in areas of productivity.

As you will read later in this chapter many, many statistical reports have been generated from top level national and regional management identifying and ranking districts and divisions within districts. I have hard copies of many of those reports as you will see in the exhibits. Now who is fooling who. Could this be part of the reason why certain top level executives are no longer with IRS, some having left prior to being eligible for retirement with no future employment lined up?

The GAO (U. S. General Accounting Office) performs various types of audits of IRS and in April 1997 GAO reported to a House Government Reform and Oversight Committee that, "The IRS's faulty computer systems and its failure to act expeditiously are to blame for the approximately $200 billion inventory in uncollected taxes."

As a result of concerns regarding IRS' ability to collect taxes and to close the tax gap, IRS implemented a pilot program by contracting with private debt collectors to track down delinquent funds. IRS found that the private collectors experienced the same problems they are faced with. The pilot was considered a failure and went down in history as another IRS unsuccessful costly program.

According to my sources, current employees, as well as newspaper articles, magazines, and congressional hearings, IRS is primarily concerned with preventing taxpayer complaints. Much time is being spent on "treating customers right". The Los Angeles Times newspaper dated January 14, 1998, contained an article, "IRS Admits It Ranked Staff Members by Aggressiveness". The article reads, "Taxation: Saying agency failed to provide 'fair enforcement of law', Chief vows to end overzealous collection practices". While this article may be true it is a sure sign collections are on the way towards being reduced.

The article in the Times newspaper discussed the use of quotas and statistics being used to evaluate the performance of employees and supervisors. It also discussed the ranking of tax collections of district offices. According to the article this is the "first time IRS has examined its' district operations across the country on the issue of statistical rankings.

The article used the Oklahoma City, Oklahoma Collection Division as an example. While I have known the current chief of that division for many years, I do not have actual knowledge of whether the allegations are true or not. However, I do know that what has been alleged to have gone on in Oklahoma City is not unique. IRS officials are known to talk out of both sides of their mouths and for them to have led anyone to believe they were not aware of statistical ranking going on is definitely untrue.

The problems of utilizing quotas and statistics are finally being identified by the public watchdogs as seen in the Internet article of Deloitte & Touche Online dated September 24, 1997, "More Problems with the IRS Described at

Hearing." IRS employees told the Senate Finance Committee that IRS agents, "have manipulated income tax return figures to increase their office or division tax collection statistics." I'm sure this is an accurate statement as I have personally known managers who did the same thing.

One branch chief I worked with as a peer received several merit pay increases at the end of the work year as the result of manipulating figures to show how well his branch was doing. In addition, one manager in the IRS Special Procedures Section illegally wrote off accounts as uncollectible in an effort to increase his closure statistics. Both of these managers were promoted up the ladder and each went to other districts as top level mangers even though their transgressions were grievous and well known throughout the district where the crimes were committed.

In the IRS Hearing, Senate Finance Committee Chairman William Roth expressed his concern regarding the utilization of statistics to rate IRS employees' performance. Roth stated, "The perceived need to fulfill quotas may be preventing tax collectors from using their best judgment."

Through the years collection divisions have been ranked year after year by all levels of management including that of national office. The success of the collection divisions has been based primarily on the amount of dollars collected. During my last year with IRS the collection division chiefs in Western Region were told fiscal year 1995 -1996 was "the year of the dollar". We were all told this in all managers meeting by the Chief, Compliance Officer in the regional office.

National and regional reports were shared with all of us and those divisions ranking high were praised while those at the bottom were verbally and emotionally "beaten up". (See Exhibit 12 for overview of the 1995 year end assessment) My district, Laguna Niguel, was rated very good for having exceeded above average dollars collected. Also in Exhibit 12 Examination Division in Laguna Niguel was ranked outstanding for exceeding the goal of assessing Form 1040 Income Tax dollars per hour.

The Los Angeles Times article mentioned that ranking "employees on their aggressiveness in collecting delinquent taxes and conducing seizures of property is in violation of laws intended to protect Americans from overzealous tax enforcement". If you read the article you might believe IRS did not know managers were being ranked. However, Exhibit 13 Quarterly Compliance Comparisons: June FY (fiscal year) 95 clearly shows a memorandum addressed to Directors of Western Region ranking all Western Region districts.

In my opinion, the use of collection statistics in determining the success of IRS, especially those used in the collection divisions, is appropriate. It is the way the statistics are used that can cause problems. As stated before I have never agreed with the IRS' stance on use of reports that measure the status of collections.

The June FY 95 memo lists all districts in Western Region and shows dollars collected as well as the percent change from FY 1994 to FY 1995. It also states under the graph on page 1, "Western leads all regions in total dollars collected, but ranks sixth in Dollars Collected per staff year. Little progress has been made since last quarter in meeting the region wide goal. Laguna and San Francisco are the only two districts which are on target."

These results were discussed extensively at the September 1995 Western Region Collection Division chiefs meeting in Las Vegas, Nevada. At this meeting division chiefs were asked to advise (in front of everyone in the meeting - about 25 -30 people) of what percent of improvement could be expected in the upcoming fiscal year. Of course being the chief of Laguna, I had it made for that final quarter of the year as well as the entire fiscal year's ending. We were at the top of the region and most of the country.

Now I ask you , if you are competitive, aggressive or assertive, and take pride in what you do, how would you feel about being at the bottom? What would you do about it? Most chiefs would go back to their divisions and take what ever steps were necessary to ensure more dollars would be collected and to ensure they did not have to face the region's public wrath again.

As I said earlier, IRS at the top talks out of both sides of its mouth, wanting more dollars collected but, wanting it done "quietly". Above all, everyone is expected to be smart enough to collect enough money to meet the objectives and to be able to keep from generating any unfavorable publicity.

The month following the meeting in Las Vegas, October 1995, a meeting was held in Pasadena, California with both district directors and managers from the districts attending in addition to executives from the region and national office. During this meeting my district director was singled out because of the great job "his collection division was doing" in increasing collections. He lapped the praise up like a dehydrated cat slurping milk. Yet, he was the one who placed many obstacles in our way because he was afraid some bad publicity would come up and prevent him from receiving his retirement. Is it any wonder IRS employees operate the way they do many times? Many policies and procedures are inconsistent based upon the way the wind in congress or the public happens to be blowing at any given time.

I decided a long time ago that I would make my own decisions regarding what needed to be done to be successful because I recognized the double edged sword I had to operate under. Here national office wanted to see increases in dollars collected. However, the director, was so conservative the divisions chief worth their salt did not go to him to discuss most of their plans as he would always, always want you to make changes in your plans.

As an example, if you had a plan to increase collections and it involved open discussions with employees about this topic he became paranoid. He wanted the collections increased, but he was very paranoid about how it was going to be done. Rather than have to go through the changes I knew he would try to take me through if I told him everything I was going to do, I decided to tell him just what he needed to know and to do what I needed to do. I always operated within the guidelines, but I took guidelines to be guidelines and not absolute direction.

A memo dated July 17, 1995, (Exhibit 14) from the Acing Chief, Compliance Officer of Western Region to District Director, Laguna Niguel, addressed issues regarding the mid-year assessment of the Laguna Collection Division accomplishments. The memo was written to "clarify our approach to assessments and to the use of value statements. It is especially fortuitous that you raised these points at this time since the Mid-Year's, in addition to giving you a mid-term report card, gave us the opportunity for a dry run at our assessment process". The phrase "in addition to giving you a mid-term report card" clearly indicates that districts were being "graded" on their accomplishments, with the major one being dollars collected.

As seen in the overview attachments to the memo, the first thing mentioned is dollars collected. Also the first chart for collection divisions attached to the memo is for dollars collected with a statement, "The district exceeded the goal 5% a very good accomplishment on a goal rated as above average". The first chart for Examination Division also deals with dollars per return.

In my opinion, the use of collection statistics in determining the effectiveness of IRS, especially those used in the collection divisions, is appropriate and needed. It is the use of the statistics that can cause problems. As stated before, I have never agreed with the IRS stand on publicly banishing statistical reports in an effort to ensure they are not used to promote unauthorized collection tactics.

In private industries employees and managers are provided with procedures and directions and they are held accountable for following them. In IRS, the perception seems to be the only way to prevent managers from abusing the rules is to keep certain information from them. I say the information needs to be shared and managers need to be held accountable for any actions contrary to procedures and directions.

Interestingly enough even though IRS officials say statistical information may not be shared with employees and should be shared with managers only at a certain level, I guarantee there are no secrets and the employees can gain access to just about anything they are interested in anyway.

As a newly hired revenue officer it was very interesting to discover the clout IRS had when attempting to collect delinquent taxes. I was truly shocked to accompany senior revenue officers to the field and see them demand payment and when it wasn't received to be able to immediately close the persons business. If someone had told me IRS had this kind of power prior to my being hired there I would never have believed it. Too much power in any area does bring with it a potential for abuse. As discussed in Chapter Two this particular area has been abused by some IRS employees.

Achieving large seizure quotas was what it was all about in the early 1970's and it wasn't discussed in secrecy. All revenue officers knew what was expected of them. Today the same thing is expected, but it is top secrecy. Revenue officers are expected to close their cases as expeditiously as possible and this means through full pay, installment agreement, and any other means possible.

Even though no one wants to talk about it seizures are part of the IRS collection system. Revenue officers should only be seizing as a last resort, but it is part of the job. If you ask most IRS executives and/or top level managers how they expect cases to be closed most of then will do every thing possible to steer away from the area of seizures. This is because it is politically incorrect to mention such a thing in today's climate. Yet, when revenue officers' cases are reviewed any manager worth their salt will direct the revenue officer to seize the taxpayer's assets if necessary. This hypocrisy is what helps to make the job difficult for employees. With such a heavy double edge sword over their heads many times they aren't sure of what is expected of them.

In the 1970's revenue officers with high seizure numbers were looked up to by other members of the group. Their annual appraisals centered around their aggressiveness in collecting money including seizing and selling property.

While out on a seizure if a taxpayer requested time to go to the bank to get the money to pay the liability, many revenue officers said no. They then closed that particular business and continued making field calls to other businesses for the balance of the day, remaining away from the office, particularly on Fridays. The taxpayer was then out of business for the weekend. Of course there were many taxpayers who were sophisticated enough to deal with these situations.

One scenario I remember hearing the senior revenue officers discuss involved small business taxpayers in east Los Angeles. This was a predominantly Hispanic part of Los Angeles and in many sections there would be half a dozen or more small businesses on any given block. The taxpayers were friends and in some cases relatives trying to make a living running small restaurants, auto repair shops, bakeries and such.

A lot of the money they made had to be put back into the business in order to survive; therefore, they did not always pay their quarterly employment taxes timely. Quarter after quarter revenue officers would receive cases on these taxpayers. When the revenue officer made a field call to demand the payment most of the business owners on the block chipped in to keep their friend or relative's business from being seized. Revenue officers working those areas came to know this so near the end of the month when they wanted or needed to get some small cases closed and to increase their collections for the month they headed out to east Los Angeles.

East Los Angeles was also an area they looked forwarded to working on Fridays. We were headquartered in the Los Angeles Federal Building in downtown Los Angeles close to the east Los Angeles area making it a short and easy commute.

Revenue officers work on an honor system with no one knowing exactly where they are when they go to the field. The revenue officer decides which cases need to be worked and goes to the field without leaving an itinerary unless some enterprising manger uses his/her discretion and makes this the rule. However, if this hasn't been done in the past and the manager decides it should be done, it cannot be implemented until it has been negotiated with the union. In most cases even after it has been negotiated it will not be accepted by the union. This then means it can't be done.

Many revenue officers want to take off early on Fridays and the best way to do this is to always have a reserve of taxpayers they knew they could collect from easily. The revenue officers' agenda would be to go out and collect four or five payments early on Friday and then take off for the rest of the day. Of course management wasn't supposed to know this, but later when I became a manager I realized most managers didn't care as long as on Monday the revenue officer had collected money and could close some cases.

When I started out as a revenue officer we were told that inspection could be out following us in the field and we could be fired if we did not work until the authorized quitting time. Many of us were really concerned about this and took precautions to assure that we had sufficient work for the entire day when we went to the field.

I do believe in the beginning inspection may have randomly selected some of us to follow, but it would have been virtually impossible for them to follow most of us as their numbers were too small compared to our numbers. The idea that Inspection might follow us around in the field was just planted in our heads to cause us to follow the rules. I came to realize that revenue officers were generally only followed when someone reported something on them. Once that happened you became a statistic, an inspection case.

My first seizure experience occurred on a case in downtown Los Angeles. The seizure was at a business located in the One Wilshire Building. This was what was called a seizure on an in-business trust fund case. The taxpayer owed employment taxes, taxes collected from employees wages, held in trust until the employment tax return was filed.

In some cases taxes are required to be paid in advance through what is known as tax deposits. The amount of the liability determines whether deposits are required or whether the payment can be made at the time the return is filed.

At the time of the seizure at the One Wilshire Building the Los Angeles District had what was known as a "knock and lock policy". Upon receipt of a delinquent trust fund tax case, the revenue officer was expected to go to the business address, demand full payment and to seize the business if full payment was not received right them. The taxpayer at the One Wilshire Building owned a very large restaurant and he was unable to pay; therefore, the revenue officer proceeded to close the business.

Closing the business consisted of providing the taxpayer with a Notice of Seizure, Form 2433 (Exhibit 15) advising the taxpayer to immediately leave the premises, taking inventory of the taxpayers' assets and calling the locksmith to change the lock. This particular taxpayer was very unhappy and non-receptive to any IRS seizure actions. He refused to allow the revenue officers entrance to his business and proceeded to block the entrance. He also threatened bodily harm to anyone who entered the premises. The revenue officer in charge called the special agents charged with protecting us and requested their assistance.

The special agents were housed in the Federal Building on Los Angeles Street about 10 to 15 minutes away, yet it took them over an hour to get there. They could not find one of the largest buildings in downtown Los Angeles. This was a building that even today has ONE WILSHIRE in huge letters at the top of the building and can be seen for miles.

When they finally arrived they had to wrestle the taxpayer down to the ground in order to arrest him. This was my introduction to increasing collections of trust fund taxes.

Even though I was a trainee it was very obvious to me that the situation was not handled right. The taxpayer was drunk and the situation was potentially explosive. The revenue officer in charge should have backed off and arranged to seize the business after it had closed for the day which was not an acceptable procedure in IRS without special approval.

In those days IRS wanted to be highly visible to non-paying taxpayers in an effort to promote voluntary compliance through fear. During that time it was considered a good thing to seize an ongoing business while customers and/or clients were there. This would send a message to other taxpayers about what would happen if they failed to pay their taxes. Today IRS wants seizures done in a low profile manner to avoid criticism from congress and the public.

IRS in California was somewhat sensitive to racial situations, particularly after the Los Angeles race riots. Therefore cases involving minority businesses, especially those with large numbers of black employees were scrutinized carefully before seizure action was taken. Managerial approval was required before seizure action could be taken. This requirement was established as a result of some unfortunate situations as in the case of a minority owned bus line delinquent in trust fund taxes.

It was decided to seize the busses as a result of the employment taxes not being paid timely. I happened to be in the group where the case had been assigned and a lot of excitement was generated regarding this case. The seizure itself was carried off okay, in accordance with procedures, without incident, but it received so much bad publicity it became front page news in the newspapers, especially the city's black newspaper.

Seizure of the busses created significant problems for many black citizens trying to go about their daily lives of going to work and school. Significant pressure was put on IRS by congressional representatives and black business groups to "work this out".

As a result of the pressure IRS allowed the company to enter into an installment agreement and the seizure was released. Ordinarily installment agreements were taboo on employment taxes during the "knock and lock" days, but this situation was seen as an exception. In this case IRS allowed public sentiment to take priority over increasing collections

Many times revenue officers being the independent operators they are and trying to do the job they thought was expected of them, created some embarrassing situations for IRS. One in particular involved delinquent taxes owed by a children's day care center. The revenue officer determined that seizing the business would not result in much money being collected as the only thing available was the real estate (the house) which was being rented by the taxpayer, and some inexpensive children's toys and furniture.

The revenue officer then decided he would go to the business on the day the parents were due to pay for the care of their children. As parents came to get their children at the end of the day the revenue officer gave them a Notice of Levy, Form 668-B (Exhibit 16) which authorized IRS to receive any payment due the owners of the day care center.

The press had a field day with this one. The newspapers heralded the fact that IRS seized the children and would only release them after receiving payment from the parents. Of course this was not exactly true, but I'm sure it sold a lot of newspapers.

Then of course there was the Volkswagen incident. When a revenue officer makes a seizure, procedures require that they back off if the taxpayer becomes potentially violent. They are then to either phone the local police or IRS special agents, dependent upon the emergency status of the situation.

In the Volkswagen situation the revenue officer was attempting to seize the automobile while the taxpayer was in it and the taxpayer would not get out. Special agents were called and they tried to physically and forcefully pull the person out of the automobile. One again this made great news for the newspapers.

While the following example is not necessarily true abuse of a taxpayer's rights it is an example of how things were done in the good ole days. During my training year, one of the senior revenue officer's had been trying for some time to get in touch with a taxpayer and/or the taxpayer's assets. He was finally able to get. the taxpayer to come into the office, the Los Angeles Federal Building in downtown Los Angeles, He interviewed the taxpayer and received information for the Form 433, Collection Information Financial Statement (Exhibit 17). Prior to the taxpayer coming into the office the revenue officer had been tracing his assets and he had received Department of Motor Vehicle information regarding an automobile the taxpayer owned.

In the downtown Los Angeles area at that time there was one large parking lot across the street from the Federal Building and so it stood to reason that anyone going to the Federal Building would park there as no parking was allowed on the street.

While one revenue officer conducted the interview another one surveyed the parking lot and upon finding the taxpayers car called a tow truck, seized the automobile and had it towed away. The taxpayer came out of the building just as his car was being towed out of the parking lot. There are revenue officers still around who joke about the taxpayer running down the street after the tow truck.

Was this taxpayer abuse? On one hand yes, on the other hand the revenue officer was doing the only thing he thought he could do to collect some seriously delinquent taxes. This was the revenue officer's method of increasing collections.

Anyone reading this will probably be appalled; however, I would ask for suggestions on how taxes should be collected from someone who refuses to pay. Once again I say everyone wants the tax money to be used for the things that make their lives better, but everyone thinks what the tax collectors are doing is awful. To my knowledge no one, including Congress, has come up with a better or even different way to collect taxes from someone who absolutely refuses to pay voluntarily.

The regional Chief, Compliance Officer required districts to submit mid-year progress reports addressing goals laid out at the beginning of each fiscal year. A copy of the compliance report for Laguna for 1995 is shown in Exhibit 18.

The IRS national office started preparing business master plans for goals and actions expected of the district offices. The regional office faxed those objectives down to the district offices and the collection divisions planned for the coming year in accordance with the plan. As seen in Exhibit 18 the goals for collection divisions included collecting a larger percentage of the tax base annually and increasing productivity.

The document goes on to show results expectations to include "increases in dollars collected through the collection processes". The collection processes include seizures, sales, notices of levy, and liens. These are all things repulsive to the public and to congress once the public complains. How can a tax collector please everyone when the only way to collect is to seize? I ask this question repeatedly only to point out how difficult the revenue officer's job is.

Exhibit 19 also includes charts showing dollars collected by regions, as well as increases and decreases, and it goes further to show Western Region collection districts and their % of change from 1994 to 1995.

Now I ask you if you were a hard working, competitive district director and you saw your collection division at the bottom in the region what would you do? And to make matters worse those documents were shared nationwide. As the director at the bottom, you would probably encourage the division chief to increase collections. If the division chiefs and managers know they have collected all they can from voluntary collections the only alternative is enforced collection activities such as levy, lien, seizure, and sale.

No matter how hard I try I continue to have difficulty with the concept of increasing productivity without inflicting pain on the taxpaying public. How can this be done? It is a known fact that there are taxpayers who refuse to voluntarily pay taxes.

This is borne out by the IRS admitting in the 1998 congressional hearings that there is a tremendous tax gap. IRS or anyone in the future who has the "duty" of collecting the taxes will have to do so from an involuntary standpoint. This means the money will have to be "taken" through processes the same as or similar to lien, levy, seizure and sale. This seems to be a common sense type of concept? However, everyone puts their head in the sand and attempts to make the problem disappear.

IRS executives realize the importance of increasing productivity and an example can be seen in a copy of a district director's Performance Plan for

1991 (Exhibit 20). The directors Senior Executive Performance Plans are contracts between the executives and their boss, the Regional Commissioner.

All IRS managers prepare contracts at the beginning of the fiscal year as part of the merit pay system. The contracts have different names depending on the level of the manager. Some are called Senior Executives Performance Plan for executives while others are Performance Management Recognition System Appraisal. The manager (employee) prepares the document with input from the manager (boss). The document usually centers around areas in need of improvement.

At the end of the fiscal year an assessment is made regarding achievement of the contract. Based on the level of results the manager may or may not get a payment increase as well as a bonus.

The larger the district the larger the bonus amount a director may receive. Since Laguna Niguel was one of the largest districts in IRS the director received anywhere from $5000 to $10,000 each year the main objectives were met.

The director in Laguna Niguel during my stint as chief, was fortunate in that he had an effective group of division chiefs working for him. We all took pride in our jobs and for the most part were quite successful. As a thanks for our hard work during the year the director took us out to lunch one year. Another year he had some food catered in (very economical food) and one year he planned to have a party at his home, but some how that never materialized.

As shown in the director's plan, the additional standard addresses a specific area; however, it shies away from stating how productivity will be increased. As stated before, IRS top executive management speaks out of both sides of its mouth. The name of the game is money, money, and more money. This plan was circulated throughout the district so that all employees would know what was expected of them.

To get more money the plan then escalates up to increasing productivity. IRS vehemently states that production is a dirty word similar to those popular unmentionable four letter words, but increasing productivity is okay.

Although IRS vehemently denies rating and comparing managers the (Exhibit 21) memo from national office - subject - Revised Draft 1995 Field Office Performance Index clearly shows a listing of all regions and districts and their successes and/or failures in major categories such as increase voluntary compliance, maximize customer satisfaction/reduce burden, and achieve quality driven productivity.

The definitions for each category are shown in the following three paragraphs of the exhibit. What is most interesting about the definitions is that most are easily understood except the goal of increasing productivity of the service. The Service always becomes quiet and almost non-responsive when discussions regarding productivity come up. This is because increasing productivity includes levy, lien, seizures and sales and no one has the "guts" to speak outwardly about this area. It is treated publicly as though it is an IRS dirty secret only spoken about behind closed doors.

Increasing voluntary compliance includes goals of collecting tax due and public recognition for ethical conduct. The goal regarding public recognition for ethical conduct is basically a goal for not receiving any negative publicity. Included in this goal are taxpayer privacy and IRS employees compliance. Protecting taxpayers privacy is measured by "% of IDRS employees disciplined. IDRS (Integrated Data Retrieval System) is the IRS computer system connecting districts with services centers where all taxpayer information is stored.

IRS employees are disciplined when they are caught accessing taxpayer information for which they do not have a need to know. IRS employees compliance is measured by the percentage of non-compliant employees. This category covers the compliance of IRS employees in filing and paying their own personal income taxes.

The objective to "Maximize Customer Satisfaction and Reduce Burden" has two goals. The first goal is to reduce the taxpayer burden which is basically measured by the length of time it takes employees to process the case work. This includes accuracy as well and covers all IRS divisions involved in working a taxpayer's case from the time a return is filed until any outstanding liability is paid and/or an audit examination is completed.

The second goal of maximizing customer satisfaction and reducing burdens is to resolve taxpayer inquiries with one contact. The goal is measured by determining how many contacts had to be made with the taxpayer to resolve outstanding issues.

Both goals of maximizing customer satisfaction and reducing burdens have never been satisfactorily met during my many years with IRS and from what I hear from both employees still working there and from media reports, the goals still are not being met.

There are many reasons why these goals are not being met with one of the most significant ones being the budgetary problems previously discussed. As everyone knows, Congress controls the purse strings and budgets come and go, many times dependent upon the whims of the congressional representatives. This was evident during the shutdown of the government a few years back.

Employee turnover/attrition rates are high in IRS and the inability to control the budget creates significant problems with the efficiency of employees working cases. While a budget is held up during a partisan feud in congress the availability of enough employees to do the job is impacted. Meanwhile cases sit and sit and sit becoming older and older with interest and penalties growing and growing to the detriment of the taxpayer.

In addition to the problem of not having enough experienced employees to work cases effectively, the National Commission on Restructuring the Internal Revenue Service released a report on June 25, 1997, which read in part, "Because of the high turnover rate for commissioners and an uncertain budget, the IRS shows a lack of continuity. The IRS also is plagued by a lack of expertise due to personnel qualification problems, pay levels, and a deterioration in the quality of training."

The report went on to recommend that, "The IRS should receive stable funding for the next three years and must address culture, operations, taxpayer education, technology and training so it can operate more efficiently, with more customer focus."

The third objective to "Achieve Quality Driven Productivity" has three goals. The first goal of reducing paper processing is one most taxpayers will be hoping will be achieved. The amount of paper processed through IRS is unbelievable. Many taxpayers are aware of some of the problems as a result of the voluminous returns they are required to file. The measurement for achieving a reduction in paper processing is the percentage of returns filed electronically. The goal is 100% which is unrealistic in light of the fact that IRS restrictions prevent most returns from being filed electronically. Few returns meet the requirements for filing electronically. Returns with several schedules attached cannot be filed electronically???

The second goal for achieving quality driven productivity has to do with achieving diversity in IRS workforce. The goal is to meet diverse customer needs and to provide a workforce that reflects the U.S. workforce. Once again IRS is dealing with a goal that is impacted significantly by the decisions made in congress. Without significant funds to hire when needed diversity goals lag on the back burner. Somehow IRS has decided to measure this goal by the percentage of EEO complaints received and by the percentage of female and minority employees promoted to grade thirteen positions (GS-13).

Overall, at the time I left IRS the goal was not being met particularly in the area of EEO complaints. As discussed in the chapter regarding labor/management relations, certain elements of the union in Laguna were continuing to stir things up by having employees file frivolous grievances and if the grievances were not resolved to the satisfaction of the union the representative then encouraged the employee to file an EEO complaint.

The third goal of achieving quality driven productivity is to increase the service's productivity. This is the goal that IRS deals with by presenting two conflicting sides at the same time. The measurements for determining whether or not the goal has been achieved are such things as the amount of dollars collected by Collection Division and the number of returns examined by Examination Division. This is the goal IRS says it wants to achieve, yet it is the goal they tip toe around in an effort to avoid media and public criticism.

At the time I began this book the IRS management positions at the top were held by some of the poorest examples of business men possible. In addition, some of the IRS Commissioners during the 1990's were so far removed from what was going on it was unbelievable. It appeared that some of them were window dressing for the organization just so that IRS could show its efforts to provide equal employment opportunity for females.

Incompetent executives were allowed to run the entire organization while the Commissioners appeared to defer to their judgment without interference. At least one of the Commissioners gave the appearance to the managers that she was not nearly strong enough to be "in charge" if it meant telling the Deputy what to do.

While another one certainly seemed to be strong enough to be "in charge" she gave the appearance she was just passing through. During one of her visitations to the Laguna Niguel District she was asked questions regarding the organization and future plans and she was totally incapable of answering them. She said she would have "to get back to us" on most questions asked of her.

The Revised Draft 1995 Field Office Performance Index memo is very inclusive in that it covers comparisons of overall region performance, region performance by major objective, regional rankings by goal, overall district performance, district ranking by SES (senior executive staff) assignment class, district performance by major objective, increase voluntary compliance, district rankings by goal, maximize customer satisfaction and reduce burden, and achieve quality driven productivity. In each case the districts, and regions are listed and the overall rank and an assigned score are shown. So much for IRS' denial of ranking managers and using numbers.

Originally this particular document wasn't intended to be shared with managers below the executive level, which is a joke as there are no secrets in IRS. There are leaks all over the place. To prepare a document of this nature many people have to be involved including secretaries, analysts and staff assistants. Many of these employees will not hesitate to share the information downward to the regions and districts. Most people in national office did after all come from the regions and districts; therefore, they are still aligned with their home districts.

In addition, many times they are hoping and planning to return to the home district in a much higher position sometime before they retire. They want to keep that alliance alive; therefore, they will willingly share any information the district office desires.

In addition to national office reports, Western Region distributed its infamous month at a glance reports. This particular report caused grown men to be on the verge of tears. Not only did the report compare collection divisions in districts, it compared them over a period of three years showing a percentage of change up or down and it listed the goal so that there would be no doubt to the reader as to how far off a division might be. (Exhibit 22).

In Exhibit 22 the current year achievements are shown in green and orange, green being trends downward and in need of improvement. The trend column shows green arrows which means the goal rates are going up. It also shows orange arrows which means improvement is not being seen and is in need of immediate attention.

The area of seizing taxpayers' property has always been an area that can increase collection dollars. It also causes great stress to IRS managers. A loose cannon (an employee) or a crook in the group can wreak havoc for the manager as well as IRS in general.

During my early days in IRS I worked for a branch chief who attempted to exert extreme detailed control over every aspect of the job. He demanded reports of everything and then double reports to check things already reported.

I was very curious as to why he was so paranoid and I found out from some of the old-timers that he had been in very "hot water" when he was a group manager. One of the revenue officer's in his group seized a bar/restaurant and large quantities of the alcoholic supplies disappeared. An investigation by Inspection determined the revenue officer had stolen the supplies. The group manager was held responsible for the revenue officer's actions. The revenue officer was fired, however, the damage had already been done to the manager's future career. It took him years to be able to move up and even then his upward movement was limited to one level, that of the branch chief position.

An example of IRS's unchecked authority can be seen in seizures of doctors' offices. When I was a revenue officer a fellow co-worker, seized a doctor's office without realizing drugs would be in the office and something had to be done with them as a cautionary measure.

Once the manager told the revenue officer he was responsible for the safe keeping of the drugs, the revenue officer realized he was not prepared to handle the situation. The only thing he knew to do was to take the drugs to the office for safe keeping and he did so. Fortunately for him and perhaps for all of us in the group the drugs remained safe until the doctor paid his taxes and was able to open his office.

Today the rules require that research is done to determine what special plans are needed before conducting a seizure and drugs are turned over to the appropriate authority for safekeeping until the seizure is resolved through full pay of the taxes or the assets are sold.

As a result of my knowledge and experience as a revenue officer when I became a manager I never felt comfortable that the rules were being adhered to the way they should have been. A special review I conducted on seizure documents validated my concerns and caused me great distress.

As a division chief I conducted random reviews on all of the groups seizure documents and often found that many, many of what should have been avoidable mistakes were made as well as many procedures overlooked or neglected. These mistakes resulted from many reasons one of which was the inexperience and lack of commitment on the part of some of the managers.

As stated before, some employees became managers as a result of management twisting their arm in a time of need, some became managers in order to get out of the field, a job many did not like. When employees are placed in positions of authority and responsibility because of the above you have to expect problems.

Even knowing this in advance there wasn't much of anything I could do because we never had time to plan in advance and to do sufficient recruiting or training because of Congress' consistent delays in approving the budget. Many, many times we had to hire large numbers of new employees and find managers for them in thirty days or less.

So much for increasing collections. I have been told recently that IRS has banned all statistical reports. I have been told also that the new Commissioner is attempting to recruit executives from private industry. I think this is a good idea; however, I have also been told that he is having extreme difficulty recruiting experienced executives because he cannot pay them anything close to what private industry can. This means he may have to recruit young, less experienced executives who will have to gain their experience while they do the job. Will this make things better for IRS. Probably not, but what is he supposed to do?

I was told by a reliable source that the new Commissioner was attempting to recruit a very experienced female from AT&T but he could only pay her $125,000 a year. He was trying to get the pay ceiling increased to $150,000 and in the meantime she got a job paying her in excess of $200,000. I do believe you get what you pay for.

I also believe IRS needs to have the means to bring executives up from inside as well as hiring from the outside, but a better structured way of doing this is needed. During my tenure in IRS, I had the occasion to see resumes of many executives and managers and I was surprised to find out that many had limited education after high school. I have a Masters Degree in Public Administration and many of the executives above me either had only a bachelor's degree or less.

While I am a firm believer that education does not necessarily mean you will be successful, it certainly improves one's ability to be successful. It also speaks of one's ability to persevere and to remain on track.

I had to go to school at night to get both my bachelor and Masters Degree while raising a family, but I thought it was important for me and my career to obtain as much education and experience as possible. In the beginning of my career I thought most employees (revenue officers and above) had college degrees. Being the competitive kind of person I am, I immediately began to continue my education even though as I said, I had to do it at night. Lo and behold, I later came to find out I was wrong about many employees as they were not the recipient's of higher education.

Ninety nine percent of IRS executives worked their way up through the organization and during the time of the newly resigned Deputy Commissioner many selected for executive positions did not have any experience in managing people. Some were special assistant types to executives, and that lack of experience in managing coupled with having no experience in the two major divisions, Collection and Examination, created a serious problem in the level of success of those executives.

After selecting those types of executives for several years, the Deputy Commissioner found out he had built in problems for the organization and he went back to the old way of selecting those with the experience and background to manage a district. By then however, the damage was done and many of those executives are out in districts trying to learn the functions of IRS' major divisions.

In an effort to increase collections and to reduce taxpayer complaints, IRS established what is called "allowable expenses". Historically IRS revenue officers would demand payment from a taxpayer and upon being told that the taxpayer could not pay in full the revenue officer had the discretion to consider allowing the taxpayer an installment agreement. To do this the revenue officer was required to collect information to prepare a financial statement which included a monthly income and expense analyses on a Form 433. This document includes a section showing total income and total expenses (Exhibit 17). The document also shows the net difference (income less IRS necessary living expenses).

Prior to establishment of the allowable expenses, the revenue officer would use what the taxpayer provided as living expenses with so called "common sense adjustments" from the revenue officer's frame of thinking. The net difference would then be the amount the revenue officer would expect the taxpayer to pay monthly on an installment agreement.

Well, the revenue officer's discretion was frequently questioned and criticized by both taxpayers and taxpayers' representatives. Therefore, the IRS established nationwide guidelines of specific amounts that must be used for certain living expenses such as one individual with gross monthly income of $830 being allowed $149 per month for food. Four persons in a household would be allowed $305 monthly for food with $830 monthly income.

After much wailing and gnashing of teeth from the public, IRS also established local standards for certain items such as rent or house payments. This was done because it was an accepted fact that housing expenses vary widely from state to state.

Revenue officers were not given discretion authority as to whether the standards could or could not be used. However, on occasion, hard line revenue officers trying to increase the collection pot disregarded the amount shown as net difference and demanded a higher monthly payment for an installment agreement.

I saw this example when I worked for Shylock Corporation in dealing with the Los Angeles IRS office. I had to advise one revenue officer that I would go to the district director to complain about the excessive amount he was demanding. He then begrudgingly allowed the appropriate amount shown on the financial statement.

There is a very frightening aspect to this situation. What has happened to taxpayers who either did not know they were not being treated right or to those who were afraid to speak up for themselves? I would venture to guess they paid whatever the revenue officer told them they had to pay.

The Los Angeles Times newspaper dated April 29, 1998 addresses an allegation of a high ranking senior executive stealing twenty luxury automobiles. These automobiles were impounded from taxpayers. According to the newspaper article, the executive who has since retired, was made to pay restitution of only $20,000. I don't have inside information regarding this specific situation; however, I do know that IRS seizures are not treated with as high security as they should be.

Upon becoming the Collection Division Chief in Laguna Niguel I became aware the division had at least one-half dozen automobiles under seizure. Some of the automobiles had been there over a year just sitting out in the open elements uncovered. Some of the automobiles were very expensive and only a year or so old at the time of the seizure.

Neither the managers nor the revenue officers had done anything on the cases since the seizures had taken place. In some situations the seizures should not have been conducted because the automobiles technically still belonged to a bank, credit union, etc. because they had not been paid for in full and IRS would not have been able to gain any money since the taxpayer had little or no equity and IRS was not going to be able to sell the automobiles.

Revenue officers are required to either go to sale promptly on seized assets or to release them back to the taxpayer. No one was controlling the automobiles and in some cases either the manager or the revenue officer had transferred to another group. In one situation the revenue officer had been fired.

It would have been very easy for the revenue officer or any other collection employee to either use the automobiles or to doctor the documents and sell the automobiles. The only controls maintained in the group are paper documents often maintained in notebooks label "seizures' with any and all employees having access to the binder, particularly when the manager is out of the office.

I saw to it that appropriate action was taken on each automobile. Most of them were released back to the taxpayer. We then went to sale on a few and received as much as possible and applied it to the taxpayers' delinquent accounts. So much for increasing collections.

Chapter Nine

LABOR/MANAGEMENT RELATIONS

Generally speaking it takes years for most managers to acquire significant experience in dealing with high profile labor - management situations. My experience and exposure were received in a very swift manner both as a first line manager and as a mid-level branch chief.

I tend to think my experience in the labor - management arena started out the way it did because heretofore the branch chiefs and union stewards were all white middle aged males and now here I come, a young black female, with little experience, new in the position and ready to take on whatever comes.

It was important to me that I was able to meet the same challenges the male branch chiefs had to meet. Even though I was always considered to be somewhat "smart", I didn't have enough smarts to know I was being thrown in a lion's den. However, I was smart enough to realize very soon that I was being tested and tried to the ultimate by the union. The most interesting and challenging situation started immediately upon my selection as a branch chief.

At the time of my selection to the position of branch chief I was assigned to what was called the Lawndale Branch. Lawndale was the name of the city in which the federal building housing most of the groups in the branch was located.

The branch initially consisted of five revenue officer groups in the Lawndale building, one in the post of duty located in Carson, California and one in Bakersfield, California. Both Carson and Bakersfield were on opposite ends of the branch and were on the fringes of the district. Neither group was attractive to branch chiefs because of the locations.

In addition, Bakersfield, California is a country town with some of the hottest weather in the summer and the coldest in the winter. The drive to Bakersfield would often be a nightmare as it was over an area called the grapevine which included some of the most dangerous highways in California.

Carson, California was located in an area considered to be populated predominantly by blacks. It was located in Los Angeles County, next to Compton, California which was known for its high crime rate and gang activity.

Needless to say none of the branch chiefs wanted either city as part of their assigned territory; therefore, as the new branch chief on the block I was given these prime locations. That was one of the prices you had to pay as a newly selected branch chief.

Interestingly enough the Carson and Bakersfield offices turned out to present my least problems. Most of the employees in the Lawndale office were new and had been hired as part of a large group of about 300 revenue officers as part of a reorganization. These employees were all a part of training groups.

When a training group was formed it usually consisted of nine to twelve trainees with one coach assigned to three to four trainees. To provide expertise to a group, two to three senior employees were also assigned to each group. At the time of the opening of a new office, senior employees were allowed the opportunity to transfer to a new group or branch based on seniority.

Dependent upon the location of the branch, senior employees would readily volunteer for transfer. You could expect the exact opposite reaction if the branch happened to be located in an undesirable location such as Carson, California. The most popular reason for willingness to relocate was the desire to be closer to home. Therefore, most white employees did not want to relocate to a predominantly black neighborhood.

This caused the Lawndale Branch to be predominantly black. However, the selection of the Lawndale Federal Building as the site for the new branch fooled a lot of people because even though it was known in advance to be the site for the "black branch" the building was actually located a mile or so away from the Manhattan Beach area, a prime location site for residences and businesses.

In addition, the building had free parking, something that was becoming hard to find in Los Angeles County. The Manhattan Beach area had lots of nice restaurants and a great shopping area therefore it was sought after by senior employees once they realized the location of the site.

In addition to being staffed with mostly new employees, most of the managers in Lawndale were newly selected or with minimum experience. None of them had ever had to deal with any union problems and they were therefore totally unprepared for what they walked into in the new branch.

The branch initially consisted of four female managers, three black and one white and two white males. Before the first year was over, Carson became part of the Laguna Niguel district and Bakersfield went to the San Jose, California district. This then caused me to have to establish two new groups as branches were required to have a certain number of groups.

The groups remaining in the branch after Carson and Bakersfield were taken away were then downsized with employees reassigned to make up the required additional two groups. Senior revenue officer positions were filled through promotional opportunities made available to employees in the branch as well as employees district wide.

I then selected two new managers and they were two white females. This left me with six females and one male manager. This may seem unusual and it actually was, but I believe it was because the managerial positions were just opening up to females.

I also believe that one of the major ways diversity is achieved is through minority and female managers having the opportunity to be involved in the selection process. People generally feel more comfortable with people like themselves. Therefore, the current situation of few female managers at that time was the result of males selecting more males. The selection of more female managers helped to improve diversity as the females were genuinely interested in selecting females for their groups.

I played a strong role in the selection process of the branch managers and insisted that since I was going to be the one having to deal with these new managers I should be the one to have the last word in the selections. I was able to convince the division chief of this theory, technically he was the selecting official.

Either I was able to convince him or he agreed because he didn't want to have to continue listing to my comments. Some might have called my comments nagging.

Three of the Lawndale managers had one to two years managerial experience and had somewhat strong personalities. The male manager had over ten years of managerial experience, but was not a very strong personality and he had difficulty dealing with the confrontations he was ultimately called upon to deal with and resolve.

The most controversial issues in the new branch were the result of an out of control union chapter president. He was a senior employee and was extremely aggressive and had been very successful in his intimidation efforts.

The revenue officer position started at grade 5 or 7 depending upon education and/or other related experience. Revenue officers then progressed up the ladder automatically to grade 9 and 11 if they were performing successfully. The top grade 12 was a position that had to be applied for through a competition process. Based on the results of a performance appraisal and an interview, the employee could be promoted to grade 12.

This chapter president I will call Brad refused to apply for a grade 12 position because he said he knew he would not be selected as a result of his relationship with management. He was probably right although he did demonstrate good knowledge in working cases. He was thoroughly disliked by all management authority that had the bad luck to have to end up dealing with him. Most managers did not have the personality to go toe to toe with Brad, but most of them would have definitely done what ever they could to deny him a promotion.

The major complaint management had about Brad was that he rarely went to the field while working his cases. Revenue officers are expected to spend significant time in the field in order to work their cases effectively and efficiently.

The cases that are assigned to revenue officers are assigned for field work because numerous unsuccessful efforts have already been made to contact the taxpayer or to locate assets. The first attempts to contact taxpayers are made by telephone and mail. Therefore the first step upon receipt of a new case is supposed to be a field trip to the last known address. Brad refused to go to the field and conducted much of his work by phone.

In addition, revenue officers were required to resolve cases in an official manner such as full payment or a formal installment agreement. Formal installment agreements were supposed to be documents prepared by the revenue officer, signed by the taxpayer and sent to the IRS service center or to an office group where the case would be monitored to assure payments were received timely in accordance with the agreement. This was to free revenue officers up so that they could move on to other cases and so that additional cases could then be assigned to them.

Managers usually monitor the size of revenue officers' inventory and assign cases as the inventory is reduced through case closure and or installment agreements. Some revenue officers attempt to defy the rules and regulations by maintaining installment agreements within their inventory. This will ensure the assignment of fewer cases as fewer cases will be reported as closed. Brad was a master at this game.

While Brad's modus operandi was a known fact, usually managers neglected to call him on it because they were too intimidated to do so. Brad intimidated managers and employees alike with his loud, bullying attitude.

He was able to attend all group meetings held by managers and to intimidate them at least once a month at these meetings He could attend these meetings as the result of the agreement between IRS and the union. All managers must notify the union within an advanced specified time prior to holding a meeting, providing the date, time, and location of the meeting.

Generally speaking the chapter president would assign attendance to the meetings to stewards; however, since Brad could not achieve what he considered a working relationship with management, he decided to personally attend all meetings so that he could take on the manager whenever he chose to.

He would challenge any direction the manager provided to the revenue officers and he could be counted on to ask the manager "Where in the Internal Revenue Manual can I find that?" He was allowed to continuously interrupt the manager by asking question such as "Who gave you the authority to do that?".

Believe it or not there wasn't anything anyone could do about his attendance or his performance. Or perhaps I should clarify that and say there wasn't anything top level management wanted to do about it so the first line manager had to live with this situation day in and day out.

That kind of action certainly intimidated new, inexperienced managers. If a manager questioned Brad as one bravely decided to do on one occasion, Brad would often stand up and rant and rave at the manager.

When Brad ranted and raved during a meeting it was reported up to me and I reported it to the division chief, but guess what, no one had the authority to tell a chapter president what to do. Not even national level management of the union. Chapter presidents were voted in by employees and did not have to answer to anyone, but the employees at the time of the next election.

Brad reduced one manager to tears in front of her employees during a meeting. She had been deluged with union grievances from Brad and his attendance and constant interruption at her meeting seemed to have been the last straw. She started to come unglued in front of her entire group. She finally stepped down out of management and went back to being a revenue officer.

Brad was assigned to a group managed by a young white female. Brad, the manager and the treasurer of the union were the only white people in that group. All of the other employees were black and in addition to all of the other union problems, racial problems were also beginning as a result of another tough, abusive black steward called Jefferson. Jefferson will be discussed in more detail later in the chapter.

Brad's manager Cherry was a woman who was very smart in books, but had questionable common sense. Even though I had said to her on several occasions, "Cherry it isn't a good idea to go to lunch with a few selected employees to the exclusion of others." In spite of my comments she continued to do so. I told her, "First of all you should go to lunch with the other managers or employees who are not assigned to your group." I also told her, "If you want to go with your own employees you need to go with all of them either as a group or rotate your presence with small groups."

Brad summoned her for lunch everyday and because she went with him and the union treasurer he did not file grievances against her. The other employees complained that she did not like them because they were minorities and at the slightest problem they filed EEO complaints.

In the meantime Brad became more and more aggressive. On one occasion while I was on vacation the person acting for me informed me, "The treasurer of the union, one of Cherry's employees, has been playing with a motorized car in the work area. Cherry is aware of this and she has not attempted to stop him."

In addition to toy playing in the work area being inappropriate, it was also a safety hazard as it could have tripped someone and made them fall. The person acting for me also told me, "I had to give Brad a direct order to stop playing with the toy while Cherry sat at her desk pretending not to be aware of what was going on."

On another occasion the union treasurer and Brad hung rag dolls by their necks in the work areas. I was told this was in direct reference to the order I had given preventing revenue officer access to the computer system.

Each revenue officer group had one computer assigned to the group and all requests for documents were supposed to go through the manager and to be obtained by the group secretary.

This rule was enforced because it had been determined that many revenue officers were abusing the system by accessing taxpayer information that was not needed as well as many, many unnecessary documents accessed that were not needed. These unnecessary documents were a waste of paper and they tied up the one computer and prevented the secretary from doing what she had been hired to do.

Revenue officers were not hired to perform clerical or secretarial duties. My order infuriated Brad and he in turn stirred up the revenue officers. Once again Cherry knew what was going on and she was too intimidated to do anything about it until I told her, "This is a direct order for you to have those dolls taken down."

In the meantime Brad became more and more aggressive. He started sending me cartoons from the newspapers with subtle comments written on the documents.

One of his mail messages was an article about homes for sale in an area called Camarillo, California. Camarillo was best known for having a hospital for the mentally ill located there. Anytime someone did something that could be jokingly considered insane, comments would be made saying the person should be sent to Camarillo.

Brad knew I had just married and had bought a new home; therefore, he knew I was not in the market for a home. Sending me the cartoons was a signal that he was saying I was mentally ill. I took the cartoons to the division chief who took them to the district director yet, nothing was done After all I was only a branch chief and no one was prepared to take on the powerful union.

Finally Brad made a mistake by sending the district director's executive assistant a copy of a cartoon with negative comments handwritten on it. He was finally taken serious and considered a potential threat to management.

The director finally said enough was enough and I was given orders on a Thursday to go to Brad's office that following Friday and transfer him to the

IRS office located in San Fernando Valley. Brad was going to be transferred as a disruptive force to management.

First of all Brad lived in the general area of the Lawndale office so the transfer was going to be out of his commute area. Secondly and probably most importantly, the labor-management agreement required at least a two week notice for transfers. Thirdly, involuntary transfers had to be based on a need and had to be done based on seniority. The district director was not going to give consideration to any of these requirements.

Management's out was the disruptive force theory. Anytime an employee became a disruptive force in a work area, management had the right to remove that person. Of course management's definition of disruptive force and Brad's definition were not in sync.

When management finally decided to be mean nothing could prevent them from winning the meanness award. Brad was being unofficially transferred into a branch of a somewhat feared branch chief and the group of a manager more feared than Brad.

That Friday morning I skipped off to the Lawndale office and I told Cherry she was going to have to transfer Brad that day. She did not want to do it and she said, "I can't transfer him without giving him proper notice." I then told her, "This is a direct order for you to tell Brad he is being transferred as of this day. If you refuse to follow my instructions you will be considered insubordinate and can be fired immediately." Deep down inside I knew Cherry was happy Brad was being transferred. She was just too afraid to have him think she had anything to do with it.

I had called her the evening before to set up an appointment with Brad for Friday to assure that he would be there. I told Cherry I would attend the meeting with her, but that I wanted her to finally stand on her two feet and do the job of a manager. She was obviously afraid.

At the allotted time we met with Brad in a conference room and Cherry told him he was being transferred. He became very upset and loud and said, "You can't transfer me." Cherry became almost speechless so I stepped in and told him, "She can transfer you and on Monday you are to report to the group in the Valley".

When I told him the group he was going to he almost turned blue. He said, "I am not going to the Valley and you do not have the authority to make me go". I told him, "Whether or not you report to the Valley will be your own decision, but you will not be working in Lawndale on Monday".

I further told him, " Cherry is going to reassign your cases Friday and there will not be any work for you in Lawndale on Monday". He ranted and raved, threatened and postured and I told him, "The final word is that effective Monday the Valley will be your assigned post of duty".

Brad made a big mistake, he did not report to the office in the Valley, but he did not return to Lawndale either. He filed various grievances and unfair labor practices against me, the division chief, and the district director all of which was pasted on the union's bulletin board for everyone to see. Then as luck would have it, he resigned.

Even though he continued his grievances and unfair labor complaints from the outside, he didn't have a chance of winning. Had he reported to the Valley and then fought management's actions he would have had a chance of winning. After all, what we did was not within prescribed requirements. Management would have had to prove he was a disruptive force in the branch. Because of the level of intimidation he had acquired in the branch many employees, including managers, would have been afraid to speak out against him because they were not sure he would not win. He just might win and return to the branch. If this happened they knew their lives would be more miserable than before.

Once he refused to follow orders and then resigned he lost out. Luck was on our side as Brad was a very disruptive force and created significant work stoppage problems. No paperwork was ever done to show the proposed transfer. It all remained hear say so that management could deny it if necessary.

All of management was relieved that Brad was gone and prepared to right all of the problems he had caused. Well, we were a tad too complacent. Management still had to deal with Jefferson and to some extent he represented a force that was as disruptive as Brad's if not worse.

Jefferson was hired during the massive hiring of three hundred plus revenue officers. He is a black male, well educated and at the time of being hired he was older than most of the other new hires. According to some sources, he had a wide variety of experience having been involved in many things including communism which at the time was viewed as questionable in the field of politics.

The IRS Los Angeles District did not have direct hiring authority to hire employees in permanent positions; however, since there was a serious need to hire them, the district got around the hiring restriction by hiring new employees in a temporary status. This temporary status would ultimately allow the employees to be converted to permanent status as soon as the expected hiring authority was received.

The district did not have hiring authority because congress would not provide the necessary funds at that time. IRS and other government agencies often get caught in situations where congress withholds necessary funds for various reasons including differences between the two major parties.

The temporary hiring status became a huge bone of contention with Jefferson, particularly because the majority of new employees in Lawndale were black. It was Jefferson's contention that the only reason the employees were not given permanent status was because they were black.

The status under which employees are hired in the government impacts on future promotions, retirement rights, and ability to apply for other jobs within the Service. Only those hired under what is called career conditional appointments are provided with all rights granted to government employees.

Temporary employment is limited or prohibited from being counted to determine seniority dates and retirement dates. Knowing this it is understandable that employees would be concerned. However, Jefferson took it to another level. He actually tried to take on the district director, writing letters, rabble rousing with the employees and becoming an unauthorized equal employment opportunity representative.

IRS as a government agency is governed by certain laws, rules and regulations regarding EEO (equal employment opportunity) All districts have their own EEO officer and specific procedures for dealing with allegations of discrimination. As I said before, Jefferson was a very well educated man and he had found an obscure law that allowed him to represent employees in EEO complaints without the employee having to go through the district EEO office.

Most of management including me were not aware of this law and were we shocked when we found out that Jefferson was absolutely correct. He had our hands tied and there wasn't anything we could do about it.

The district was up in arms and extensive research was conducted in an effort to discredit Jefferson and prove him wrong. It was unbelievable that a newly hired employee and a temporary one at that, would start his career by challenging his employer's authority and alleging discrimination on behalf of other temporary employees. He bypassed the EEO office and utilized his own investigative skills in dealing with employee problems. He went about the business of initiating class actions without a class or category of victims.

Jefferson's role in the EEO process was so unbelievable because it enabled him to deal with all levels of management, all the way up to the district director. In the normal process of an EEO complaint the first step is for the employee to contact the EEO OFFICE at which time an EEO counselor is assigned to the case and the counselor works on an informal basis in an effort to resolve the complaint.

Experience has shown in IRS that most initial complaints are the result of miscommunication and can be resolved at an early stage. Counselors are selected from within the IRS district where the complaint has been filed. The counselor is ultimately charged with attempting to obtain some agreement between the complainant and the alleged accused. If an agreement is reached the complaint is closed at the informal stage. If not, a formal complaint is filed and an investigator is assigned.

Counselors are selected from within the district workforce (e.g. revenue officers, revenue agents, etc.) with investigators being selected from outside of the district, but many times from within the region.

The informal stage of the complaint is the responsibility of the district EEO office while the formal stage becomes the responsibility of the regional office. The rules for handling EEO complaints are designed to attempt to have selected counselors at a level somewhat comparable to that of the accused member of management. This is done so that the counselor will not feel intimidated when dealing with a high level management official. In Jefferson's case he was a newly hired temporary employee setting up meetings with top level executives.

Jefferson decided to take complete responsibility for all EEO complaints within the branch and within the district if possible. He had established a lot of clout within the branch because he was a member of the branch.

In addition, he was very aggressive and had the nerve to say what many trainees would like to say at some period of time about their training program. Also, in a rough earthy way he was an attractive man. Here you had a newly hired employee, one who had not completed the first year training program and yet he was taking on all levels of management in IRS, questioning things even the most seasoned employees did not have the nerve to do.

Jefferson was able to drum up plenty of business because he worked in the predominantly black office in Lawndale and he was able to incite many of the employees with his rhetoric. He told the employees the district director could convert them to career conditional appointments if he wanted to, but that he wasn't going to do it because they were black.

This was an untrue statement because the district director could not do anything without approval from the region. However, many of the employees chose to believe Jefferson and everything that happened to them was viewed through jaundiced eyes.

A large number of employees hired at the time Jefferson was hired represented what I considered to be a new breed of government employees. Many were well educated, but were highly militant.

They came to the job with the attitude that they were owed something and they did not hesitate to demand what they thought was owed them. They were totally different from many minorities who were hired by IRS in the 1970's and 80's during the time I came on board.

I and a lot of black employees were very happy to have the job and we worked hard to achieve whatever success was possible. Of course, the public approval of the government was higher then than it is today. Coming out of the love-flower, Black Panther era of defiance, these employees had what seemed to be a general distrust for authority and particularly for that of the federal government.

The new breed of employees looked up to Jefferson and freely sought his advice. He led them to believe he was indestructible and willing to die for a cause. He had marched with Dr. Martin Luther King, had been arrested and gone to jail. During his arrests for participating in the civil rights movement, he had shared jail cells with some of the other employees who worked in other branches.

Having such a close alliance with employees dispersed throughout the district enhanced his power base as those employees appeared to be happy to spread his word. If you believe many people are looking for a leader, you can easily believe that most of these employees thought they had found one in Jefferson.

Jefferson's advice was always centered around the belief that the district management was in a discrimination mode. Many, many EEO complaints had to be addressed to the extent they interfered with the training program for the new employees.

Time spent in drafting complaints and meeting with managers going all the way up the chain of command was very time consuming. The EEO complaints became a full time job for Jefferson. He refused to accept any resolution for the complaints unless it was exactly what he had asked for. In addition to trying to right what was perceived as a wrong, Jefferson always wanted a monetary resolution.

Jefferson's background was very interesting. At one point he had played a significant role in the civil rights movement. It was also alleged that he had ties with the communist party. He had worked for a major corporation prior to being hired at IRS and had been fired for rabble rousing and trying to start his own union. How do I know this? Jefferson told me himself. Interestingly enough there were times Jefferson volunteered to work with me "off the record" on one racial allegation or another.

Jefferson volunteered to work with me sometime because he was consistently "hitting on me", asking me to go out with him. First of all he was my employee and I never even entertained any personal thoughts about him. Secondly, I didn't consider his offer as something special since he was "hitting on" any female in the branch who would listen to him.

On one occasion a number of black employees were poised to file an EEO complaint against a black female manager and Jefferson was all prepared to back them up. I asked Jefferson to meet with me in a conference room to discuss the situation.

I appealed to his sense of blackness by asking him why was he so ready to take the employees side in what was a blatant attempt to wrongfully discredit the manager. I told him we had few black managers and here he was talking out of both sides of his mouth about trying to help black employees, yet he was trying to help railroad a black manager out of her job for accusations that he knew were untrue.

He suddenly seemed to remember he was black and agreed with me and told me he would see what he could do to resolve the situation. I was never really sure exactly what he did except I was told that the complaint had been dropped. It appeared that Jefferson had decided to play fair in this particular incident.

Behind closed doors he agreed with me on numerous occasions and I have to say I did agree with him some times. I also advised him that what he was trying to do was impossible. I told him right or wrong, IRS would never allow him, a black man to take down or discredit a white district director particularly when the black man was wrong in his accusations and I did believe Jefferson was wrong.

The director during Jefferson's employment was a career employee with over twenty years of service and he was the director of one of the largest districts in the United Sates. I told Jefferson he was going to be the one on the losing end if he continued to go after the director. Of course Jefferson discounted what I said and he told me he wasn't afraid of being fired. He said he had been fired from better places than IRS.

Shortly after Jefferson started his own EEO procedures he started trying to build his own union in IRS. This action immediately started a war between Brad and Jefferson with management in the middle. Many of the things that happened in the Lawndale office were very unprofessional and most of them were the results of Brad and Jefferson. Through all of their antics, management did nothing until the situations became unbearable.

Jefferson had the office in such a turmoil the executive assistant to the district director (a black male) became aware of the issues and the unprofessionalism that was being demonstrated. He met with some black managers, including me and a black union steward and arranged to have a meeting with black employees after hours at a local church.

The primary focus of the meeting was to attempt to reach the black employees and to garner some unity, self-respect, and professionalism. We all discussed the fact that for the first time in the history of the Los Angeles IRS district the employees had significant representation of black managers, a black branch chief (me), a black assistant division chief, and a black executive assistant and here they the black employees were doing everything they could to focus on the negative. Fortunately the objective was achieved and things became better in the office with employees and managers engaging in more open effective communication.

Even though improvement was seen the office continued to experience some problems and a significant bone of contention became the relationship of a former division chief and a union steward.

This former division chief had experienced significant problems in another district and was taken out of his job. Since he was close to retirement it was worked out that he would go to the Los Angeles district for the remaining year to two years of his career and to work as a group manager. Unfortunately for all of us this man was assigned to a vacant position in the Lawndale office.

This man we will call George was very gun shy and apparently very concerned about doing anything that would cause him to lose his retirement.

He was a nice enough person and supposedly had been a very strong division chief in his day. Evidently whatever he had been found guilty of was serious as he was demoted down two levels.

He arrived at the Lawndale office planning to operate on a very low key level. He obviously did not want any problems. Well, the union was waiting on him. The union representatives have a strong network and they knew of this man's reputation and they were prepared to take him on.

I actually felt sorry for George although he was the cause of enormous problems for me. Everything he did in his daily duties was questioned by the union and particularly by the bully union steward that was assigned to his group.

If he did not acquiesce to everything the union wanted they immediately filed paper (grievances) against him. He would then give in to prevent the grievance from escalating above him. The steward assigned to George's group, Jack Curns, was the most obnoxious one in the branch. Jack was given his marching orders from Brad to work this man over. They smelled blood and like sharks went after it.

Since I wasn't there every day you might wonder how I obtained so much inside information. There are always people willing to work both sides of the street and to leak information. I have always been able to maintain my sources. Then too I had been a revenue officer in the Los Angeles district and had worked with some of the revenue officers still there.

Jack Curns rode George day in and day out until finally one day George had had it. Near the end of a trying day Jack took it upon himself to go into George's private files and George caught him. Supposedly George caught Jack with his arm in the file cabinet he had opened and George pushed Jack and slammed the drawer on his arm in plain sight of the entire group. Jack was not seriously injured, but all hell broke out with the union making a grand federal case out of the incident, filing grievances and unfair labor practices against George and posting all of them on the bulletin boards.

The result of this incident consumed significant time of union officials and management away from the primary work IRS was paying employees to do. Many meeting were held and the paper flowed like a faucet. Time has a way of taking care of many things and because George was right at retirement's door by then, he took leave until the magic retirement date and then he officially retired.

The union used George's situation as a major publicity campaign and posted notice of the whole ordeal in their words on all bulletin boards. Basically they said, one down and so many more to go.

One major irritant for management was that the union could put almost anything on the bulletin boards, true or untrue, and management could not stop them. The official agreement between IRS and the union allowed the union so much space for their bulletin boards with carte blanche authority for posting.

Many a manager has been thoroughly embarrassed because the union posted something totally untrue about them and they have actually used the manager's name. By looking the other way and allowing this to happen, top level management gave the appearance of sanctioning this kind of behavior with total disregard of how it might make the managers feel.

Jack Curns continued his reign of terror for a year or so but, once Brad was transferred out of the building management took him on. So much heat was put on his failure to work cases he voluntarily transferred to another district out of state. It takes an average or better performance appraisal for another district to accept an employee on transfer; however many a manager has given an undeserved positive appraisal to someone they wanted to get rid of and in this case Jack Curns must have looked real good on paper because he was accepted on transfer.

Back to Jefferson. He continued to operate and to stir up problems. At one point he invited the only male manager in the branch out in the parking lot to resolve problems in what probably would have been a serious physical situation had the manager had the nerve or used the bad judgment to go to the parking lot. However, the manager was actually afraid and so obviously did not accept the challenge.

This threat was reported up the management chain yet nothing was done other than a lot of wasted discussions between layers of management. Management was still not ready to take on the union and particularly not ready to take on Jefferson. Any action on the part of management would have opened up the doors to many unwarranted EEO complaints and grievances. Management as usual shied away from any bad publicity.

Jefferson's undoing came about as a result of his refusal to work cases. Union stewards, EEO counselors, investigators, and all other employees assigned to non case related duties, commonly called collateral duties, are allocated certain amounts of time to work on those other assignments. As a result of this allocation of time an employee's case load is usually reduced. However, the employee is expected to continue working cases albeit on a limited basis.

My advice to my subordinate managers was that whenever the employees picked up a case they were expected to do something substantial. They were expected to set deadlines for taxpayers and for themselves and were expected to meet those deadlines or take what ever appropriate action was necessary.

A major problem created by the union was to take a non-performing employee and assign that person to a steward's job. This would generally be an employee management had started to document as failing to perform satisfactorily. The union would then see to it that the employee had so much union work they didn't have the time to do IRS case work.

This was an ongoing battle between IRS and management even at the time I retired and from what I hear from my sources it remains a problems. The union contends they have the right to select stewards on an as needed basis and to have the steward work on union business as appropriate. If the steward did not have any time left over for IRS cases, so what.

This means stewards are out there doing what some low level union official decides is appropriate and no one has the authority to challenge it. On occasion management feels its oats and does challenge these situations. It doesn't happen often so when it does it is memorable.

The labor-management agreement outlined the amount of time that could be used on union duties and even required union representatives and officials to prepare time reports and to turn them in to management. The labor relations section of IRS is supposed to monitor the reports to assure when the time allocated has run out and to notify the union that no more time can be used by that particular steward.

Believe it or not, even though this was very important to management, few reports were ever actually received and fewer still were monitored. Many stewards refuse to prepare time reports either through outward refusal or procrastination. Either way management did nothing other than on occasion to ask for the reports.

Jefferson reached the point where he told his manager and all the employees in the group he didn't have time to work any cases. He wanted her to take his entire case load away. She refused, but he still did not work the cases.

Deadlines, statutes, and receipt of money were in jeopardy with Jefferson's refusal to work the cases. In addition, he was jeopardizing morale among the other employees. When employees see one person not holding up their end and management fails to remedy the situation the other employees start to mimic the negative behavior. This puts the manager in an impossible situation of trying to insist that employees do what everyone knows the manager is letting one employee get away from doing. The employees had first hand knowledge that Jefferson was not working his cases as his manager had transferred his cases to other members of the group.

I reported Jefferson's refusal to work cases to the division chief and he had me arrange a meeting with Jefferson and him. Jefferson told me that at this meeting he told the division chief, "I am not going to work anymore cases". He said when the division chief told him, "Failure to work cases is an act you can be fired for. Refusing a direct order is even worse and can be considered insubordination, something you can be fired for immediately" He advised the chief, "I have been fired from jobs far better than IRS". The chief never shared this information with me. He may have been embarrassed.

After all Jefferson had done or had failed to do, according to him this statement incited the chief more than anything else. He told Jefferson, "I am giving you a direct order to continue working your cases or I will start action to remove you from the job". Jefferson told the chief again, "I am not going to work anymore cases". With those comments the chief evidently started action to remove Jefferson from the job as a result of insubordination. It was a long drawn out ugly battle, but Jefferson finally failed to return to work.

At one point prior to Jefferson's failure to report for duty, he was able to obtain a favorable resolution to an EEO complaint filed by an up and coming young female revenue officer. Upon advising the complainant of the resolution, she thanked Jefferson and he advised her if she really wanted to thank him she could go with him to get a room at a motel down the street from the federal building. This information was provided to me by the young woman, the complainant. She also advised me she not only told Jefferson no but hell no she was not going to a motel or any where else with him.

At the time Jefferson advised the young woman of the resolution of her complaint, he advised her to not accept the proposed resolution unless the chief agreed to pay her a monetary sum for her "pain and suffering". She was appalled and advised Jefferson she only wanted a right remedied and wasn't looking for money. In her case she was complaining because she was bypassed on a promotion list. The chief agreed she should not have been bypassed and he agreed to promote her.

While working at IRS Jefferson was quite the ladies man. He was attractive in a rough sense, very personable when he wanted to be and as mentioned earlier, well educated and he gave the appearance of being very worldly. As a result of these points there were a number of women vying for his attention. He dated several during the same period of time, supposedly broke a few hearts and ended up living with one of the female revenue officers.

After Jefferson was fired from IRS I was told that he was accused and convicted of child molestation. It was alleged that he was convicted of molesting his own female child and the female child of his live in lover. He was found guilty and sentenced to serve time in prison. While I am not 100% sure of the charges I know he did serve prison time. He actually had the gall to write me a letter from prison. It was just a hello, how are you kind of letter, but I was surprised to receive it and I certainly did not reply.

It is still amazing to me that people like Brad and Jefferson were able to control management in IRS and were allowed to waste many, many taxpayers dollars. That says a lot about IRS management particularly those at national office level as they condoned union activities by failing to do anything to improve damaging situations until they got completely out of hand.

A few years after the Brad and Jefferson episodes I was promoted to assistant chief in Laguna Niguel. I left the Los Angeles district, but I didn't leave labor-management problems. They seemed to haunt management everywhere in IRS and particularly in the southern California districts.

The worse example of money wasted by the union was seen in the actions of a chapter president in the Laguna district. This chapter president had been inducted into the union as a steward when he started to demonstrate work performance problems. A former chapter president took this revenue officer under his wings in an effort to thwart management's plan to take adverse action against him.

Once he became a steward the chapter president saw to it he had sufficient union work (grievances, unfair labor practices, meetings, etc.) to prevent him from having time to work his cases. While this was not a legitimate reason for not working cases, the Laguna district was far behind the Los Angels district in holding the union to the nationally agreed rules outlined in the

Labor/Management written agreement. At the time no one in Laguna Niguel was willing to take on the union.

We will call this union steward Shannon. He had more nerve than anything else. He was willing to take on anyone and he often did whether it was just or unjust, right or wrong. After a few years Shannon ran for chapter president and won. Winning this position enabled him to become more and more aggressive. It was not too difficult to win an election as few employees were involved enough in union politics to vote. The key was to frighten those employees whose work was substandard into thinking their jobs were on the line and that they were in desperate need of the support of the person who was running for office.

While all of this was going on the other chapter presidents were working towards not having to work caseloads. Mind you there were five chapter presidents in the Laguna district as well as a chief steward. The chapter presidents during most of my stint in Laguna were all from Collection Division and they were all senior revenue officers being paid at the top of the salary chart. While they were involved in union duties almost full time, the division was minus six senior employees and we could not fill the positions because they were considered employees of IRS.

One of the primary reasons for all of the chapter presidents coming out of collection division was because the revenue officer job is so demanding it generates much more need for union representation than other divisions. This then causes more involvement by collection division employees in union activities as mentioned above with collection employees always receiving more votes than other divisions' employees.

In addition, few employees showed any type of interest in running for office. On some occasions only one person ran. Thus the selection of Shannon as chapter president.

I don't have a problem with union activity in the workplace and I actually believe there is a need for it as there are many people who are not able to speak for themselves. The problem I had in IRS was that a number of the union officials in my district did not play by the rules.

This failure to play by the rules then caused some members of management to harbor resentment and to take reprisal action whenever possible The negative action of both parties eventually caused a covert war and all of this was at the expense of taxpayer dollars.

I call it a covert war because while everyone knew it was going on it was denied by both sides with secret agendas being played out every day. Not only was IRS paying the salary of six senior employees who were not working cases, their inventories were often sitting because they either refused or were crafty in finding ways to avoid working cases.

The former chapter president who initially supported Shannon moved to another office taking a higher ranking position. This move gave him significantly more clout which then legitimized Shannon giving him clout in his never ending battles against management.

The level of the chapter presidents stock depended upon their reputation as a full time revenue officer. If they were able to demonstrate expertise and a good solid work ethic in their jobs they were respected by other employees and were then held in high esteem as chapter presidents.

Shannon continued to be re-elected as chapter president because he would take on management and fight whether the employee had a valid complaint or not. He supposedly never counseled employees on the merits or non-merits of their complaints. There were chapter presidents who on occasion advised employees that they were wrong or that they did not have a winning case. Shannon never did this. He would take on any case even when it was blatantly obvious that he could not win it. I think he did this to aggravate management and to be sure he had so much work he could continue to try to justify not being able to work cases.

Shannon was not held in high regard by employees nor management and his reputation for working cases was very poor. The few cases he had worked were of such poor quality it was obvious he did not know the job well. More than likely he would have been fired if he had not been protected by the union and he was aware of this.

Even if a union official was not held in high esteem by employees if that official happened to be the only game in town, the only union official in the building, they would still be sought out by employees who were afraid they might lose their job. This is how Shannon was able to remain in office because he saw to it that any employee criticized by management was advised that management was out to fire the employee.

It just happens that Shannon was not held in high esteem by the other chapter presidents. He was not trusted and therefore did not have the ear of the district director the way a few chapter presidents and the chief steward did. The others were able, on some occasions, to meet with the director and have off the record discussions in an effort to resolve complaints. Shannon was known to lie and not deal in good faith; therefore, the director would not go off the record with him.

The chief steward in Laguna, Jim, was initially held in high esteem by both management and employees. He was an effective and efficient revenue officer at one time and even though he had an ax to grind with management he was able to restrain himself sufficiently enough so that he could work well with management to resolve issues.

Many years before the Laguna experience this chief steward had been interested in a position in management. He was given numerous long term acting assignment in a particular position. He was led to believe he was going to get the position on a permanent basis once it was announced.

I was well aware of this situation because even though he and I both did not have much experience in IRS we were both interested in management and I was given the opportunity to fill in behind him on one of his acting assignments when he went on vacation for a short period of two weeks.

He did not get the position when it was announced and he was embarrassed and furious about it. He told me he believed the current chief of the division in which he was acting had double crossed him. He felt he had been used. He then turned to the union a few years down the road and when the opportunity arose he showed his vindictiveness against the person he believed had betrayed him.

At the time he was acting in the position she was the Chief, Taxpayer Service Division and she soon afterward became the Chief, Collection Division in the Los Angeles District. We were all part of the Los Angeles District at that time. This was prior to the district splitting and establishing Laguna Niguel District. As mentioned earlier, this chief steward was the one who took on the division chief, writing negative articles in the union's newsletter.

Jim had a reputation for dealing fair in Laguna and he did not hesitate to tell employees when they were wrong. He represented the employee as best he could if the employee insisted but he did advise them up front of their chances of winning. Even with this kind of reputation, he took any available opportunity to embarrass IRS.

One grand opportunity became available during the IRS Hearing in the 1980's. Jim testified against IRS and its seizure practices. His testimony centered around IRS establishing seizure quotas and management's practice of forcing employees to take seizure action. He did a grand job of embarrassing IRS.

In the early 1990's something seemed to have happened to Jim. He did not seem to be his own man anymore. A chapter president who became Chief of the Joint Counsel seemed to have usurped his authority and demonstrated a much more dominant personality than Jim did. All of a sudden Jim almost disappeared from day to day life in the union and in IRS. As the chief steward he was the only union official authorized to work full time on union matters.

IRS agreed to provide office space for chief stewards and Jim went into his office, closed the door and seemed to have disappeared. He did attend important meetings sometimes and on occasion you might glimpse him in the hall way in Laguna but there was no mistaken that this Chief of the Joint Council was in charge. All of the chapters formed together made up the joint council and that made this person an important person in the union. Not only was he chief of the council, he was also still a chapter president.

For years Shannon said that the district director discriminated against him. While I did not see any out and out discrimination against Shannon I would not have been surprised if it existed because no one wanted to have to deal with him.

I do believe he tried hard to either change his feelings or to hide them because he worked with the others as best he could and he never outwardly made a difference in dealing with any of them.

Shannon complained to the national level union president regarding the alleged discrimination from the district director. He felt he was being left out of many things going on in the district while the director included both the chief steward and the chief of the joint council.

He was right for at least two reasons. First, he was working in the a part of the district away from the headquarters while both the chief steward and the chief of the joint council were in the same building and were right down the hall from the director. Secondly, as stated before the director had no intention of having off the record discussions with him.

The national president put pressure on the director to work with Shannon by complaining to the IRS national level management. National level management did discuss this issue with the director and he denied the allegations.

When this tactic failed to get Shannon the involvement and recognition he wanted he declared war on the district and particularly the collection division.

Because the chief steward Jim and the chief joint council Ron worked so closely together and were housed in the same office it was Shannon's contention that they were operating as Chapter President and Assistant Chapter President although there wasn't an assistant's position. Also, with all of the duties of the chief council and chapter president position Ron was given some unofficial leeway in working a very small caseload. This meant that basically neither Jim nor Ron were working caseloads while the division had started to turn up the heat under Shannon in a effort to make his work cases.

A precedent had been set in the Los Angeles District with Jefferson having been fired for not working cases. Shannon started to work a few cases while he fought the director tooth and nail trying to have his case inventory taken away and to force him to allow him to have an assistant chapter president. The director refused both requests. This problem became a well publicized, well discussed issue throughout the district as it was in the union's best interest to tell employees how bad management was. It was even published in the union's newsletter and posted on the bulletin board.

It was then that Shannon took her problems to her clout wielding friends in the national level union. The national level president made a special trip, at taxpayer's expense, to the Laguna District to meet with the district director and to discuss Shannon.

I say at taxpayers expense as IRS funds all union travel whether local management likes it or not. As long as they, the union can say it is business related, IRS gets the bill. Nothing was resolved at the meeting between the union president and the director other than for the union president to leave the district angrier than he was before he arrived there.

As mentioned before in the discussion regarding the union's treatment of the former Los Angeles Collection Division chief the union had a habit of printing negative, libelous statements in their newsletters and even though management was horrified at times there wasn't anything that could be done about it. Management refused to take the union on and put something in writing to dispute the lies. Even if it ruined the reputation of a manager, top level management would not do anything about it. While there are many examples of the under handed methods used by the union, the one that stands out in my mind more than others had to do with libelous articles written in the union chapter newsletter.

As a result of my meetings with employees as spelled out in Chapter Two, a chapter president, Ann decided to take me on personally. In my mind it almost appeared to be dejá vu with what had happened to the Los Angels division chief. (Chapter Two). As I mentioned in the chapter about her, a union steward started her downfall with his notorious articles defaming her. I refused to be a negative statistic resulting from libelous statements from the union; therefore, when I read the newsletter (Exhibit 2) stating I lied about statements made by the national president and that I did not care about my employees I became incensed.

I considered the statement libelous and I called the chief joint council and asked him if the union as a group supported what was written in the chapter newsletters. After hemming and hawing, he appeared, by his tone, to become suspicious and cautious and he asked why did I want to know. I decided to throw caution to the wind and told him I found the statements in Ann's newsletter to be libelous. I further told him if it did not discontinue I was going to sue whoever was responsible. Well, not surprisingly, he quickly advised me each chapter was responsible for its own newsletter and anything it contained.

I believed him because while I did not completely trust this person, on occasions he and I had off the record discussions and on occasions he had confided in me. He was a black male and he appeared to feel that he and I shared some of the same concerns at times. This was true but, I never felt very comfortable with him as I always knew he was out to feather his own nest and if he had to step on me on his way up he wouldn't hesitate to do so. All in all, on the surface I had a decent working relationship with both the chief steward and the chief joint council and I knew definitely that they did not like nor respect this chapter president. On that issue we were in total agreement as we had all laughed at her foolishness behind her back.

I then went to the director and the assistant director's office and told them I was going to warn Ann and that if she printed any additional libelous statements against me I was going to sue her. I let them know this would be my own personal action as IRS would never, ever take action against the union no mater how bad it got.

Interestingly enough, neither the director nor his assistant had a problem with my potential actions. As a matter of fact each told me separately they thought it was a good idea. Each gave me the idea they wished they could take some kind of action against the union for some of their cruel action against management.

I then called Ann and told her I found her statements to be libelous and if they were not discontinued I was going to sue her. Ann, being the coward she was, told me one of her stewards had written the article. She said it was her newsletter but she had nothing to do with what was written in it. I told her it would be wise for her to advise the steward to be sure of his facts because I refused to allow the union to undermine me and to make my employees think I did not care about them.

Sometime later the assistant director visited my office and told me once again that he agreed with what I had told Ann. He then went on to say that he had had to go outside of the agency and get an attorney regarding some travel expenses that were disallowed. So much for IRS showing compassion for employees. This is the same feeling as that of another assistant director who moved to Laguna from another state for the "good of the Service" only to have his wife treated very shabbily.

When managers or even employees are moved for promotions or any job related reasons at the request of the Service, the Service finds a job for the spouse if the spouse is also employed by IRS. In this case the only job they made available for this executive's wife was a clerical job in the Los Angeles District which is about sixty or more miles from Laguna where they were living. The wife attempted to make the commute but couldn't keep it up; and so she took a leave of absence. Months later she was given a job in the Laguna IRS Legal Counsel's office. The counsel employees were technically not a part of the district, but were part of the regional office. Technically speaking a spouse cannot work for a spouse and so to get around that obstacle most executive's spouses are given jobs in regional offices, counsel or appeals, all a part of the region although located in Laguna.

I was told counsel did not want her in their office because they thought she would be reporting back to the director what was going on in their offices. On occasion counsel and the director disagreed vehemently on issues and obviously counsel did not want a member of the enemy camp on their staff.

I was told the chief counsel treated the assistant's wife very bad, even putting her on what was called a leave letter for supposedly abusing leave. This was unheard of treatment of an executive's wife. This is just an example of how IRS treats its own so how can the public taxpayers expect to be treated better. IRS' treatment of employees and managers alike, as well as a lack of concern for their welfare is another reason why recalcitrants like Brad, Jefferson, Shannon and Ann were allowed to operate without restrictions.

About a month or so after my conversation with Ann regarding her newsletter, we had a labor- management relations committee meeting. These meeting were generally attended by all of the chapter presidents, the division chief, assistant division chief, the division staff assistant and a labor relations specialist. Minutes were taken at these meetings and were disseminated through out the division with a copy to the director. The meetings were held in what management hoped was a good faith effort to resolve potential concerns before they were blown out of proportion.

At this particular meeting I was sitting across from my assistant and the labor relations specialist. My assistant handed me a note that said "Ann is taping this meeting." Sure enough there was what looked like a small tape recorder on the table. This was definitely not allowed. The Service does not allow anyone to tape anything without advising the other party in advance. Any revenue officer worth their salt knows this. In addition, it is illegal.

As I've said through out this book, I am very outspoken and up front. Therefore, I asked Ann right out if she was taping the meeting. She immediately turned red and started to sputter. She finally said she had not taped anything but had the recorder there in case she needed it because I had threatened to sue her.

Everyone, including the other chapter presidents were amazed that even Ann would stoop so low. The labor relations specialist spoke up and told Ann we would have to cancel the meeting as what she was doing was illegal. I then spoke up and said no we would not cancel the meeting, we would take a brief recess so that management could get a tape recorder and then we would reconvene.

A labor relations specialist always attended meetings held with union officials and employees, especially when dealing with union matters and adverse actions. They would be there to provide legal advice to management. The taping incident was just one of many examples of the lying and underhanded actions Ann was caught in.

During the break from the meeting, several of the other chapter presidents castigated Ann behind her back, It was said that taping the meeting was a new low even for Ann. They also said that was why they did not trust her. We, management, did bring in a tape recorder and taped the balance of the meeting; however, nothing significant was said during the time remaining for the meeting.

Another deplorable example of Ann's actions can be seen in the trouble she started between the director and national level union with me in the middle. It appeared Ann had nothing but contempt for the director and she went out of her way to show him her feelings. She contacted the national level union president in writing (Exhibit 23) and advised him that I had quoted her in saying that he had joined the IRS Deputy Commissioner in supporting collections efforts to improve dollars collected.

She specifically said I quoted the union president by saying "The top executives and the union's national president have pledged their support for management's efforts to increase dollars collected this year. Collection of dollars is a national problem. If we don't increase dollars collected there will be contracting out of collection functions."

First of all Ann misquoted me. I did make a similar statement saying, "It has become a necessity that the division improves in the areas of dollars collected and overall productivity. In the not too distant past there has been discussions about contracting out and I wonder whether at sometime in the future it might be considered more efficient to contract the work out rather than to continue the current collection efforts".

Naturally the union would object to any contracting out and I can understand why; however, my statement became true because in 1996 and 1997 collection cases were contracted out to a collection agency on a trial basis. I have since been told that IRS decided that the contracting out was not successful and that the concept had been abandoned.

All managers and management officials in the know in IRS know that few tests succeed because IRS often does not give the test enough support nor enough time. The National Academy of Sciences conducts reviews on IRS from time to time and they have said on several occasions that IRS fails many times because they will move on to something new before they assess the success of the current program.

My comments quoted by Ann were actually based on comments printed in a newsletter from the IRS Chief Compliance Officer. In his newsletter (Exhibit 24) he printed a direct quote from the union president in response to a question regarding how the union would be accountable for helping IRS increase collections, "NTEU is also laying its credibility on the line with Congress. In testimony earlier this year, I made a pledge to Congress: Give IRS an additional $405 million for jobs and training and we, NTEU and IRS will produce results – greater revenue collection and greater service to taxpayers. Partnership is the essential means for improving the Service and NTEU and IRS are both accountable to Congress for its success."

At the top levels in the union the officials were saying they wanted IRS to be effective; however, the wild actions of some union officials would lead you to believe they were operating at cross purposes. Ann worked diligently to get everyone involved in things totally non-job related yet IRS continued to pay her salary and all of her travel expenses.

Management was at the top of ineffectiveness and inefficiency during that time. I often asked myself who was running the shop. As said before the local union officials had carte blanche to do whatever they wanted to do and no one, absolutely no one with authority questioned them.

Many, many, many, hours were spent dealing with frivolous and ridiculous accusations. Allegations would start somewhere. They would then be sent up or down the chain depending on where they started, sometimes through three or four levels of management. The responses would then go back up or down the chain taking many, many hours away from job related actions.

The personnel office had an entire full time section to deal with labor/management problems. There were six, seven, or more full time employees assigned to support each of the two large divisions. With several others assigned to support the other four divisions. THE TAXPAYERS DOLLARS PAID FOR THIS FOOLISHNESS.

Sometimes it was understandable that the union had concerns, complaints, and questions. Sometimes it was very clear to everyone that some member of management had screwed up. Many, many times it was very clear to everyone it was just Ann's way of getting even with management as a whole and the director in particular. Even the other chapter presidents said behind her back that she was a loose cannon. They actually seriously criticized her off the record when talking to division chiefs. Yet once again, NO ONE DID ANYTHING ABOUT IT. Management was definitely not in control of the district.

The allegation regarding my misquoting the national president was one of the most blatant, openly ridiculous allegations Ann ever made. Ann had not gone to any special lengths to pick on me, she just happened to be in my division and my division was the second largest in the district and the largest collection division in the country.

She wrote the national president and informed him of my statements as though they were totally off base. After having made the statement and having them put in print at national level, the national president wrote a letter to the Deputy Commissioner as though my comments were lies and were totally off base.

The Deputy Commissioner wrote the Regional Commissioner who wrote the district director who called me in. The Chief Compliance Officer works directly under the Regional Commissioner and he is the one who reported the comments made by the union president in his newsletter. Apparently the national president had said he supported IRS but he either forgot he said it or he did not want the chapter president to go against him because she thought he was buying in with IRS.

The newsletter of the Chief Compliance Officer was circulated throughout collection divisions in Western Region yet the union had the audacity to deny the comments. To make matters even more interesting, the Leaders Digest , Fall 1994, (Exhibit 25) printed an entire interview with the national president and he made similar comments that were even more at odds with Shannon's philosophy.

The Leaders Digest is a magazine published quarterly for IRS managers. In the Fall 1994 issue the national president was quoted as saying the following, "As for accountability in the NTEU internal structure, as mentioned earlier, NTEU local and national officers are accountable to their members.

If union members don't like what their elected leaders are doing, they can vote them out at the next election." He continued to say, "NTEU is also laying its credibility on the line with Congress" followed by the exact quote shown above.

Both the Chief Compliance Officer's newsletter and the Leader's Digest were printed in November 1994. The letter of complaint from the union president is dated November 24, 1994. Now who was fooling who? What king of games were these people playing at government expense. See my response to this foolishness (Exhibit 26) written for the director's signature.

I composed the response, a duty usually done by my secretary or staff assistant. This was one duty I wanted to take care of personally. Do you think anything was done or said to Ann or to the union president regarding this shameful waste of government expense? Absolutely not.

Part of the union's problem with the comments published in the newsletter and the Leaders Digest was that they were caught between a rock and a hard place. IRS and the union were in the midst of trying to secure a partnership agreement. The agreement meant joint efforts were necessary. Since the union represented the employees it was necessary to do everything to provide job security yet they were criticized by employees each time they were found to be in agreement with management on any issue.

Ann's camp was totally against any agreement with management unless management gave in completely. Her actions caused reactions from management and the work environment became unbearable for many.

Management definitely did not respect nor like her and I have to admit it was obvious there were times management could have agreed with her, but refused to do so because of her attitude. This caused every concern to go through the grievance procedure.

To get an idea of the time spent in resolving grievances you need to know the steps involved. First the complainant meets with the union steward to express concern about some kind of treatment regarded as undeserved or unjust. The steward then arranges to meet with the manager to discuss the allegation and supposedly in an attempt to resolve it. This is considered a first step meeting and along with the other steps is required by the IRS/NTEU Agreement.

If the problem is not resolved at the first step the steward then arranges to meet with the branch chief at what is known as the second step. Failure to resolve the matter with the branch chief results in the chapter president meeting with the division chief at the third step. The grievance is then elevated to the director for the fourth step if it has not been resolved.

Failure to resolve the issue with the director can lead to the union taking the matter to arbitration for resolution. All along the way a labor relations specialist is involved, preparing the file, preparing written responses at each level and advising of whether management is in agreement with the union's proposed settlement. The employee is allowed time on the clock to prepare for the meetings. Both the employee and the employee's union representative attends all meetings.

Failure to resolve the matter through the fourth step then requires involvement with an agency attorney to prepare for an arbitration hearing. An arbitration hearing requires many, many, hours of time from the employee, the union, management, labor relations, the agency attorney, witnesses, and an arbitrator. All of this is at the government's expense.

Some times the above actions are necessary because management refuses to right a wrong. Many times, particularly with union representatives such as Ann the grievances are frivolous. She had a reputation for taking every unresolved grievance to arbitration. She had the authority to do this. Chapter presidents have the sole discretion to spend the government's money in the manner in which they choose in situations such as this.

Some oversight committee needs to remedy this kind of blatant atrocity. Most of the chapter presidents do not have any training that provides expertise in handling grievances. Some of them land in the position as a result of poor work performance and/or unresolved feuds with management. They are then given a blank check to do what ever they decide to do. What with

Congress sanctioning this how can they have the audacity to criticize IRS, as they so often do, or any other government agency for utilization of budget funds.

The games that were played, the time and money wasted, were unbelievable. If the public knew how much latitude the union has in IRS and how much unchecked authority they have been provided by IRS in their so-called agreement, many questions would be asked.

Again, no one has authority over the chapter presidents. The national president can try to keep them in line but if they don't like what he says they don't have to listen. If he keeps trying to pull them in line, the chapter presidents can cause the national president problems and can make it difficult for him to be re-elected as he is also voted in office.

The Leader's Digest Fall 1994 contained an article, "Partnering with NTEU to Influence Outcomes" in which both the national union president and the IRS national level Labor Relations Director were interviewed. The director was asked to describe the new partnership agreement and he stated the following in part, "The new partnership arrangement between NTEU and the Service is an extension of the Vice President's National Performance Review (NPR), entitled Creating a Government That Works Better and Costs Less."

I can't believe Vice President Gore is aware of the high costs being incurred by labor/management problems. If he were told I would be willing to bet he would automatically lay the problem at the feet of IRS management. IRS management would be advised to fix the problem and NTEU would be allowed to continue operating, business as usual.

In an effort to gain the unions viewpoint, this same article reports on an interview with the national president. One question to the national president was, "What has NTEU given up to get benefits from the partnership?" The national president responded, "Partnership means abandoning the safety of the status quo. By changing our primary role from management adversary to management partner. NTEU local and national leaders have made themselves vulnerable to charges of "sleeping with the enemy" "from our membership. In effect, we have pledged that an IRS-NTEU partnership will improve employees' work lives. Now we will have to deliver on our promises or risk losing membership, which is the power base for every union."

Perhaps the union president meant what he said during the interview; however, if he did, he evidently did not know how out of control Ann and her cohorts were in the Laguna District. Believe me folks it was like walking on a battlefield every single day in some groups. If the union decided to take on a manager in the branch in which Ann worked, that manager's life became unbearable. At any rate, there wasn't any way Laguna Niguel district and NTEU were going to reach any effective partnership agreement.

During those hectic times IRS nationwide was in the process of implementing a total quality concept. The concept was designed to make changes that would enable the IRS to improve in areas such as systems management, labor relations, quality of worklife and empowerment to name a few. Before the concept could be established, both NTEU and IRS had to agree on a plan and have the plan certified by both the regional and national management. The overall plan had been agreed to and signed off on by both a national level IRS executive and a NTEU executive.

Near the time I retired, other districts were implementing Total Quality Organization processes yet Laguna Niguel district and NTEU were at totally opposite ends of the pole. The district and NTEU were not able to agree on what was needed in the plan. Many hours were spent going over and over the plan only to come together with NTEU and to find that the chapter presidents all disagreed with each other. The plans for the TQO process were over three years old by the time I retired and Laguna Niguel was still fighting over even getting together to plan for implementing the process.

The major problem came about as a result of the process requiring the district to conduct a self-assessment and prepare a multi-year plan to achieve the goals of the plan. The plan had to be agreed to by both management and labor and that was not about to happen in Laguna Niguel. The last update I received in 1998 regarding the plan was that it was still being worked on. Exhibit provides a copy of a memo from the executive level of management and labor addressed to all joint quality councils of IRS with the subject being "TQO Certification Process".

The entire environment was very hostile on both sides to the extent the director had to hire an outside intervention expert to come in and try to bring us together. This was a very costly process not only the fee for the intervention expert, but all the cost of two to three hundred managers having to attend meeting after meeting with the expert to provide feedback so that she could determine what the problems actually consisted of. (See Exhibit 27 Laguna Niguel/Santa Ana POD Assessment Report) The Assessment Report provides examples of both management and the union's perspective.

The other division chiefs and I stayed late many evenings trying to identify and work out our hostility towards NTEU. In the meantime NTEU chapter presidents had their own internal problems. The Chief Joint Council had been the speaker for the chapter presidents, but in 1995 the council disintegrated.

First, Ann pulled out of the joint council. This caused major problems for the director. Having one joint council group meant that major concerns of the union came through one person who had the majority consensus of the chapter presidents. With Ann pulling out war was truly on between Ann and the remaining members of the joint council and Ann and the district. She would not accept decisions made by the remaining joint council and she definitely did not want to meet with management except from across the grievance table.

One of the major problems was that the rules and regulations required the director to only have to share concerns and conduct business with the spokesperson of the joint council, the chief, who in turn would advise the chapter presidents. Ann refused to accept this way of doing business and the director being the kind of person he was did not want to muddy the waters. Instead of holding Ann to the rules, he played it her way. This fiasco caused many things to have to be done twice, once with the remaining members of the joint council and once with Ann. Keep in mind though, the expense for this came from the district's budget, not the director's nor the union's pocket. So why should he or Ann care?

Once the director realized he would never get agreement between the warring factions, Ann and the council, he started to stall and to ignore requests to negotiate on issues raised by both Ann and the council. On November 21,

1995, the Chief Joint Council filed an unfair labor charge against the director (Exhibit 28).

By November the council as originally set up, was no longer operating as a group because national IRS and national NTEU had entered into an agreement whereby "NTEU Chapters were not required to belong to a joint council where two or more union chapters existed within a district.

Each chapter could decide to fashion a direct relationship with the district director, negotiate agreements with the district etc. This meant that a district, such as Laguna Niguel, could have a joint council and an independent chapter in the same district. Each body has equal representational and institutional standing in the district." The director had basically abdicated his responsibility where NTEU was involved and was ignoring both the independent chapter and what was left of the joint council.

During the time the joint council problems were surfacing, in an effort to improve overall quality within the district the director formed a Joint Quality Council. This was not done out of the goodness of his heart, but was yet another mandate from national office. The council was composed of division chiefs, the chief steward, chapter presidents, the director, and the assistant director.

Meetings were scheduled once a month at which time the group got together and discussed any issues pertaining to quality. After establishing the council, on many, many occasions the director was not available for the meetings. He was out of town, on vacation, had other priorities, etc. As a result of his frequent absences, the union was very critical of the district and not cooperative in working towards certification.

The district was required to come up with a written plan to achieve a certain level of quality and the plan had to be certified at national level. Total quality certification was expected to be completed in December 1994. All of the division chiefs thought that date was a joke. The union officials frequently made negative comments to us behind the director's back while during face to face meetings they sucked up to him, showing the two-faced creatures they were.

I suppose I should also say that we, the division chiefs, were also two-faced as we also criticized the director behind his back, both in conversations with the chapter presidents and among ourselves. Although we were on friendly terms on the surface, the chapter presidents failed to cooperate with us and refused to say why. They just plain refused to take us seriously.

They started not showing up at scheduled meetings as a group and to state that it was very difficult, if not impossible, to be available for dates on which we tried to schedule meetings. I remember once we were in a meeting and at the end we were attempting to schedule the next meeting. We went through at least three months of dates and could not find a time the union would be available. This was a travesty on the part of management and the union. What a travesty and at the government's/taxpayers' expense.

Most of the district experienced labor/management problems. However, some of the offices experienced more problems than others.

For a time the collection branch located in Long Beach, California became the district's major problem. The Long Beach office had originally been located in Carson, California in what was thought of as a predominantly black area. This is the area mentioned earlier where most white employees did not want to work.

The employees in Carson did not experience any more crime related problems on an individual level than any other office. However, the building was broken into on numerous occasions and this caused serious concern about having to be in the building when it became dark.

The office had initially opened with concerns expressed by employees as in the beginning it was located in an area with several vacant lots adjacent to the building. It was also located in an industrial area that lent an atmosphere of isolation to the area.

Prior to IRS moving in the building a dead body had been found dumped in one of the vacant lots. Ten years or more after the body was found it was still being discussed as a problem and a blemish on the location. It was apparent that the person had been murdered somewhere else and had been brought to the vacant lot.

The IRS employees, particularly the white ones, never stopped speaking of their fear of the location. Therefore, the office was predominantly black. There were a few brave white souls who lived closer to the Carson office than to offices that were predominantly white and they refused to drive long distances just to get away from a building with a so called "bad" reputation.

As a result of the bad publicity Carson received there was a difficulty recruiting the best managers to work there. There were many fine employees located in the Carson office, but most of them did not want to be managers.

Therefore, when a vacancy occurred managers could sometimes be recruited for the office if a promotion was involved. If they went there on promotion they lived for the day they could promote out to another area. Unfortunately this caused a number of managers selected through the years who really were not strong enough to manage strong minded employees. The office experienced many problems because the employees were stronger than the managers and they were virtually running the groups.

There was also a problem with professionalism, both in the way some employees treated taxpayers and in the image they created in the manner in which they dressed. A number of employees were selected from the groups to become the manager for the same group. This caused numerous problems as it is difficult many times to manage people who have not been co-workers, but it becomes extremely difficult to have to say no to a friend or a co-worker.

In addition, some of the employees being managed knew things about the manager that were undesirable traits for managers, things that management did not know or the person would never have been selected as a manager.

When the office was moved to Long Beach it was located in a new federal building, a few doors down from the World Trade Building. The area was metropolitan with many people in the area dressed professionally and carrying themselves in a professional manner. The IRS employees for the most part rose to the occasion with most of the ones who had started to let them selves go down in regards to professional dress in Carson starting to take pride once more in the way they looked. This was the most positive part of the move.

While in Carson the union had a black chapter president and he was known for trying to work with management all up and down the line when trying to resolve an employee's complaint. One of his stewards had to be pulled back in line on occasion, but he met the challenge and kept her in line.

Just before the move to Long Beach the mood of the collection branch in Carson turned ugly. Several black employees became very unhappy. I had started to change the work habits of the non-performers and to turn up the heat and since these employees were the seniors in the branch and were black they fought back with a vengeance. Since the chapter president was friendly with management, the employees voted him out. The new chapter president was aware that she had only been selected because she was supposed to give management hell. And did she try!

Next to Ann the Long Beach union tactics were the most aggressive in the district. It was obvious in my one on one conversations with the chapter president Jean that she did not inwardly support many things the employees complained about; however, she did want to stay in office and she knew the senior employees, a group of women, would dump her in a second if she did not fight the way they wanted her to.

In the beginning it appeared Jean was someone the managers could work with. She had always seemed to be a reasonable person and it was felt by management that she knew and understood when her constituents were in the wrong. She even went so far as to attempt to resolve issues through discussion rather than immediately filing grievances. Management believed she even had the nerve to tell her constituents when they were wrong; however, with the employees being as anti-management as they were they refused to allow the chapter president to work anything out amicably.

To ensure that Jean believed them when they told her they would vote her out many low rated actions were taken by some of the members to humiliate and embarrass her. One of their actions can be seen in a document distributed throughout the office when Jean had failed to please some of her constituents (Exhibit 29).

Jean gave the appearance of having difficulty understanding what was being said or what was going on. Management often wondered whether it was because of her inability to understand or her stubbornness.

The feeling about this was one of the few things shared by employees, other union officials and management. She really wasn't smooth but she was sharp enough to have a professional image. However, she dressed more like someone going out to do manual labor instead of a professional. She was always neat and clean but she always wore casual, wash and wear type pants along with high top black tennis shoes. According to gossip provided by the other chapter presidents, she even dressed in this manner when attending national office meetings where everyone else was decked out trying to impress each other.

The ugliness in Long Beach escalated in August 1995 when a memo entitled "Jean Must Go" (Exhibit 30) was distributed by an anonymous author. Around that time it was believed that the chief steward and the chief Joint Council were trying to gain control of the Long beach chapter. Their main method of doing this was to low rate and down grade the chapter president. Many believed the chief steward was the author of the document although he vehemently denied it.

Jean became incensed, and rightfully so as far as I was concerned, and she solicited the support of the national president. The national president arrived at the conclusion that the chief steward was the one who wrote the castigating document. He alleged that he had a handwriting analysis conducted (See Exhibit 30) and that it was determined the handwriting on the envelope was that of the chief steward.

He then issued a "cease and desist order" to the chief steward ordering him to cease and desist from all future similar activity against the chapter president. He wrote a general letter to all members of the Long Beach chapter supporting the chapter president (Exhibit 31). Needles to say the chief steward and the chief joint council both told the national president to go take a flying leap.

In the meantime management sat back observing this unbelievable fiasco that was taking place at government's expense. During this particular time IRS was experiencing budget problems and we had been told to tighten our belts and to economize where ever possible. All travel except case related travel was curtailed yet the union continued to travel at their own discretion and continued to take aim at each other while being paid government dollars.

Ordinarily all of the foregoing might be interesting reading material, not particularly relevant to most people's lives; however, this is just another example of something that impacts all taxpayers whether they know it or not. Hours and hours are spent by management and the union dealing with non-job related issues. Many, many memos are written using government supplies, numerous meetings are held with employees, union, management, labor relations specialist, and many others in attendance.

Management's actions are outrageous many times, but at least every manager has to answer to a higher authority. Union officials who are voted into office don't have to answer to anyone. If they are out of control, so be it. They exist on unchecked power. Memos from the national president are meaningless. There's nothing he can really do to stop anything from happening.

Meanwhile with all of the above going on the work environment in Long Beach became unbearable to the extent an outside consultant had to be brought in. In an effort to resolve the management-employee-union (35 to 40 people) problem and to attempt to improve the relationships the consultant Turner Stevens held separate meetings with all managers, all employees, the director, the assistant director, labor relations specialists, Chief, Human Resources and me.

Workshops were conducted for days at a time for all employees. Many, many dollars and hours were spent attempting to resolve the "at war" attitudes of both management and the union. This went on for at least six months before I retired and was sill going on six months later.

In the meantime taxpayers cases were sitting in drawers with no work being done. I know that the taxpayers were not anxious to hear from IRS; however, the longer the cases were allowed to sit the more interest and penalty accrued. This is always the case and is a grave injustice to the honest taxpayer who wants to resolve their issues with IRS.

Why have I spent so much time discussing management-union problems? One of the major criticisms leveled at government agencies is their waste of money, yet national level management accepts, for the most part, without question, the tremendous waste in dealing with these problems. Is it the unions fault? Certainly not. It is both management and the unions fault.

I'm sure most people reading this chapter will have difficulty believing the tremendous waste taking place day in and day out; however, nothing is going to be done about it if left up to the current IRS national level management.

I certainly don't have all of the answers to this major problem and I do believe that unions have the right to exist and that many times they are needed by employees. I do believe that IRS has abdicated authority and thrown caution to the wind in entering into agreements with the union.

How can they be allowed to operate so independently and so unchecked? My suggestion would be for congress to appoint someone such as an ombudsman to look into this problem and to provide oversight and major assistance to IRS when negotiations begin for the next agreement.

IRS-NTEU agreements are negotiated for a specific period of time and sometimes prior to the expiration of the current agreement, negotiations are started for the next one. Management throughout IRS have difficulty believing each agreement when they are made aware of it. It always appears that the system is more political than anything else. The former Deputy Commissioner appeared to have preferred to enter into something acceptable to the union regardless of what it meant to the organization rather then hold NTEU accountable for their actions.

As recently as November 1998 NTEU in Laguna was still holding the district hostage although the acting District Director at that time was attempting to wrest control from them. Reliable sources have advised me of a situation wherein the district scheduled a meeting for all managers and the union in the never ending situation of attempting to enter into a partnership agreement. All parties involved were scheduled to stay in a hotel close to the Laguna office; however, the union refused to stay there and made their own reservations to stay in another hotel. Even though IRS was paying the entire bill for the meeting the union was determined to slap management in the face.

Word has it that the current Commissioner is very concerned that IRS provides individual offices for NTEU representatives within the quarters of IRS. IRS pays the bills for the offices yet NTEU has its own financial resources acquired from the thousands of dollars collected from the dues paying members. IRS pays salaries for all of the union stewards, officials, Chapter Presidents, etc. provides space so that they have private offices, telephones, furniture and all of the trimmings necessary to run an office; however, IRS has absolutely no say over what any of the officials do.

A new contract was recently entered into between IRS and NTEU and supposedly management is attempting to enforce the rule of NTEU having to report all of their union time to management. NTEU has historically been granted a specific amount of time to work on union matters and once that time is used up they would have to cease or work on their own time.

Management being as disillusioned as it has been about top level management support in union matters has seriously failed to make NTEU report their time. Since the time is not reported accurately or not at all, NTEU officials are using twice as much or more of the time than they are allowed.

Attempting to make the union officials report their time is an uphill battle since it has not been done in the past. NTEU is notorious for bringing up the rule that once IRS allows something to be done they can't stop because the past practices rule prevents them from doing so.

As of this writing a few things are looking up for IRS. I was told that the notorious former chief of the joint council has been accused of sexual harassment by one of the employees in his territory. In the meantime his fellow union members called a meeting and gave him a vote of no confidence.

The former chief then resigned from his position with the union and supposedly after a brief stint of working cases as a professional revenue officer he resigned from IRS. I know from personal experience with him that he was capable of working cases effectively if he had chose to do so. However, with many managers having had negative dealings with him in his role as a union official, he may have decided he was going to be in for a rocky road without the union backing him up. Rather than face that for the rest of his career, he resigned.

In addition to the former chief of the joint council resigning his position, his toughest, most feared steward was temporarily taken out of her job based on an allegation of fraud. According to the Los Angeles Times newspaper article dated October 1, 1999 she has been working with a firm that represents taxpayers seeking Offers in Compromise. The article says the firm would receive checks from taxpayers that were supposed to be paid over to IRS, yet they kept the money and the steward would then show the account as uncollectible. This steward has about 20 years of IRS service and she has been indicted and faces many years in prison if she is found guilty.

This steward is basically a nice person on a personal level; however, she is tough to deal with when it comes to union matters and some managers fear her and would prefer that she not be around. She was finally found guilty and was fired as well as having to face a criminal trail.

Again, in my opinion, the former national level executive leaders in IRS are responsible for mismanagement of IRS. Many managers saw one in particular that they watched as he climbed the IRS ladder and they have found it very difficult to believe he was ever selected for such a highly responsible position. There is a general feeling that he was incapable of leading such a large organization as IRS and that everyone should have known it. His incompetence may well have led to the major problems publicized regarding IRS in the 1990's.

Chapter Ten

EMPLOYEE OUTREACH EFFORTS

Most of the feedback I have received over the years regarding the perception of IRS by the public has been and still is negative. Most people react very negatively to the idea of IRS. Even in my personal life my friends and acquaintances have nothing but negative remarks to make about IRS. Even when I know they think highly of me as an individual they still express overall disdain for IRS in general.

On one occasion I was invited to a party at my brother's girl friend's home. During the course of the evening the girl friend's brother appeared to have had too much to drink and he started asking me questions about IRS. At first I paid him the courtesy of answering his questions because after all I saw it as an opportunity to attempt to spread some truth (as I knew it) and goodwill regarding my place of employment.

Well, unfortunately this person had some misconceptions about how IRS operates and he was more than willing to express them loudly. The party was small enough that everyone could hear any conversation going on unless it was whispered and needless to say this one wasn't whispered.

It seems as though this person had a personal problem with IRS; however, rather than discuss his problem he chose to find fault with hearsay information. After asking me several innocuous questions he then started talking about how terrible it was for IRS to take taxpayer's welfare payments. I assured him that wasn't true and that IRS had procedures for hardship situations and welfare recipients certainly fell into that category.

He refused to accept what I had to say and gave the appearance he was steadily becoming more and more angry at something and/or someone. Being the kind of person I am I decided it was past time for me to leave before I became more hot under the collar than I already was.

Unfortunately for the hostess, I decided to get up right in the middle of this person's conversation and asked for my coat and that of my guest. The hostess asked me why I was leaving and her brother spoke up immediately and said "She's not leaving because of me." To which I immediately replied, "I am leaving because of your brother. I refuse to stay anywhere and allow someone to insult me." The hostess asked me to stay and my brother asked me to stay but I refused and gathered up my coat and my guest and exited the premises.

Again, unfortunately for the hostess, she and my brother got into an argument about how I had been treated and they severed their relationship that night never to get back together again. Maybe one or both of them just used that night to get out of something they were already unhappy with; however, on the surface you could say they ended their relationship as a result of misinformation regarding IRS.

Most citizens do not know much about the inner workings of IRS and most probably never stop and think about the people employed there. The only frame of reference many taxpayers have comes from their own personal dealings with IRS employees or information they receive from the news media or their personal acquaintances. Most of this kind of information is automatically negative. However, there is a very large population of employees working in IRS, somewhere in the hundred thousands nationwide. If you stop and think about it surely all of those people would not be cruel and evil, taking delight in making taxpayers lives miserable.

Unfortunately, there probably are some cruel, evil employees in IRS the same as anywhere else, but most employees are simply people trying to live their lives the best they can and they just happen to be working for IRS. These people have families, suffer tragedies, and enjoy happiness in the same manner as the rest of the world.

During my time with IRS I have to say I had the privilege of working with some of the best people I could have ever known. I have had many secretaries through the years and they were all stellar people who all with the exception of one moved up to jobs of higher responsibility. The one who failed to make it failed as a result of personal problems.

Most of the people who worked closely with me did not hesitate to work more than the regular eight hours if it became necessary. I never asked anyone to work beyond their regularly scheduled hours unless I could authorize overtime; however, there were many occasions when I had to actually make some of my employees leave for the day. If I had an expedite they always wanted to complete it before they left for the day.

At the time I retired IRS was using a merit pay system to authorize pay raises and awards for managers. The merit pay system was supposed to pay managers in accordance with the level of quality work they did; however, the system was so flawed and the budget was so limited it never worked out that way. An entire book could be written regarding the faulty merit pay system, but I will stick to my subject regarding outreach efforts of IRS employees.

Prior to the merit pay system IRS in Los Angeles District utilized what was known as the District's EEO (Equal Employment Opportunity) Plan. This plan was drawn up to identify areas within IRS that were in need of improvement regarding equal employment opportunity. The plan was IRS' effort to eliminate and break down barriers to equal employment.

I first became aware of the plan when as a relatively new manager I was assigned to the Carson post of duty. As mentioned in prior chapters, the Carson post of duty was located in Carson, California in the county of Los Angeles. It was an area with a high population of Blacks. It was also adjacent to Compton, California, which at the time was a predominantly Black populated city.

As a result of the population in the area it was determined that the people employed in the Carson branch should include one outreach item in their EEO Plan that would target Black students.

IRS is a very large organization and is very wide spread with many offices in outlying areas, some at significant distances from the headquarters where the District Directors are headquartered. To ensure smooth effective operations are not hampered by the absence of the Director in a particular office IRS designates managers to act for the director.

These mangers are generally called RDD's (Representative of the District Director) or DDR's (the District Director's Representative). This responsibility is rotated among managers for terms around two years or so. Many managers do not want this added responsibility because not only do they become responsible for the entire building they also retain all of the responsibilities they previously had as a manager. Most IRS buildings contain

200 or more employees and the person assigned the responsibility of acting for the district director then becomes the building manager in all things pertaining to IRS.

At any rate, during my stint in the Carson building the RDD would meet with all of the managers from all divisions at the beginning of the fiscal to assess the prior years success and to plan for the coming year. I was a manager in the Carson building as well as being given the RDD responsibility for three years.

During this meeting the RDD and the group would decide on the areas they wanted to be come involved in during the course of the coming year. Specific plans would be written up with specific goals documented. Each manager had the opportunity to volunteer to assume responsibility for any portion of the plan they chose. The manager was then assigned that particular area and the plan was drawn up and documented to show all necessary information including the person assigned the responsibility.

This group known as the EEO Committee met on a quarterly basis to discuss the current status of the plan and at that time changes could be made if necessary. The plan was set up so that it could show accomplishments on a quarterly basis. Once the district went to the merit pay system each manager's contribution to the EEO Plan was considered to be that manager's accomplishment of merit pay in the area of EEO. Most merit pay plans contained three parts, program management and accomplishment, management of resources, and implementing and managing EEO (See Exhibit 32).

Two of the major areas of the Carson EEO Plan involved local predominantly minority schools. These areas consisted of programs put on by IRS managers with a significant number of employees volunteering to participate. One of the reasons it was so popular was that the majority of the employees in the Carson branch were Black and some of them had attended the local schools.

One program was known as the "Stay in school program." The RDD and certain managers met with school administrators and arranged to have students bused to the Carson building where presentations were made by the employees.

First of all, the employees were broken up into small groups and given a tour of the premises and shown where the IRS employees worked. Then they were all brought together at which time representatives from each division,

Collection, Examination, Taxpayer Service, Criminal Investigation, and Inspection made presentations.

Each of the employees advised the students of the kind of work done in each division as well as the opportunities available for them once they had finished school. Special emphasis was placed on the advantages of being hired once a high school diploma had been obtained. The students were shown the additional advantage of the difference in job opportunities available for those with college experience and/or degrees versus those who only had completed high school.

While we were never able to actually track the future of the students, the program was successful in that all of the local schools were interested in participating and the visible level of interest demonstrated by the students was high. The program was so successful participants were given awards (plaques, certificates, etc.) by the city of Carson at very impressive awards ceremonies at the end of the year.

The second major program also involved students and it was put on in the students' classrooms. Participants from IRS visited the classrooms and made presentations regarding the responsibility of citizens to file and pay taxes.

One of the reasons this was a successful program was that a lot of students worked during the summer or after school and on weekends and if they filed tax returns they often received tax refunds. So of course this went over big with the students.

The IRS employees provided instructions on preparing tax returns and also provided the actual forms for the students. The students were told in advance they would be able to file their tax return if they brought the necessary information with them on the day of the presentation. Once the returns were prepared the IRS employees had the students sign them and they took them with them back to office and filed them with the Service Center.

This method of providing instructions for preparing tax returns was not only a service to the taxpaying public but was a good way for IRS to be introduced in a positive way to future taxpayers. It also provided a significant benefit by allowing future taxpayers to interact with IRS employees in a positive way and to show them that people who work for IRS were just like them.

Many, many hours of IRS employees own personal time was used in outreach programs by helping taxpayers to prepare their tax returns. Many taxpayers can not afford to pay tax preparers to prepare their returns yet they do not know how to prepare them for themselves. Many of these taxpayers are senior citizens.

VITA (Volunteer Income Tax Assistance) programs are put on in many places by volunteers from the public with IRS participating by having employees work with them. While it was against the rule to have employees work on their own time without compensation, IRS employees often volunteered to give up part of their weekend to assist taxpayers and they were then given compensatory time off during the week.

IRS employees participate in numerous important outreach activities. Although few districts contribute as much time as the Laguna Niguel District did towards outreach programs most districts offer some form of outreach to the public. Some of the activities include Collection modules for Small Business Workshops, support for Government Days, town hall meetings and support for Federal Emergency Sites.

The Collection modules for Small Business Workshops are information and training programs provided by IRS employees for taxpayers owning small businesses. These sessions are ways for IRS to inform small business taxpayers of their tax responsibilities including timely filing and paying requirements. It is also a time when these taxpayers are introduced to all necessary tax documents so that they may meet the requirements.

Many cities have what is called Government Days programs. These programs include introducing school children to the various government agencies and even allowing some of them to perform in the positions of some of the managers of the government agencies. IRS often participates in this program.

Town hall meetings are conducted nationwide by IRS management. The meetings provide opportunities for taxpayers to meet with IRS management from the District Director on down the line. The taxpayers have an opportunity to ask questions in person and many times the sessions are broadcast on the radio and taxpayers call in with their questions. These sessions provide an opportunity for the taxpayers to meet IRS employees and to see that they are people trying to do the best job possible. Also, it provides the opportunity for taxpayers to get answers to some of their tax problems.

The Federal Emergency Site program offer services during times when disasters hit cities. Most recent ones have been earthquakes, tornadoes, hurricanes, etc. Taxpayers are given reprieves from having to meet normal deadlines for tax returns. IRS prepares lists of taxpayers living in such areas and employees are made aware that no enforcement action is to be taken regarding these particular taxpayers.

Additional outreach programs supported by IRS employees include seminars on understanding taxes and tax counselling for the elderly. IRS' commitment to taxpayer education is outstanding. I know this is hard to believe because the tax system itself is so cumbersome. However, in spite of this, IRS works hard to assist taxpayers in an effort to help the taxpayer and to make the job easier for IRS employees.

During certain times of the year IRS participates in such programs as Black History Month, Hispanic Heritage Week, as well as various programs regarding women and Asian Pacific citizens. During these programs IRS invites outside speakers to address issues regarding these subjects.

These programs go over big as efforts to improve the relationships of various minority groups. The speakers share information regarding their particular ethnic or gender group and employees are given the opportunity to set up display tables for artifacts and/or information regarding their group.

The employees are able to dress in the clothing of their ethnic origin. They are also able to bring in samples of food unique to their ethnic origin. All of these efforts are shared with everyone in the branch. This goes a long way in enabling employees to get to know and better understand cultures other than their own. The employees work very, very hard on these programs and they take great pride in their success.

In an effort to improve relationships with the taxpaying public, the director in Laguna Niguel established a group composed of IRS division chiefs and enrolled agents. Enrolled agents are tax preparers, accountants, and attorneys who have been authorized by IRS to practice before the IRS in representing taxpayers.

This group met once a quarter and exchanged concerns and ideas. The director and the division chiefs would start off the meeting by sharing current changes within IRS and allowing the enrolled agents the opportunity to ask questions and to express their concerns about any problems they were seeing in their relationship while working with IRS employees

Immediately following the meeting all in attendance would sit down to a luncheon provided by the enrolled agents. IRS could not pay for the enrolled agents lunch because it would have created the appearance of preferential treatment as all enrolled agents did not attend the meetings. The ones attending were ones belonging to formal groups of enrolled agents such as the California Society of Enrolled Agents.

The luncheons gave both sides the opportunity to interact and to discuss business or anything else they chose. This provided the opportunity for both sides to get to know each other better and to realize that both sides were human. It also eased future situations by enabling the enrolled agents to feel welcome to contact one of the division chiefs if they encountered a problem they could not resolve with individual employees or managers.

The generosity of IRS employees was consistently demonstrated within the organization when donations were taken up as the result of a death or some hardship experienced by employees. In addition, employees were strongly encouraged on an annual basis to contribute to charitable organizations such as the Combined Federal Campaign.

The willing and sometimes unwilling generosity of managers was demonstrated by the purchase of savings bonds, contributions to charitable organizations, and contributions to the organizations leave bank program.

The leave bank program was one that was established to provide contributions of annual leave (employees' vacation time) to employees who were off duty as the result of extended illnesses and/or injuries. Employees could donate what they may consider access annual leave to be converted over for the use of a co-worker.

I say unwilling generosity of managers because many times we did not have a choice as to whether we contributed or not. I can remember when I was a group manager and my branch chief would personally visit each manger in the branch to advise that they should purchase savings bonds or contribute to charitable organizations through payroll deduction. Most managers would be willing to voluntarily contribute; however, this branch and many others did not leave it up to chance and the participation of each branch was noted by top level management.

As an up and coming Division Chief I was advised that the Regional Commissioner had expectations that anyone desiring to move up in the organization would donate to the leave bank program. This was not an especially difficult thing for many employees, particularly branch and top level management because believe it or not many ended up at the end of the year with annual leave that had to be used or it would be lost. But just the idea that the Regional Commissioner would coerce managers to donate left a bitter taste in many of our mouths.

Government employees receive eight hours of sick leave each month and a range of four hours of annual leave a pay period up to eight hours a pay period depending on the length of time they have been in the service. Both of the leave categories may be accumulated with no restrictions on sick leave. Annual leave may be accumulated up to 240 hours a year and can be carried over to the next year; however, by the end of the last pay period of each calendar year all annual leave in excess of the 240 hours must be used or it will be lost.

Many IRS managers are so tied into their jobs they find it difficult to use the five weeks of annual leave they receive at the beginning of the year; therefore, they end up running out of time in December. As a result of this situation I have personally known subordinates and peers with excess leave that they were more than willing to donate for the use of a co-worker who was experiencing some misfortune. The spirit of giving was always apparent in IRS.

One of the most noticed demonstrations of giving was at the time of the bombing of the Oklahoma City Federal Building. IRS was one of the fortunate organizations in that we did not have any of our offices in that building. We were housed in another building not too far away.

Upon hearing about the disaster, IRS went into action nationwide and established a means for accepting and delivering contributions for those who were in need. The outpouring of generosity was overwhelming.

Throughout the year IRS participates in blood banks and employees who donate their blood are given some hours off from work that day. Many employees line up to donate their blood in the blood mobile that visits IRS each year. Even though employees are given the time off I have seen many employees return to work to finish some incomplete project they were responsible for.

While none of the above examples are out of the ordinary they are being shared to bring to the mind of the readers that IRS employees have hearts and are true hard working human beings like many other American citizens. They simply put on a different hat when they go out to collect taxes.

I personally believe the relationships between the taxpaying public and IRS would improve if each side had the opportunity to see each other in their outside lives. It might help to remember that donations collected by the Red Cross and blood collected in blood banks throughout the nation contain donations and blood from citizens from many walks of life including IRS employees.

Chapter Eleven

IRS TODAY

After all is said and done the IRS is still in operation with the same major responsibilities, that of examining tax returns, securing delinquent tax returns and collecting delinquent taxes. Much to do has been made over how these very important tasks should be undertaken in the future.

For the most part the changes are supposed to have a significant impact on the treatment of taxpayers. Of course the newer and smarter IRS is shying away from phrases such as "a kinder and gentler IRS". We all know that public relations program was a total fiasco. Now IRS is going after the same results without all of the words that failed before.

The IRS has always had a so called mission and a mission statement. The statement of today is quite different from the one used during my career. Today the IRS Mission statement reads, "Provide America's taxpayers top quality service by helping them understand and meet their tax responsibilities and by applying the tax law with integrity and fairness to all."

At the time I retired in 1996 the mission statement read, "The purpose of the Internal Revenue Service is to collect the proper amount of tax revenue at the least cost; serve the public by continually improving the quality of our products and services; and perform in a manner warranting the highest degree of public confidence in our integrity, efficiency and fairness."

I'm sure you readily noticed that the current statement leaves off any mention of collecting taxes. Let's not fool ourselves. The major function of IRS, the bottom line function, is to collect taxes. All efforts put forth in IRS all arrive at the bottom line of collecting the amount of taxes owed. All efforts put forth by employees examining returns is to find out whether the proper amount of taxes have been reported. All efforts put forth by employees who provide information about accuracy in tax preparation is to assure that the proper amount of taxes have been reported. It all gets down to assuring that the proper amount of taxes have been reported and finally that the proper amount has been collected.

Is IRS attempting to fool the public? I believe the IRS commissioner is sincerely interested in applying the tax law with integrity and fairness to all; however, he is also deeply interested in seeing that taxes are collected.

The IRS continues to have a formidable task. How do you collect money from the delinquent public and make them like it? Admittedly there is a small percentage of the entire population with delinquent taxes, but also, admittedly that percentage is made up of a large portion of taxpayers who do not intend to pay taxes unless made to do so.

I believe IRS would have higher credibility by admitting that there is a serious problem with the tax gap rising every year and that its major responsibility is to collect the delinquent taxes. IRS needs to advise the public of what authority it has and to admit that it will be used when necessary.

The most important aspect of this scenario is how IRS is going to do that. Appropriate oversight of management and congressional representatives can curb IRS abuse. The hiding of heads in the sand and eliminating words regarding collecting taxes from the mission is not going to solve the IRS problem.

What's wrong with being upfront and saying what the problem is and what will be done to those who refuse to pay their share of taxes? IRS has always tiptoed around problems, working hard to resolve them while denying the methods needed and the methods used to resolve them.

As stated earlier rather than discuss the problems of insufficient collections by employees IRS chose to deny that numbers are important. All the while IRS executive level management and Congress were zeroing in on the amounts that needed to be collected. If IRS cannot be upfront with its own employees about what is needed how can the public expect high integrity? High integrity includes honesty, lack of deception.

To be fair I have to say that I believe IRS management believes its own words. However, to have a collection division and a collection responsibility and to go out of the way to avoid talking about the need to collect more money is deceptive.

During the reform hearing of 1998 Senator Roth stated that IRS, "has admitted to using quotas and statistics and -standards of measurement that pit IRS employees against taxpayers in adversarial and potentially destructive confrontations." Most assuredly, the only quota IRS should use is one to collect all outstanding delinquent taxes. However the sharing of statistics, if used appropriately, can be an incentive to employees to do the best job possible. For executives and management to use statistics and to intentionally deceive employees denying its use is deceptive.

Senator Roth continued in his remarks by making the profound statement that, "The many short comings, abuses and inefficiencies we are discovering within the IRS are not solely the fault of the agency itself. Congress and the Administration must share in the blame. Consequently, necessary change will not be made by internal efforts alone. We need legislative remedies. We need real enforcement, disciplined Congressional oversight, and a long-term change in culture and attitudes."

I applaud the senator for his profound remarks. It is the first time I have ever heard anyone remotely connected to Congress accept any of the blame for the IRS and its shortcomings. It will be interesting to see how Congress reacts to the drop in IRS collections. History has a way of repeating itself in IRS. Every single time IRS has taken a "kinder, gentler attitude" the amount of money collected has been reduced. Those hard core taxpayers who refuse to pay their taxes without enforcement action always use the "kinder, gentler attitude" to suit their purposes.

As soon as IRS announces it new attitude the hard core group and even the less hard core group of procrastinators start to complain about employee treatment in an effort to stall collection efforts. That strategy works and overall collections fall. IRS employees become confused and unsure of what is expected. Rather than risk the wrath of management resulting from taxpayers complaints many employees start to hold back on enforcement action.

IRS has implemented what is called the 1203 rule which provides for all taxpayer complaints against employees to be investigated by the Inspection Division of the Treasury Department. During my time in IRS Inspection was part of IRS. As a result of the numerous problems within IRS it was decided that Inspection can perform much more objectively working outside of the IRS. This is probably true because Inspection Division worked so closely with the other divisions we always seemed to be one big family.

My connections back in my old division have advised me that this new rule has created an unbelievable fear in the hearts of employees. According to my contacts, employees are feeling a tremendous amount of stress. This is one major way to reduce the efficiency of IRS employees which will ultimately reduce collections. The pendulum continues to swing in IRS and continues to confuse employees. One year the pressure is on to collect more and more money. The next year customer service becomes the priority.

During my tenure at IRS employees were running scared of being investigated by inspection or internal audit. I am being told this feeling of dread has not changed. Once employees start to believe taxpayers' complaints are going to go directly to Inspection, the employees will go out of their way to be accommodating to taxpayers which often mean not doing the necessary job of collecting money.

Years and years of experience has shown me that this becomes a vicious circle with Congress cracking the whip to collect more money, the Revenue Officer assuming a get tough attitude, the taxpayers complaining, an IRS Hearing being conducted, IRS becoming kinder and gentler, collections going down, Congress starting all over again. The current status is one of IRS collections falling and the tax gap widening. Guess what happens next.

I certainly don't pretend to have all of the answers; however, I do strongly believe IRS needs to have a firm but fair policy that is clearly understood by employees, the public and Congress. IRS management needs to feel comfortable discussing the necessity of increasing collections. They also need to hold all managers and employees accountable for any mistreatment of taxpayers and accountable for doing the job they are paid to do. Then and only then will we, the public, have a tax agency we can trust.

EXHIBITS

Exhibit 1

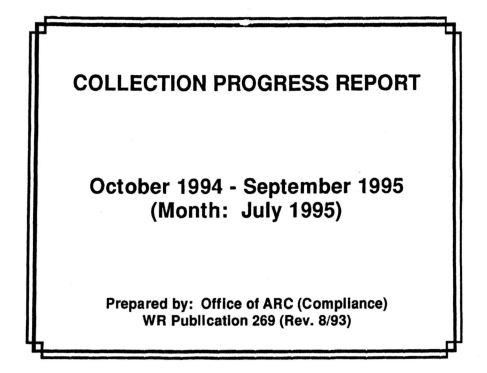

COLLECTION PROGRESS REPORT

October 1994 - September 1995
(Month: July 1995)

Prepared by: Office of ARC (Compliance)
WR Publication 269 (Rev. 8/93)

PAGE 1

CFf CUMULATIVE COLLECTION PERFORMANCE INDICATORS

CUM OCT 94 - JUL 95

DISTRICT-CFf	$ Collected per Staff/year (000)		Inventory Turnover (Weeks)		TBA Dispositions (CFf+9)		TBI Dispositions (CFf+9)		TBA Inventory (CFf+9)		TBI Inventory (CFf+9)		Delinquent Return Secured * (CFf+9)		Total Dollars Collected (000)	
	Base 9/94	Cum 7/95	Base 9/94	Avg 7/95	Base 9/94	Cum 7/95	Base 9/94	Cum 7/95	Base 9/94	7/95	Base 9/94	7/95	Base 9/94	Cum 7/95	Base 9/94	Cum 7/95
ANCHORAGE	$284	$290	54.8	51.3	7,776	5,559	1,811	1,152	10,857	9,510	2,277	2,156	1,948	0	$23,209	$19,02ε
BOISE	$347	$322	49.5	46.6	6,270	4,705	907	623	8,233	7,692	1,930	2,012	1,234	0	$19,477	$14,49ε
HONOLULU **	$549	$377	50.8	54.8	4,134	3,560	1,869	5,006	14,520	13,893	5,846	2,381	2,169	0	$29,745	$21,59ε
LAS VEGAS	$437	$399	37.2	40.5	14,758	11,910	3,291	2,507	29,955	28,114	6,873	6,250	2,871	0	$52,350	$45,11ε
PORTLAND	$491	$447	37.1	35.0	18,000	16,567	4,493	4,426	23,860	20,582	7,884	6,135	5,365	0	$65,516	$51,41ε
SACRAMENTO	$377	$355	50.3	44.3	33,532	33,984	10,559	5,806	67,909	51,973	12,993	10,055	6,613	0	$109,622	$95,11ε
SAN FRANCISCO	$366	$463	41.7	43.1	23,769	20,785	11,127	4,298	37,041	34,940	7,098	6,142	4,815	0	$81,315	$85,07ε
SAN JOSE	$352	$332	52.0	52.3	34,311	43,842	16,399	11,930	99,543	79,607	16,616	9,210	8,247	0	$126,097	$112,95ε
SEATTLE	$432	$419	43.6	38.4	38,921	28,489	10,009	6,235	40,360	33,968	10,873	9,768	9,279	0	$110,559	$91,81ε
LAGUNA NIGUEL	$338	$406	51.5	43.8	75,939	107,767	37,169	24,677	199,283	152,788	33,752	22,525	16,755	0	$226,794	$245,35ε
LOS ANGELES***	$411	$415	65.9	55.4	38,982	49,475	27,421	18,072	129,231	108,403	31,861	21,836	11,420	0	$202,849	$205,56ε
REGION	$363	$394	48.6	44.0	296,392	326,643	125,055	84,732	666,772	543,470	138,003	98,470	70,716	0	$1,047,529	$987,52ε

* Delinquent Returns Secured data not available on ERSS.
** Large number of TBIs disposed in error for Honolulu.
*** Los Angeles - $7.5 million collected in July 1995 on form 1120.

Exhibit 2

Bill thought you might like a copy of this

NTEU CHAPTER 92
SPECIAL BULLETIN
FOR REVENUE OFFICERS

NTEU SETS THE RECORD STRAIGHT ON INCREASING PRODUCTIVITY

Recently you may have heard Collection Division Chief Yvonne Wiley and other management officials tell you that NTEU supports management's current actions being taken to increase dollars collected and productivity. She has stated that a meeting took place between District Director ‎ and NTEU Joint Council Chair ‎ and the Chief Steward of chapter 108, 117 and 234 ‎ where they discussed the Service's need to increase the amount of revenue that we bring in. Wiley has stated that ‎ and ‎ have come out in full support of management's efforts.

It has come to the attention of Chapter 92 President and Chief Steward ‎ that revenue officers in San Diego and Kearny Mesa believe that NTEU is supporting the heavy-handed tactics that management is utilizing to judge the performance of revenue officers based on individual stats on dollars collected and cases closed. NTEU *does not* support the methods management is currently using to determine who is performing and who is not. NTEU *does* support the goal of the Annual Business Plan to increase the dollars collected.

In fiscal year 1994, NTEU President

hearing regarding the budget and funding of the Internal Revenue Service. We were instrumental in obtaining funding for 5000 additional compliance positions nationwide. In exchange for that, funding commitments were made to increase compliance and dollars collected in FY 1995. It is no secret that in past years when additional positions were tied to increased compliance, we have experienced shortfalls. Congress is watching the Service closely and expects that we will increase productivity or face potential consequences. NTEU acknowledges the business decision to increase the dollars collected, and we support the concept. NTEU stands firm however, that employees must not be given quotas to collect specific dollars or close a specific number of units in order to assess whether individual revenue officers are working.

The current practice of compiling weekly group figures on dollars collected is a mine field when assessing management's compliance with policy statement P-1-20 and certain provisions of the Taxpayer Bill of Rights. The Policy states that, "Tax enforcement results tabulations shall not be used to evaluate an enforcement officer or *impose or suggest production quotas or goals.*" It further not only to protect employees from adverse impact of quantitative goals, but also to protect taxpayers against possible inequities. In the discharge or his/her responsibilities, but subject to the above prohibition, a manager may raise questions with an individual about the number of cases he/she has processed, the amount of time he/she has been spending on individual cases, or the kind of results he/she has been obtaining."

Tax enforcement results are defined as all case actions taken by enforcement personnel which are counted, measured or tracked by management to evaluate program effectiveness. Some examples of results are:

* lien, levy and seizure rates
* Dollars collected, full pay rate, returns secured rate
* Dollars collected with secured returns
* Any production/participation rates or norms

This list is not all-inclusive. The policy applies to *any* numerical or quantitative measure relevant to actions taken on taxpayer casework, or actions which effect those actions, or the manner in which taxpayers are served.

In additional statements made by management officials such as Ms. Wiley, you may have been told that NTEU National President Robert Tobias also supports management's efforts to increase dollars and supports changing the policy statement P-1-20. NTEU Chapters have received no such information from Washington on a change in policy. Mr. Tobias does understand the need for increasing dollars, but it is certain that he does not support management's scare tactics and efforts to target employees for discipline based on failure to meet dollar quotas

case closure quotas.

The Collection Division Chief as stated to NTEU that she has identified 25 percent of the revenue officers in this district who don't want to work or otherwise refuse to work. We have reports that revenue officers have been given specific quotas for case and unit closures and dollars collected per month. Managers are telling revenue officers what the quotas are and whether individuals are meeting them. This is clearly a violation of policy and the law.

NTEU plans to vigorously fight management's 25 percent target rate and compiling and using individual enforcement statistics. We need your help to keep NTEU informed as to what is happening to you so that we can assess the full extent of the problem to ensure that we fully cover everyone. If you are subjected to specific scrutiny concerning a specific number of closures expected or achieved, dollars collected or expected (this can also encompass an implied dollar figure. Or, if you feel that you have been identified as one of the revenue officers targeted in the 25 percent, you need to let us know immediately. Write down the specific incident or violations and when they occurred. Get that information to your area steward or send it to the Chapter 92 address at NTEU Chapter 92 P.O. Box 2190 San Diego, Ca. 92112.

We are also tracking all group meetings, either scheduled or unscheduled (such as stand-up meetings) to determine management's compliance with proper notice to NTEU. Please advise us a written note of the date, time and place as well as the subject matter as soon as possible. We will periodically issue these BULLETINS to keep you up to date.

Exhibit 3

Answer Sheet for Exercise 5

Daily Report of Collection Activity	Name/Grade (print or type) (YOUR NAME)								Employee No. 1417			Type (check one) FVO ☒ PR ☐ Other ☐		Initials (YOUR INITIALS)	Date 10/17/86	Page 1 of 1
					Complete and Incomplete Cases and Collections											

PART 1

Taxpayer (a)	Type of Case (b)	IMF BMF (c)	TDA (d)	TDI (e)	O (f)	FTD Alert (g)	IA (h)	RO (i)	E (j)	OI (k)	Taxpayer Case Disposition (l)	Delinquent Returns Secured (m)	Amount Collected (n)	Receipt Number (o)	Remarks (p)
▬▬▬	F		✓										$ 75.00	1003XX-21	PP 30-8412
▬▬▬			I										650.00		FP 30-8512
▬▬▬			✓										150.00		PP 30-8512
▬▬▬	F				I						C	I	100.00		FP 30-8412
▬▬▬				✓								2			30-8512/8412 DLTR DUE
▬▬▬			I								C				53 01-8512
▬▬▬			I	I							R				TRANSFER ▬▬▬
▬▬▬	F		✓												
▬▬▬	F		✓												
▬▬▬	F				✓										
▬▬▬	F				✓										
1. Totals	▨▨		**3**	**2**							**3**	**3**	**$975.00**	▨▨▨	

PART 2

Inventory Summary	Total Tax-payers (a)	TDA (b)	TDI (c)	Total del. OI's (d)	Total del. OI's (e)	OIC (f)	FTD Alert (g)		ACP in				BTF UI		7. Verified By (MMDD)	Date
													LBADP	EXAM :NV	**8. Remarks**	
2. Balance Forwarded	93	104	31	I	3											
3. Received Today	2	3	I	—	—											
4. Subtotals	95	107	32	I	3											
5. Disposed Today	3	3	2	—	—											
6. Balance on Hand	92	104	30	I	3											

PART 3

Hours			Balance Due						Del. Return				ADP				
	TDA OI 101	DA Not 102	DA ACS 103	DA OI 104	FTD 105	OIC 106	MRP 107		TDI OI 201	DR Not 202	DR ACS 203	DR OI 204	301	301	301	301	301
Forward	46			3					23								
Today	4			I					3								
To Date	50			4					26								

		BTE			Overhead			Detail	Total								
	Direct Exam 4014	Legal & Dev. 4018	Proce-dural 4010	MGT 810	ACM 811	TRN 812	LV	HV	T6								
Forward										9		80					
Today										—		8					
To Date										8		88					

Form 795 (Rev. 9-98)   Dispose of all prior issues   Department of the Treasury—Internal Revenue Service

A-3

Exhibit 4

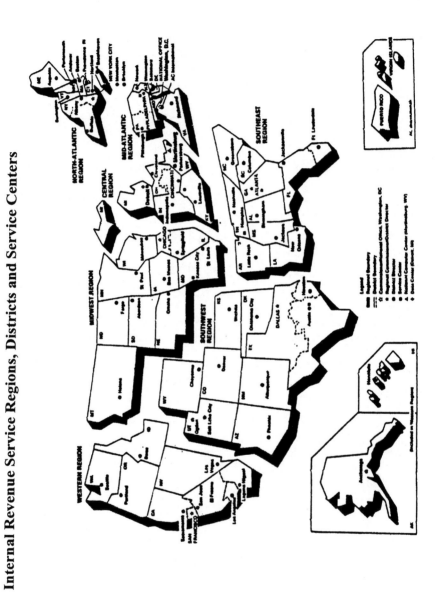

Internal Revenue Service Regions, Districts and Service Centers

Exhibit 5

 # Internal Revenue Service

Mission

The purpose of the IRS is to collect the proper amount of tax revenues at the least cost to the public, and in a manner that warrants the highest degree of public confidence in our integrity, efficiency and fairness. To achieve that purpose, we will:

Encourage and achieve the highest possible degree of voluntary compliance in accordance with the tax law and regulations;

Advise the public of their rights and responsibilities;

Determine the extent of compliance and the causes of noncompliance;

Do all things needed for the proper administration and enforcement of the tax laws;

Continually search for and implement new, more efficient and effective ways of accomplishing our Mission.

Exhibit 6

Module H

TDI's

<u>TOPICAL OUTLINE</u>

LESSON 1. Investigating TDI's

LESSON 2. Interpreting Codes on TDI's

LESSON 3. TDI Closing Codes

LESSON 4. Completing a TDI

<u>INSTRUCTIONAL OBJECTIVES</u>

By the end of this lesson, the trainee should be able to:

201. Explain the TDI investigation process.

211. Interpret the coded information on a TDI.

221. Determine TDI closing codes to report the results of your investigation.

231. Complete the necessary sections of a TDI to close the investigation.

<u>TIME REQUIRED</u>

6 hours

<u>ASSISTANTS</u>

None

<u>SPACE REQUIRED</u>

Classroom

<u>REFERENCES</u>

IRC 6020(b)
IRM 5(11)00 and IRM 5(18)00
Policy Statement P-5-133

<u>TRAINING AIDS</u>

Chalkboard
Overhead Projector

H-1

Exhibit 7

CONTENT OF LESSON	NOTES TO INSTRUCTOR

GENERAL INTRODUCTION TO MODULE

Tie-in to Previous Module

In Module G, you learned the steps the IRS
follows in resolving delinquent accounts.
Similarly, if a taxpayer fails to file a
required return, the Service Center sends
a series of notices to the taxpayer
requesting the return. If the taxpayer
does not respond to these notices, then a
Taxpayer Delinquency Investigation (TDI)
is issued and eventually worked by a
Revenue Officer.

Preview of General Content

1. The TDI investigation process.

2. Interpreting the information encoded on
    a TDI.

3. Using TDI closing codes to report the
    results of a TDI investigation.

4. Completing all actions necessary to
    close out a TDI investigation.

Why This Module Is Important

TDI's can represent a significant portion
of a Revenue Officer's inventory. TDI's
are potential accounts receivable and
have the potential of producing large
amounts of revenue. The quality of work
that a Revenue Officer puts into the TDI
area has a direct bearing on increasing
the potential revenue yield.

From your experience,
give examples of TDI's
leading to significant
tax liabilities.

H-3

Exhibit 8

Internal Revenue Service

Detroit Computing Center
Enrolled Practitioner Program

Department of the Treasury

P.O. Box 33968
Detroit, MI 48232

Number of this Letter: 1683(NO)
Date of this Letter:

Dear Applicant,

We are pleased to inform you that we have approved your application to practice before the Internal Revenue Service. We have enclosed your enrollment card and a copy of Treasury Department Circular 230 that contains the regulations governing practice before the IRS. You should become familiar with these regulations and comply with them in your practice.

The regulations in Circular 230 contain several restrictions that apply to former government employees who practice before the IRS. The restrictions involve any matters you were significantly involved in or had official responsibility for during your last year of government employment. (See section 10.26 of Circular 230.)

There are some other restrictions that may apply to your practice -- for example, the regulations issued by the Office of Government Ethics (5 CFR Part 737) and Title 18 US Code, section 207. We are calling your attention to these restrictions because violating them may make you subject to disciplinary action or criminal penalties.

To maintain active enrollment to practice before IRS, you must review your enrollment every three years. (See section 10.6 of circular 230 for complete information.)

Please note: You must use the "96-" prefix followed by your enrollment number on all declarations, powers of attorney and any correspondence you send us. You must also advise us promptly of any change in your address.

We hope your enrollment will help to maintain the highest standards of tax practice and will be beneficial to you and your clients.

Sincerely,

Joanne L. Wiegand
Chief, Program Analysis & Review

Enclosures

Letter 1683 (NO) (Rev. 11-95)

Exhibit 9

Certificate of Enrollment

This Is
To Certify That

YVONNE THERESA WILEY

Is Enrolled
To Practice
Before The

INTERNAL REVENUE SERVICE

Effective The   **14th**
Day Of   **March, 1996**

Enrolled Agent
Number   **59891**

Department of the Treasury
Internal Revenue Service

Director of Practice

Exhibit 10

Lesson 2
PREPARING COLLECTION INFORMATION STATEMENTS

You should generally secure a collection information statement promptly after you have demanded payment and the taxpayer indicates that he or she cannot full pay immediately. You should secure the appropriate form on your first contact with the taxpayer. You should not grant an extension of time to pay until you've gathered enough information to plan a course of action if the taxpayer defaults on any commitments made.

OBJECTIVE

At the end of this lesson, you will be able to:

- Complete Form 433-A and Form 433-B.

CONTENTS

General Rules
How To Complete Form 433-A
   Information About Employment
   Personal Information
   General Financial Information
   Analysis of Assets and Liabilities
   Analysis of Monthly Income and Expenses
   Certification
How to Complete Form 433-B
   Information About Owners and Other Individuals
   Accounts and Notes Receivable
   Analysis of Income and Expenses
Summary

GENERAL RULES

As a rule, it is best that you personally interview the taxpayer and record the information on the CIS. You can make notes or clear up any ambiguities by asking incisive questions as you go from item to item. Phrase your questions carefully, making sure that the taxpayer understands each of them. Avoid questions that can be answered "yes" or "no." Avoid leading questions. Taxpayers tend to give you more information if you ask open-ended questions.

Figure Q-1

Form **433-A** (Rev. April 1989)	Department of the Treasury — Internal Revenue Service **Collection Information Statement for Individuals**

NOTE: Complete all blocks, except shaded areas. Write "N/A" (not applicable) in those blocks that do not apply.

1. Taxpayers' names and address (including County)	2. Home phone number (XXX) 826-1764	3. Marital status MARRIED

County DENVER | 4. Social Security Numbers | a. Taxpayer 159-XX-1173 | b. Spouse 306-XX-0419 |

Section I.   Employment Information

5. Taxpayer's employer or business (name and address) DENVER, CO 80110	6a. How long employed	6. Business phone number (XXX) 916-0421	7. Occupation SALESMAN
	6b. Number of exemptions claimed on Form W-4 2	8. Paydays FRIDAYS	9. (Check appropriate box) ☒ Wage earner ☐ Partner ☐ Sole proprietor
10. Spouse's employer or business (name and address) N/A	10a. How long employed	11. Business phone number ( ) ———	12. Occupation HOUSEWIFE
	10b. Number of exemptions claimed on Form W-4	13. Paydays ———	14. (Check appropriate box) ☐ Wage earner ☐ Partner ☐ Sole proprietor

Section II.   Personal Information

15. Name, address and telephone number of next of kin or other reference

(xxx) 948-0122

DENVER, CO 80202

16. Age and relationship of dependents (exclude yourself and spouse) living in your household

DAUGHTER, 14 YRS. OLD

17. Date of birth ▶	a. Taxpayer 01-11-51	b. Spouse 01-15-54	

Section III.   General Financial Information

18. Latest filed income tax return (tax year) 1989	19. Number of exemptions claimed 3	20. Adjusted Gross Income $ 36,256—	

21. Bank accounts (include Savings & Loans, Credit Unions, IRA and Retirement Plans, Certificates of Deposit, etc.)

Name of Institution	Address	Type of Account	Account No.	Balance
UNITED BANK	17th & STOUT DENVER, CO 80216	CHECKING	146-XXX	$850—
Total (Enter in Item 28)			▶	$850—

Form **433-A** (Rev. 4-89)

Figure Q-2

Section III — continued	General Financial Information				

32. Bank charge cards, Credit Unions, Savings and Loans, Lines of credit

Type of Account or Card	Name and Address of Financial Institution	Monthly Payment	Credit Limit	Amount Owed	Credit Available
MASTER CARD	FIRST BANK OF AURORA 19801 E. 14th ST., DENVER	47-	800-	750-	50-
A VISA	DENVER FED. CREDIT UNION LAKEWOOD, CO 80211	25-	500-	200-	300-
Totals (Enter in Item 34) ▶		72-	1300-	950-	350-

33. Safe deposit boxes rented or accessed (List all locations, box numbers, and contents)

NONE

34. Real Property (Brief description and type of ownership)	Physical Address
a. 3-BED ROOM, SPLIT LEVEL, BRICK TENANTS IN ENTIRETY	15 PEPPER CORN LANE DENVER, CO 80216 County DENVER
b.	County
c.	County

35. Life Insurance (Name of Company)	Policy Number	Type	Face Amount	Available Loan Value
EQUITABLE LIFE	1102169	WHOLE LIFE	$25,000-	NONE
Total (Enter in Item 30) ▶				-0-

36. Other information relating to your financial condition. If you check the yes box, please give dates and explain under remarks.

a. Court proceedings	☐ Yes ☒ No	b. Bankruptcies	☐ Yes ☒ No
c. Repossessions	☐ Yes ☒ No	d. Recent transfer of assets for less than full value	☐ Yes ☒ No
e. Anticipated increase in income	☐ Yes ☒ No	f. Participant or beneficiary to trust, estate, profit sharing, etc.	☐ Yes ☒ No

Remarks

FAMILY HEALTH GOOD
INCOME STABLE

Form 433-A page 2 (Rev. 4-80)

Figure Q-3

Section IV.					Asset and Liability Analysis			
Description	Current Market Value	Liabilities Balance Due	Equity in Asset	Amount of Monthly Payment	Name and Address of Lien/Note Holder/Obligee	Date Pledged	Date of Final Payment
27. Cash			100—				
28. Bank accounts (from Item 21)			850—				
29. Stocks, Bonds, Investments			-0-				
30. Cash or loan value of Insur.			-0-				
31. Vehicles (Model, year, license, etc)							
a. '83 SUN BIRD T82-1172	4360—	2000—	2360—	113—	GMAC, DENVER, CO	6/88	6/92
b.							
c.							
32. Real property (From Section III, Item 24) a.	76,000—	59,200—	16,800—	568—	FIRST NAT'L BANK, DENVER	5/82	5/2012
b.							
c.							
33. Other assets							
a. ALPINE CAMPER	4200—	3500—	700—	150—	UNITED BANK, DENVER	9/86	1/92
b. HOUSEHOLD FURN.	3800—	-0-	3800—				
c.							
d.							
e.							
34. Bank revolving credit (from Item 20)		950—	—	72—			
35. Other Liabilities (Include judgments, notes, and other charge accounts) a. PERSONAL LOAN		4200—		143—	ASSOCIATED FINANCE	2/89	2/92
b.							
c.							
d.							
e.							
f.							
g.							
36. Federal taxes owed		5000—					
37. Totals			$23,660	$1046—			

Internal Revenue Service Use Only Below This Line

Financial Verification/Analysis

Item	Date Information or Encumbrance Verified	Date Property Inspected	Estimated Forced Sale Equity
Personal Residence			
Other Real Property			
Vehicles			
Other Personal Property			
Gross Employment (Husband and Wife)			
Income Tax Return			
Wage Statements (Husband and Wife)			
Sources of Income/Credit (D&B Report)			
Expenses			
Other Assets/Liabilities			

Form **433-A** page 3 (Rev. 4-91)

Figure Q-4

Section V. **Monthly Income and Expense Analysis**

Income

Source	Gross	Net
38. Wages/Salaries *(Taxpayer)*	$ 3129–	$ 2211–
39. Wages/Salaries *(Spouse)*		
40. Interest - Dividends		
41. Net business income *(from Form 433-B)*		
42. Rental income		
43. Pension *(Taxpayer)*		
44. Pension *(Spouse)*		
45. Child Support		
46. Alimony		
47. Other		
48. Total	$ 3129–	$ 2211–

Necessary Living Expenses

49. Rent (Do not show mortgage listed in item 32)	$ —
50. Groceries (no. of people 3)	370–
51. Allowable installment payments *(IRS use only)*	896*
52. Utilities (Gas $ 20– Water $ 25– Electric $ 50– Phone $ 12–)	107–
53. Transportation	110–
54. Insurance (Life $ 10– Health $ — Home $ 10– Car $ 16–)	36–
55. Medical *(Expenses not covered in item 54)*	15–
56. Estimated tax payments	-0-
57. Court ordered payments	—
58. Other expenses (specify)	—
* CAMPER PAYMENT OMITTED	
59. Total *(IRS use only)*	$ 1534–
60. Net difference (income less necessary living expenses) *(IRS use only)*	$ 677–

Certification Under penalties of perjury, I declare that to the best of my knowledge and belief this statement of assets, liabilities, and other information is true, correct, and complete.

61. Your signature	62. Spouse's signature *(if joint return was filed)*	63. Date
George Brewer	Nancy Lee Brewer	6/9/90

Internal Revenue Service Use Only Below This Line

Explain any difference between item 60 and installment agreement amount:

Additional information or comments:

Name of Originator and IDRS assignment number	Date

Form **433-A** page 4 (Rev. 4-89) U.S. GPO: [illegible]

Exhibit 11

FULL-SERVICE					Fixed Fee Agreement

I,_____
("CLIENT") hereby hires			Associates Inc. (		to represent the
following taxpaying entity(ies):

_____

_____("TAXPAYER").

All communications with CLIENT can be made at:

Address: _____

City:_____

State:_____ZIP:_____

Telephone: (B)_____

Telephone: (H)_____

Fax: (B)_____Fax: (H)_____

SSN or EIN of taxpayer:_____

1. SCOPE OF REPRESENTATIONS:

shall represent CLIENT (Check appropriate box):

A. ☐ in the negotiation of an Offer-In-Compromise ("OIC") and/or an Installment Agreement ("IA"), whichever one, in · · · ' sole judgement upon reviewing the CLIENT's situation with the CLIENT and the appropriate Tax Agency ("TA"), becomes the most likely solution to the CLIENT's tax problem. ` ' shall prepare an application for an OIC or IA and submit the application along with all necessary documentation to support such application. ` 'shall also respond to requests from the TA regarding the OIC or IA and, if required by the TA, attend an on-site interview with the CLIENT.

Whenever		attends an on-site interview, provided that the interview is conducted outside of		office, there will be an additional charge of $150.00 which must be paid in advance at least five (5) working days prior to the scheduled date of that interview, or		can decline to attend.

In addition, if · · · attendance at on-site interview would necessitate airline travel costs and/or overnight accommodation costs, CLIENT is responsible for payment of all such costs.

B. ☐ for the following services, rather than an OIC or IA (describe):
_____

C. · ` ·  shall assign a Tax Manager to handle the CLIENT's matter. The Tax Manager shall keep CLIENT advised of all developments regarding the matter. · ` · ~epresentation of CLIENT is expressly limited to the following tax liabilities and tax agency(ies):

TAX	AMOUNT	PERIODS
IRS Payroll Taxes (940 & 941)	_____	_____
IRS Trust Fund Penalty (6672)	_____	_____
California EDD Payroll Taxes	_____	_____
IRS Federal Income Taxes (1040)	_____	_____
California Income Taxes (540)		

D. ·		shall not participate or advise with regard to any judicial proceedings under this Agreement. · ` · ~ is not engaged in the practice of law and is not authorized to perform legal services on behalf of or provide legal advice to CLIENT.

E. If the scope of		representation is limited to an OIC or IA, such OIC or IA is subject to the consent and agreement of CLIENT. The goal of		services shall be a settlement or repayment agreement acceptable to the TA based upon CLIENT's financial ability to pay. However,		cannot guarantee the success of any application for an OIC or an IA. By signing this Agreement, CLIENT acknowledges that . ` ` has made no representation or promises regarding the outcome of this matter and that any opinion expressed by		in the future will not constitute a guarantee of any particular results.

F. The scope of		· representation does not include the preparation of delinquent or future tax returns, unless otherwise indicated in #1B herein.

2. CLIENT'S DUTIES:

A. CLIENT shall make prompt payments and file returns timely for all taxes that become due after the date of this Agreement. CLIENT understands that " ` ~ representation is conditioned upon CLIENT staying current on all future tax liabilities as they become due. CLIENT further understands that if CLIENT cannot or does not stay current and in compliance with filing of returns and payment of taxes subsequent to this Agreement, CLIENT's Application for an OIC or IA may be rejected and		.bility to effectively represent CLIENT will be substantially impaired.

B. CLIENT shall respond promptly and fully and within ten (10) calendar days, to all information and document requests by ` .and shall attend meetings at · ` ~`* office on adequate notice. If CLIENT fails to respond to		request for information or documents, or if this matter is not resolved during the Primary Period as defined in the attached Full Service Fee Schedule, and CLIENT elects not to extend		representation,		may, at its sole discretion, terminate this Agreement and cease to perform any future services on behalf of CLIENT.

C. By signing this Agreement, CLIENT agrees and acknowledges that		has advised CLIENT of CLIENT's obligation to fully and accurately disclose the nature and extent of CLIENT's assets and liabilities. CLIENT further acknowledges that		has advised CLIENT that the failure to disclose the existence of assets or the understatement of the value of the CLIENT's assets on the financial forms submitted to the TA may (1) invalidate any OIC or IA ultimately entered into, and (2) may lead to the imposition of additional civil or criminal penalties upon the CLIENT.

D. CLIENT, by signing this Agreement, agrees to pay		fees for its services as indicated in, and under the terms and conditions of the Full Service Fee Schedule (attached hereto) and thereby made a part of this Agreement.

Fee Schedule

■ Fee Schedule

In accordance with the terms and conditions of the Full Service Fee Agreement, for the first twelve (12) months of ＿ representation (the "Primary Period"), CLIENT agrees to pay a Primary Fixed Fee of $＿＿ determined by the amount of the tax liability, including penalties and interest, as shown on ＿ fee schedule in effect as of the date of this Agreement, and at the option of ＿ may be increased if the liability, in ＿ sole judgment, is materially understated. Plus special services: $＿＿ = Total Fixed Fee: $＿＿

For purposes of computing this Primary Period, the first month begins on the first day of the next month immediately following the month this Agreement was signed by the CLIENT and continues thereafter until the end of twelve (12) consecutive calendar months, including the first month.

At the conclusion of the Primary Period, CLIENT at its sole option may elect to extend ＿ representation, at a monthly fee, payable in advance equal to one-twelfth (1/12) of the Primary Period Fixed Fee.

Such election by client to extend ＿ representation beyond the Primary Period will not directly nor indirectly be construed either as an increase or addition to ＿ scope of representations as described in paragraph #1 of the Fixed Fee Agreement. Payment is to made in accordance with the method selected as follows (check one):
☐ in full with this Agreement, or
☐ on an installment basis as follows: $＿＿ Down Payment

    $＿＿ x ＿＿ Installment Payments

■ Postdated Check Policy

Each installment payment is to made by POSTDATED CHECKS all of which are to be presented upon execution of this Agreement. These payments are to be made in accordance with the Installment Payment Schedule attached to, and made part of, this Agreement. In the event any check presented to ＿ is returned by CLIENT's financial institution for insufficient funds or any other reason, will impose a $20 charge for each return item.

No services shall begin until CLIENT's initial payment has cleared ＿ bank as collected funds, and this Agreement is accepted by a ＿ principal. If CLIENT does not make timely payment or perform as promised (e.g., make current deposits or supply information or a CLIENT's check is returned to ＿ for insufficient funds), in its sole discretion ＿, at its option, may terminate all services and withdraw its representation immediately and without further obligation to render services. CLIENT further agrees that ＿ may withhold submission of CLIENT's application for an OIC or IA if CLIENT is not in compliance with this fee payment agreement.

■ Miscellaneous Policies

In the event (1) additional tax liabilities are assessed or discovered during the term of this Agreement; (2) CLIENT elects to appeal a negative decision with respect to CLIENT's Application for an OIC or IA, or (3) there is a significant change in CLIENT's circumstance, additional fees will be due. If this Agreement is terminated prior to the completion by ＿ of the services contemplated by this Agreement, CLIENT may be entitled to a partial refund of amounts paid to ＿ The amount of the refund, if any, will depend, in part, on the amount of work performed by ＿ and will be determined as follows.

Nonrefundable base charge for administrative costs: $750. Thereafter the amount of the remaining fee paid in excess of the nonrefundable base charge applicable for refund will be a percentage based upon the time expired since the file was opened as follows: 2 weeks or less = 60%; 2 to 4 weeks = 25%; more than 4 weeks = 0%. The date the file is opened shall be determined to be the date on which CLIENT's initial payment has cleared ＿ bank as collected funds, and this Agreement is accepted by a ＿ principal. For purposes of determining the amount of a refund, if any, due to CLIENT, ＿ representation of CLIENT will terminate upon receipt by ＿ of a written notice of termination from CLIENT. CLIENT and ＿ agree that this schedule is designed to estimate, in advance, the value of the services rendered by ＿ to CLIENT.

Installment Payment Schedule
To be paid by postdated checks.

Payment Dates:	Amounts:
1.	1.
2.	2.
3.	3.
4.	4.
5.	5.
6.	6.
7.	7.
8.	8.
9.	9.
10.	10.
11.	11.
12.	12.
13.	13.
14.	14.
15.	15.
16.	16.

Installment Payment Chart

For Primary Fixed Base Fees. Applies to Full Service Fee Schedule only. Does not include Special Services Fees which must be paid in full and are nonrefundable.

Base Fee	Minimum Down Pay	Balance	Weekly Payments (based on 16 weeks)
$3,450	$1,194	$2,256	$141.00
4,250	1,370	2,880	180.00
4,450	1,554	2,896	181.00
4,750	1,662	3,088	193.00
5,150	1,806	3,344	209.00
5,450	1,898	3,552	222.00
5,850	2,042	3,808	238.00
6,150	2,118	4,032	252.00
6,550	2,294	4,256	266.00
6,850	2,402	4,448	278.00
7,250	2,546	4,704	294.00
7,550	2,654	4,896	306.00
7,950	2,782	5,168	323.00
8,150	2,854	5,296	331.00
8,650	3,034	5,616	351.00
8,950	3,126	5,824	364.00
10,000	3,504	6,496	406.00

■ 10% Prepay Discount:

Clients who pay in full in advance may take 10% off the Total Fee. This applies to the Primary Fixed Base Fee only, not to Special Services Fees.

■ Payment Policies

FULL PAY: Balance due before work begins. INSTALLMENT: Down payment is required before work begins. Client also agrees to pay the financed amount with postdated checks in accordance with the Installment Payment Schedule attached. See chart on reverse side. About Special Services: Payment of this fee is not refundable and payment does not, in any way, guarantee results. About Primary Fixed Base Fee: Includes analysis of taxpayer situation, preparation of all required forms (excluding tax return preparation), submission (excluding Special Services issues), negotiation and mediation, excluding Appeals.

CLIENT: Please sign here after you have read and understand the information printed on both sides of this agreement.

By:＿＿＿＿＿ Date:＿＿＿

By:＿＿＿＿＿ Date:＿＿＿

         . Sherman Oaks, CA 91403

By:＿＿＿＿＿ Date:＿＿＿

Accounting Approved, Recorded By:＿＿＿＿＿

File No:＿＿＿＿＿ Date:＿＿＿

Principal's Acceptance By:＿＿＿＿＿ Date:＿＿＿

By:＿＿＿＿＿ Date:＿＿＿

Exhibit 12

To:	District Director, Laguna Niguel
Fax:	714-643-4029
From:	Chief Compliance Officer, Western Region
Date:	October 13, 1995
Pages:	19, including cover sheet.

RE: FY 95 Year End Assessment–DRAFT

Attached for your review is our draft assessment. Please distribute this document to all affected Division Chiefs. The arrow indicator (➡) identifies RAOP items. If there are problems with the FAX transmission, contact

fax

From the desk of...

RAOP Manager
Office of Chief/Compliance, Western Region
1650 Mission Street, Room 404
San Francisco, CA 94103

415-556-3154 or VMS 1004
Fax: 415-556-0826 or -5639

Internal Revenue Service

memorandum

1284

date: OCT 1 3 1995

to: Directors
Western Region

from: Chief Compliance Officer C
Western Region

subject: Draft Year-End Business Review Report

Attached is the draft of the Compliance function input to the Year-End Business Review of your office, along with a copy of my August 28 memorandum describing our use of value statements.

Please share this draft with your Chiefs, Collection, Compliance, DORA, and Examination Divisions, as applicable. If there are areas of concern, the Chiefs should discuss these by telephone with the appropriate Executive Assistant on my staff. If there are no concerns, no contact is necessary. All differences must be resolved by COB Wednesday, October 25. Please do not respond in writing; our time constraints do not allow for an exchange of correspondence.

This draft is based upon August data unless otherwise specified. The final document will reflect September data if available; no second draft will be sent, but if a conclusion is changed by the September data update we will contact the affected Chief to explain the change.

While differences must be resolved with the Executive Assistants, procedural questions may be directed to

Attachments

Chief Compliance Officer
FY95 Year-End Assessment
Laguna Niguel District

Overview

Collection operations improved significantly in FY95.
Accomplishments include meeting or exceeding dollars collected,
TDA/TDI dispositions, and inventory turnover goals in CFf,
introducing an aggressive in-business trust fund policy, and
training 125 Revenue Officers and Revenue Representatives.
Offer processing and bankruptcy dollars collected per staff-hour
improved, and the UIR/VPC program was fully supported. ACS
programs were maintained while the Call Sites downsized. In
FY96, the District should continue this upward trend by
processing Offers timely, increasing dollars collected with
delinquent returns secured, using ACS residual staff
appropriately, and resolving one million dollar cases earlier in
the Collection process.

All major aspects of the Tax Auditor program improved; dollars
and hours improved significantly in FY95. Corporate dollars per
return decreased significantly. The Revenue Agent Nonfiler
closure goal was not met; this hindered the District's TCMP
preparations. Revenue Agent Nonfiler dispositions, 1040 cycle
time, and 1120 dollars per hour need improvement.

The District FedState program is extremely active. It is one of
the drivers behind implementing plans to improve joint compliance
through five distinct strategies: market segment research, joint
collection, sharing interagency information, joint training, and
taxpayer/preparer education.

BMP Action IP13 Compliance Productivity

CFf Productivity - Dollars (000) Collected per Staff-Year

Very Good. The District exceeded its above average CFf dollars collected per staff-year goal by a significant margin. Performance was well above the regional average. Actions taken by the District in the past two years to improve productivity, including increased communication concerning goals and performance, reduced overhead, conducting accountability reviews, and using Revenue Representatives have generated good results.

Suggestions for fine tuning?

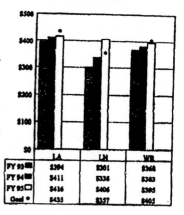

	LA	LN	WR
FY 93	$394	$301	$368
FY 94	$411	$336	$363
FY 95	$416	$406	$395
Goal	$435	$357	$405

ACS Productivity - Dollars (000) Collected per Staff-Year

Poor. ACS results are well below the goal and prior year's performance, and were negatively impacted by the Service Center's Early Intervention ACS hours charged to the District. Both Laguna Niguel Call Sites experienced unprecedented attrition and operated in a downsizing mode during the second half of the fiscal year. At the Region's request, the District provided instructors and coaches to the Early Intervention training program, pulling skilled technicians off line in support of this priority program.

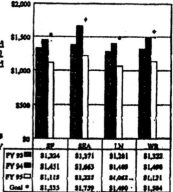

	SF	SEA	LN	WR
FY 93	$1,224	$1,371	$1,281	$1,323
FY 94	$1,451	$1,663	$1,489	$1,498
FY 95	$1,115	$1,233	$1,062	$1,131
Goal	$1,335	$1,732	$1,490	$1,384

Dist is complemented for actions taken in redeploying — assisted region in re-directing

2

Revenue Agent 1040 Productivity - Dollars per Hour

Outstanding. The District is
exceeding its above average goal by
28% and leads the Region with the
highest Revenue Agent 1040 dollars
per hour.

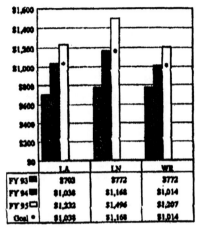

	LA	LN	WR
FY 93	$703	$772	$772
FY 94	$1,038	$1,168	$1,014
FY 95	$1,232	$1,496	$1,207
Goal	$1,038	$1,168	$1,014

Revenue Agent 1120 Productivity - Dollars per Hour

Fair. The District is at 48% of its
above average RA 1120 goal.

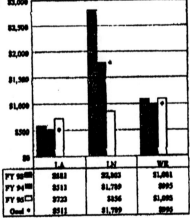

	LA	LN	WR
FY 93	$383	$2,303	$1,081
FY 94	$511	$1,789	$995
FY 95	$723	$856	$1,895
Goal	$511	$1,789	$995

DE$Y Delivery

➜ **Fair.** The District delivered 306.39 RA DE$Ys representing 93% of the plan. The underrealization is due to an underrealization of the FY95 Examination Plan staffing level of 4.07 staff-years and overrealization of non-DET (almost all categories) by 22.01 staff-years.

	FY 95	Plan	% of Plan
RA	306.39	367.78	93%
TA	61.18	72.90	93%

➜ **Fair.** The District delivered 61.18 TA DE$Ys, representing 93% of the plan. The underrealization is due to a failure to achieve the FY95 Examination Plan staffing level and overrealization of training time.

	Region	Los Angeles	Laguna Niguel
RA	1,374.22	370.05	306.39
% of Plan	93%	93%	93%
TA	286.98	74.13	61.18
% of Plan	104%	103%	93%

BMP Action IC2 Close TDAs/TDIs

Dollars Collected

➜ **Outstanding.** The District exceeded its above average CFf dollars collected goal. This accomplishment was due to proactive efforts such as explicit communication to employees of goals and results, accountability reviews, effective utilization of Revenue Representatives, and lowering overhead.

	FY 93	FY 94	FY 95	Goal	% of Goal
CFf (000)	$172,280	$226,794	$269,343	$219,849	123%
ACS (000)	$282,957	$278,861	$232,119	$294,913	86%

➜ **Poor.** ACS dollars collected are well below the goal and prior year's performance. Heavy attrition forced management to use all available technicians to handle incoming calls, allowing inventory to age. Downsizing and the ACS Transition were the focus during the second half of

	Region	Los Angeles	Laguna Niguel
CFf (000)	$1,084,651	$225,343	$269,343
% of Goal	107%	115%	123%

	Region	San Francisco	Seattle	Laguna Niguel
ACS (000)	$673,782	$207,978	$233,685	$232,119
% of Goal	92%	94%	95%	86%

Exhibit 13

Internal Revenue Service   Laguna Niguel
memorandum

                              1284
date: FEB 2 4 1995

to: Directors
    Western Region
    (Simultaneous copies to Chiefs, Collection, Compliance, DORA,
    Examination, and Quality Assurance Divisions)

from: Chief Compliance Officer   C
      Western Region

subject: Quarterly Compliance Comparisons - December FY 95

        Attached are graphs depicting Regional and District
results through the first quarter of FY 95.

        These graphs focus on key measures of productivity for
both Collection (dollars collected per staff-year) and
Examination (dollars recommended per hour). There are also
graphs showing total norm for Collection and 1120 no change
rate for Examination. In addition, there is a graph which
shows criminal fraud referrals in relation to Examination
closures. Finally, there are tables showing EQMS and CQMS
effectiveness rates.

        We intend to provide these comparisons quarterly as a
supplement to the Month-at-a-Glance. For the March quarter
we hope to add Nationwide data, for those comparisons where
it is available, for additional perspective.

        As always, we welcome your comments.

Attachments   INTERNAL REVENUE SERVICE
                                  RECEIVED:

                              MAR 0 3 1995

                        COLLECTION/TECHNICAL AND SUPPORT ...
                        LAGUNA NIGUEL DISTRICT

		A	C	I
C				✓
C:AC				✓
C:SA			✓	
C:TR				✓
C:FB-I				✓
C:FB-II				✓
C:FB-III				✓
C:FB-IV				✓
C:FB-V				✓
C:FB-VI				✓
C:FB-VII				✓
C:ACS I				✓
C:ACS II				✓
C:SPS				✓
C:TSB				✓
RETURN TO:				

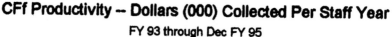

CFf Productivity -- Dollars (000) Collected Per Staff Year
FY 93 through Dec FY 95

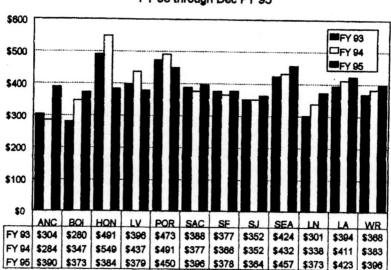

	ANC	BOI	HON	LV	POR	SAC	SF	SJ	SEA	LN	LA	WR
FY 93	$304	$280	$491	$396	$473	$388	$377	$352	$424	$301	$394	$368
FY 94	$284	$347	$549	$437	$491	$377	$366	$352	$432	$338	$411	$383
FY 95	$390	$373	$384	$379	$450	$396	$378	$364	$457	$373	$423	$396

Percent Change Dec FY 95 over Dec FY 94

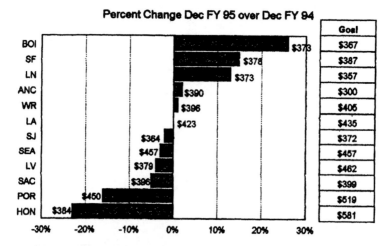

Goal
$357
$387
$357
$300
$405
$435
$372
$457
$462
$399
$519
$581

Regional CFf dollar productivity increased in FY 94 over FY 93, and the trend continues in the FY 95 first quarter. Comparing first quarter FY 94 and FY 95 results, four Districts improved over last year while six Districts' results declined.

ACS Productivity -- Dollars (000) Collected Per Staff Year
FY 93 through Dec FY 95

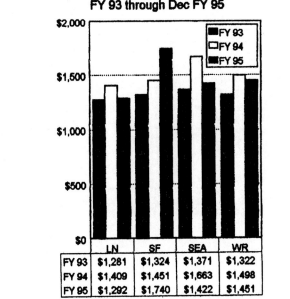

	LN	SF	SEA	WR
FY 93	$1,281	$1,324	$1,371	$1,322
FY 94	$1,409	$1,451	$1,663	$1,498
FY 95	$1,292	$1,740	$1,422	$1,451

Percent Change Dec FY 95 over Dec FY 94

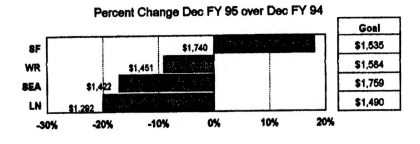

	Goal
SF	$1,535
WR	$1,584
SEA	$1,759
LN	$1,490

Regional ACS dollar productivity has declined in the first quarter of FY 95, compared with FY 94 and with the first quarter FY 94. Only the San Francisco District posted a gain.

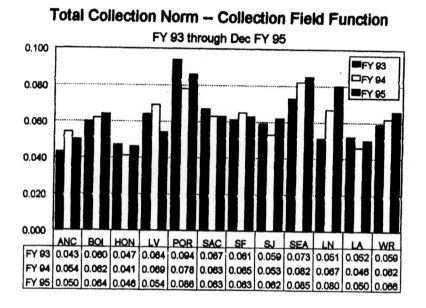

Total Collection Norm -- Collection Field Function

FY 93 through Dec FY 95

	ANC	BOI	HON	LV	POR	SAC	SF	SJ	SEA	LN	LA	WR
FY 93	0.043	0.060	0.047	0.064	0.094	0.067	0.061	0.059	0.073	0.051	0.052	0.059
FY 94	0.054	0.062	0.041	0.069	0.078	0.063	0.065	0.053	0.082	0.067	0.046	0.062
FY 95	0.050	0.064	0.046	0.054	0.086	0.063	0.063	0.062	0.085	0.080	0.050	0.066

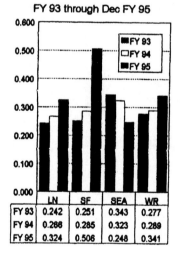

Total Collection Norm -- ACS

FY 93 through Dec FY 95

	LN	SF	SEA	WR
FY 93	0.242	0.251	0.343	0.277
FY 94	0.266	0.285	0.323	0.289
FY 95	0.324	0.506	0.248	0.341

The Region's Total Collection Norm (combined TDA and TDI closures divided by total direct and overhead hours) are improving for both CFf and ACS. Comparing FY 95 first quarter results with FY 94, seven CFf and two ACS operations show improvement.

Tax Auditor 1040 Productivity -- Dollars Per Hour
FY 93 through Dec FY 95

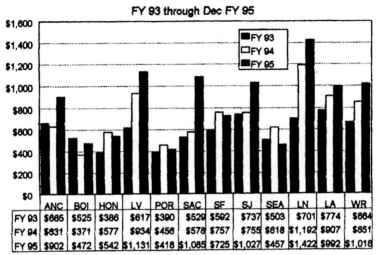

	ANC	BOI	HON	LV	POR	SAC	SF	SJ	SEA	LN	LA	WR
FY 93	$665	$525	$386	$617	$390	$529	$592	$737	$503	$701	$774	$664
FY 94	$631	$371	$577	$934	$456	$578	$757	$755	$818	$1,192	$907	$851
FY 95	$902	$472	$542	$1,131	$418	$1,065	$725	$1,027	$457	$1,422	$992	$1,018

Percent Change Dec FY 95 over Dec FY 94

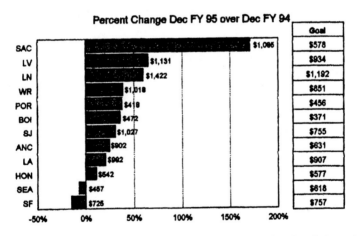

		Goal
SAC	$1,065	$578
LV	$1,131	$934
LN	$1,422	$1,192
WR	$1,018	$851
POR	$418	$456
BOI	$472	$371
SJ	$1,027	$755
ANC	$902	$631
LA	$992	$907
HON	$542	$577
SEA	$457	$818
SF	$725	$757

Regional Tax Auditor productivity continues to increase; In six Districts first quarter FY 95 results exceed both FY 94 and FY 93. Laguna Niguel District, which had the highest productivity in FY 94 is again leading in FY 95. Comparing results for the first quarter FY 95 against the same quarter last year, all but two Districts posted gains, with Sacramento's increase being by far the largest.

Revenue Agent 1040 Productivity – Dollars Per Hour

FY 93 through Dec FY 95

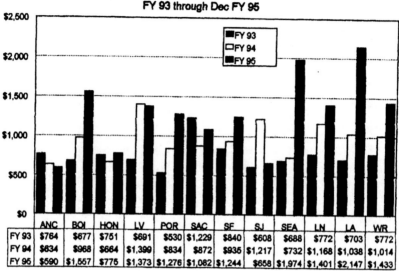

	ANC	BOI	HON	LV	POR	SAC	SF	SJ	SEA	LN	LA	WR
FY 93	$764	$677	$751	$691	$530	$1,229	$840	$608	$688	$772	$703	$772
FY 94	$634	$968	$664	$1,399	$834	$872	$935	$1,217	$732	$1,168	$1,038	$1,014
FY 95	$590	$1,557	$775	$1,373	$1,276	$1,082	$1,244	$658	$1,974	$1,401	$2,147	$1,433

Percent Change Dec FY 95 over Dec FY 94

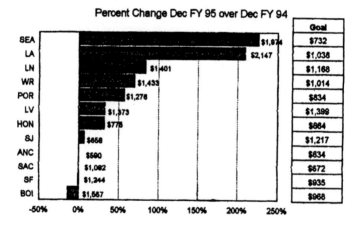

	Goal
SEA	$732
LA	$1,038
LN	$1,168
WR	$1,014
POR	$834
LV	$1,399
HON	$664
SJ	$1,217
ANC	$834
SAC	$872
SF	$935
BOI	$968

Regional Revenue Agent 1040 productivity is up over the two prior years; first quarter FY 95 results exceed both FY 94 and FY 93 in seven Districts. Comparing results for the first quarter FY 95 against the same quarter last year, seven Districts posted gains, with Seattle and Los Angeles both increasing over 200%.

Exhibit 14

Internal Revenue Service
memorandum

1284-LN

Copy to Chief, Exam
Chief, Coll.
Jeff
Keith
Yvonne ✓

date: JUL 1 7 1995

to: District Director E:PSP:PA
    Laguna Niguel

from: Acting Chief Compliance Officer C
      Western Region

subject: Mid-Year Assessment
         URMEM dated June 13, 1995

      Thank you for sharing your thoughts concerning our Mid-Year Assessment of District accomplishments. I am pleased that you took the time to do this, because it affords us the opportunity to clarify our approach to assessments and to the use of value statements. It is especially fortuitous that you raised these points at this time since the Mid-Years, in addition to giving you a mid-term report card, gave us the opportunity for a dry run at our assessment process.

      My position is that assessments must focus on results while acknowledging contributing factors. Accordingly, value statements (outstanding, very good, good, fair, poor) must reflect the result rather than the effort or the obstacles encountered. My memorandum of February 22, 1995, Dictionary of Summary Value Statements, discusses this approach. That memorandum states that the factors to be weighed are "past performance, performance of like Districts, and relative difficulty of the goal"; thus, if a goal had been rated as above average, a more generous value statement might be assigned than if the goal had been rated lower The February 22 memorandum goes on to say that "we will mention in our narratives significant factors not within your control that inflate or deflate results"; thus, it is in the narrative that we acknowledge circumstances rather than in the value statement itself.

      I have reviewed our use of value statements in your Mid-Year Assessment and find that they are essentially appropriate. However, there were two instances where we could have done better on this. The rating of "very good" for ACS TDA dispositions considered the inventory reduction assistance provided by Oklahoma City and Fresno; a rating of "outstanding" should have been assigned and the assistance cited in the narrative. The rating of "fair" in ACS dollars collected per staff-year considered attrition and other issues; a rating of "poor" should have been assigned. These two instances point to the need for us to more diligently focus on outcomes when assigning value statements, avoiding the temptation to be swayed by circumstances, and to be more complete in our narratives. The review triggered by your comments also points

District Director E:PSP:PA
Laguna Niguel

out the value of the field offices' self assessments and the need for us to fully consider
the circumstances reported to us.

You indicated you do not anticipate charging any more time to the Voluntary
Payer Compliance initiative. As indicated in our previous memoranda and discussed
between _____ , of my staff and _____ , VPC is a Congressionally mandated
initiative funded in your Examination plan. Your District has in place an action plan to
achieve that expectation and should make every effort to do so.

I agree the District had a challenging nonfiler disposition goal. The District
was offered the opportunity to reduce inventory in October 1994 by returning excess
inventory to the Service Center, but returned only 1000 cases with bad addresses.
This opportunity was given in order to allow more time in FY95 to prepare examiners
for TCMP.

Thank you again for the opportunity to clarify our approach to the assessment
process. Also, this review has shown the need for more effort within my staff at
uniform results-focused application of value statements. Finally, a procedural
difference between the Mid-Year and Year-End processes will enable us to improve
in our assignment of value statements and the writing of narratives: there will be an
opportunity for field offices to review and comment on drafts before the Year-Ends
and finalized.

If you wish to discuss this further, please call me at

Chief Compliance Officer
FY 95 Mid-Year Assessment
Laguna Niguel District

Overview

Outstanding TDA dispositions and reductions in TDA\TDI inventories have resulted in increased
dollars collected at this point in the fiscal year. Continuing attrition in ACS has frustrated the
District's ability to deliver some of the ACS RAOP goals. The declines in LOS, turnover time,
dollars collected per staff-year, dollars collected, and ACS TDA Inventory are not surprising.
Total dispositions of ACS TDAs/TDIs and limiting dispositions to the queue have resulted in
ratings of "very good." The District has not completed a CMIS project in FY 95, and its
reporting of status and implementation of earlier-identified improvement opportunities is good.

Special credit should be given to the District for its efforts to deliver the Compliance initiative
hires. It has demonstrated a high level of commitment in overcoming redeployment problems,
poor selection certificates, and training challenges to deliver its goals timely.

Tax Auditor dollars have improved significantly over FY 94 results. Emphasis must be placed
on Nonfiler closures as the District has the greatest impact on the Region and is far from its goal.
Early elimination of this inventory will allow Examiners more time to prepare for TCMP. There
has been some confusion about the District's role in IC6 with regard to the Voluntary Payer
Compliance initiative, which is a Congressionally mandated initiative. The expectation is that
the District will meet its target of applying 5 RA FTE, 2574 RO hours, and 1430 Other hours
(Collection) by Sept. 30, 1995. The District has a specific plan of action in place to meet its
objective.

The report that follows encompasses both RAOP and BMP actions and performance indicators,
and contains value statements describing performance as outstanding, very good, good, fair, or
poor. All FY 95 data are as of March unless otherwise indicated. To identify which
performance indicators are included in the RAOP, each value statement pertaining to a RAOP
performance indicator is preceded by a pointer (⇒).

Exhibit 15

Figure R-12

Notice of Seizure

Department of the Treasury
Internal Revenue Service
Form 2438 (Rev. March, 1988)

Name and Address

Under the authority in section 6331 of the Internal Revenue Code, and by virtue of a levy from the District Director of Internal Revenue of the district shown below, I have seized the property below for nonpayment of past due internal revenue taxes.

Due from	Amount	Internal Revenue District (City and State)
	$ 3,500.93	Richmond, VA

Description of property

1	LIQUOR LICENSE
16	ROUND DINING TABLES
164	WOODEN CHAIRS
1	ABC CASH REGISTER
21	CASES OF BEER (24 - 12 OZ. BOTTLES)
6	LITERS OF GIN
10	LITERS OF VODKA
11	LITERS OF SCOTCH
11	LITERS OF BRANDNAME WHISKEY
7	LITERS OF BRANDNAME RUM

Signature of Revenue Officer making seizure	Address	Date 7/7/89
Signature of accompanying employee	Address	Date 7/7/89

Part 1 — Taxpayer Copy

Form 2438 (Rev. 3-88)

2-19

Exhibit 16

Figure R-8

Form **668-B** (Revised July 1989)			Department of the Treasury — Internal Revenue Service **Levy**			
Due from						
			Originating Internal Revenue District *(City and State)* Richmond, VA			
Kind of Tax	Tax Period Ended	Date of Assessment	Taxpayer Identification Number	Unpaid Balance of Assessment	Statutory Additions	Total
941	12-31-88	03-20-89	54-00X3456	$ 3,125.38	$ 463.55	$ 3,588.93
				Total amount due ▶		$ 3,588.93

The amounts shown above are now due, owing, and unpaid to the United States from the above taxpayer for internal revenue taxes. Notice and demand have been made for payment. Chapter 64 of the Internal Revenue Code provides a lien for the above tax and statutory additions. Section 6331 of the Code authorizes collection of taxes by levy on all property or rights to property of a taxpayer, except property that

is exempt under Code section 6334. Therefore, under the provisions of Code section 6331, so much of the property or rights to property, either real or personal, as may be necessary to pay the unpaid balance of assessment shown, with additions provided by law, including fees, costs, and expenses of this levy, are levied on to pay the taxes and additions.

Dated at ____ Falls Church, VA ____   July 7 ____, 19 89

Signature of Revenue Officer	Telephone Number (XXX) 222-3333	Date 7/7/89
Concurrence — Signature of Group Manager		Date 7-7-89
Signature of District Director or Asst. District Director (Taxpayer's principal residence is to be asked, unless Collection is in jeopardy)		Date

____ *(Taxpayer's Name)* ____ was asked to be present during inventory. ____ *(Revenue Officer Signature)*

____ *(Taxpayer or Taxpayer's Representative's Name)* ____ was present at inventory.   ☒ Yes ☐ No

Part 1 — SPf Seizure File   Form 668-B (Rev. 7-89)

2-2

Exhibit 17

Section IV.					Asset and Liability Analysis			
Description	Current Market Value	Liabilities Balance Due	Equity in Asset	Amount of Monthly Payment	Name and Address of Lien/Note Holder/Obligee	Date Pledged	Date of Final Payment
27. Cash			125-				
28. Bank accounts (from item 21)			1420-				
29. Stocks, Bonds, Investments			-0-				
30. Cash or loan value of insur.			2500-				
31. Vehicles (Model, year, license, tag#)							
a. 1989 PIMA VAN	7600-	7000-	600-	225-	FIRST FEDERAL	12/89	1/93
b.							
c.							
32. Real property (From Section III, Item 34) a.	70,000	50,000	40,000	560-	FIRST FEDERAL	1978	2008
b.							
c.							
33. Other assets a. 16-FT. SAILBOAT	900-	—	900-				
b.							
c.							
d.							
e.							
34. Bank revolving credit (from item 22)							
35. Other Liabilities (Include Judgments, notes, and other charge accounts) a. MEDICAL	1200-			100-	DR. LAMAR	OPEN	
b. SIGNATURE LOAN	900-			80-	KNOX FINANCE CO.	1/89	1/91
c.							
d.							
e.							
f.							
g.							
36. Federal taxes owed	3500-						
37. Totals			45,545-	965-			

Internal Revenue Service Use Only Below This Line

Financial Verification/Analysis

Item	Date Information or Encumbrance Verified	Date Property Inspected	Estimated Forced Sale Equity
Personal Residence			
Other Real Property			
Vehicles			
Other Personal Property			
State Employment (Husband and Wife)			
Income Tax Return			
Wage Statements (Husband and Wife)			
Sources of Income/Credit (D&B Report)			
Expenses			
Other Assets/Liabilities			

Form 433-A page 3 (Rev. 4-90)

Section V. Monthly Income and Expense Analysis

Income			Necessary Living Expenses	
Source	Gross	Net		
38. Wages/Salaries (Taxpayer)	1600—	1200—	49. Rent (Do not show mortgage listed in Item 23)	300—
39. Wages/Salaries (Spouse)			50. Groceries (no. of people___)	250—
40. Interest - Dividends			51. Allowable installment payments (IRS use only)	230—
41. Net business income (from Form 433-B)		200—	52. Utilities (Gas $ ___ Water $ ___	
42. Rental Income			Electric $ 105 Phone $ 20)	125—
43. Pension (Taxpayer)			53. Transportation	100—
44. Pension (Spouse)			54. Insurance (Life $ ___ Health $ 80	
45. Child Support			Home $ ___ Car $ ___)	80—
46. Alimony			55. Medical Expenses not covered in Item 54)	25—
47. Other			56. Estimated tax payments	
			57. Court ordered payments CHILD SUPPORT	200—
			58. Other expenses (specify)	
48. Total	1600—	1400—	59. Total (IRS use only)	1310—
			60. Net difference (income less necessary living expenses) (IRS use only)	90—

Certification Under penalties of perjury, I declare that to the best of my knowledge and belief this statement of assets, liabilities, and other information is true, correct, and complete.

61. Your signature | 62. Spouse's signature (If joint return was filed) | 63. Date *today's*

Internal Revenue Service Use Only Below This Line

Explain any difference between Item 60 and installment agreement amount:

Additional Information or comments:

Name of Originator and IDRS assignment number | Date

Form **433-A** page 4 (Rev. 4-88)

Section I — continued   **General Financial Information**

12. Real property

	Brief Description and Type of Ownership	Physical Address
a.	NONE	County _____
b.		County _____
c.		County _____
d.		County _____

13. Life insurance policies owned with business as beneficiary

Name Insured	Company	Policy Number	Type	Face Amount	Available Loan Value
NONE					
			Total (Enter in item 18) ▶		-0-

14. Additional information regarding financial condition (Court proceedings, bankruptcies filed or anticipated, transfers of assets for less than full value, changes in market conditions, etc.; include information regarding company participation in trusts, estates, profit-sharing plans, etc.)

15. Accounts/Notes receivable (Include current contract jobs, loans to stockholders, officers, partners, etc.)

Name	Address	Amount Due	Date Due	Status
ALPINE CORP.	106 ELM ASPEN, CO	$2036—	4/30/90	CURRENT
ELECTRIC, INC.	10106 22ND ST. DENVER, CO	753—	4/15/90	CURRENT
WOODRUFF CRAFT CO.	606 S. BROADWAY DUMAS, TX	1102—	3/31/90	CURRENT
	Total (Enter in item 18) ▶	$3891—		

Page 2   Form 433-B (Rev. 4-88)

Figure Q-6

Form **433-B** (Rev. April 1989)	Department of the Treasury — Internal Revenue Service **Collection Information Statement for Businesses** *(If you need additional space, please attach a separate sheet)*

1. Name and address of business

County ALAMO

2. Business phone number (XXX) 221-5880

3. *(Check appropriate box)*
☐ Sole proprietor
☐ Partnership
☒ Corporation
☐ Other *(specify)*

4. Name and title of person being interviewed
JOHN BROWN

5. Employer Identification Number 43-234X567

6. Type of business MANUFACTURING

7. Information about owner, partners, officers, major shareholder, etc.

Name and Title	Effective Date	Home Address	Phone Number	Social Security Number	Total Shares or Interest
JOHN BROWN, PRES.	10/4/82		486-3216	346-XX-6662	50%
MARY BROWN, V.P.	10/4/82			062-XX-1616	50%
ADAM BROWN, SEC.	11/15/86		486-5126	436-XX-0124	-0-

Section I.   **General Financial Information**

8. Latest filed income tax return ▶

Form	Tax Year ended	Net income before taxes
1120	8809	$45,000 —

9. Bank accounts *(List all types of accounts including payroll and general, savings, certificates of deposit, etc.)*

Name of Institution	Address	Type of Account	Account Number	Balance
FIRST STATE BANK		CHECKING	21-4567	$1600 —
		Total *(Enter in item 17)* ▶		$1600 —

10. Bank credit available *(Lines of credit, etc.)*

Name of Institution	Address	Credit Limit	Amount Owed	Credit Available	Monthly Payments
FIRST STATE BANK		$5000 —	$5000 —	-0-	$275 —
Totals *(Enter in items 24 or 25 as appropriate)* ▶		$5000 —	-0-		$275 —

11. Location, box number, and contents of all safe deposit boxes rented or accessed

NONE

Page 1   Form 433-B (Rev. 4-89)

Figure Q-8

Section III.		Income and Expense Analysis	
The following information applies to income and expenses during the period 2-28-90 to 3-31-90		Accounting method used CASH	
Income		**Expenses**	
28. Gross receipts from sales, services, etc.	•10,522—	34. Materials purchased	•2252—
29. Gross rental income		35. Net wages and salaries Number of Employees 3	3286—
30. Interest		36. Rent	2962—
31. Dividends		37. Allowable installment payments (IRS use only)	546—
32. Other income (Specify)		38. Supplies	200—
		39. Utilities/Telephone	125—
		40. Gasoline/Oil	386—
		41. Repairs and maintenance	—
		42. Insurance	410—
		43. Current taxes	682—
		44. Other (Specify)	
33. Total	▶ •10,522—	45. Total (IRS use only)	▶ • 10,849—
		46. Net difference (IRS use only)	▶ • <327-7>

Certification Under penalties of perjury, I declare that to the best of my knowledge and belief this statement of assets, liabilities, and other information is true, correct, and complete.

47. Signature pres.	48. Date 4/21/90

Internal Revenue Service Use Only Below This Line

Financial Verification/Analysis

Item	Date Information or Encumbrance Verified	Date Property Inspected	Estimated Forced Sale Equity
Sources of Income/Credit (D&B Report)			
Expenses			
Real Property			
Vehicles			
Machinery and Equipment			
Merchandise			
Accounts/Notes Receivable			
Corporate Information, if Applicable			
U.C.C. : Senior/Junior Lienholder			
Other Assets/Liabilities:			

Explain difference between item 46 (or P&L) and installment agreement amount: (if Form 433-A is not used)

Name of Originator and IDRS assignment number	Date

Page 4 Form 433-B (Rev. 4-89)

Exhibit 18

Internal Revenue Service

memorandum

1276-1

date: NOV 2 3 1994

to: Directors
Western Region
(Simultaneous copies to Chiefs Collection, Compliance, and Examination Divisions)

from: Chief Compliance Officer C
Western Region

DISTRICT DIRECTOR
LAGUNA NIGUEL DISTRICT

INTERNAL REVENUE SERVICE
RECEIVED
NOV 2 8 1994

subject: Office-Specific Compliance FY 95 RAOP Goals

Attached for your information and use as points of reference is an advance copy of the FY 95 RAOP office-specific numeric goals for all Compliance components in the Region.

These goals were developed during June with input from each Division Chief and dialogue between the Chiefs and the Executive Assistants. Unfortunately National Office has not yet confirmed our RAOP or the Regional goals, so there remains some doubt that the attached goals are final. However, in view of the passage of time since their development and the fact that some goals were orally negotiated after the field offices' original submissions, we decided to issue the attached which is our best information to date. Once the goals are finalized, they will be confirmed formally by the Regional Commissioner.

We expect that when the goals are formally issued we will be able to include along with each goal a simulated rating of average, above average, or below average, assessing that goal's relative contribution to the Regionwide effort. In the future these ratings will provide perspective in the assessment of accomplishments; however, since the idea of providing them developed too late in the goal-setting process to adequately communicate it, we have delayed full implementation until development of the FY 96 goals. Thus the ratings for FY 95 will be simulated, illustrating how each goal would have been rated had the technique been applied.

The attachment provides the goals for all offices, along with data for FY 93 and FY 94, and the percent difference from the baseline period (FY 93), but without the simulated ratings. Where the percent difference is shown with a minus sign (-) this represents less desirable performance, but not necessarily a declining number since for some performance indicators (e.g. cycle time) lower is better.

Attachment

cc: Chief, Compliance Division, Ogden Service Center
Chief, Quality Assurance Division, San Francisco District
Chiefs, DORA, Laguna Niguel, Los Angeles, San Francisco, San Jose, and Seattle Districts

Exhibit 19

ACTION IC2				6
PERFORMANCE INDICATOR				
Total Dollars Collected CPf (000)				
DISTRICT	FY 93 BASELINE	FY 94 ACTUAL	FY 95 GOAL	% CHANGE FROM BASELINE
Ano	24,409	21,882	26,000	6.50%
Bol	15,503	17,758	20,900	34.80%
Hon	25,362	26,938	28,800	13.60%
LN	172,280	192,450	184,000	6.80%
LV	40,428	46,354	42,000	3.90%
LA	180,559	177,957	189,340	4.90%
Por	57,730	61,570	58,700	-1.80%
Sac	101,267	96,669	105,000	3.70%
SF	77,009	70,934	78,500	1.90%
SJ	110,874	108,980	116,418	5.00%
Sea	95,704	97,007	98,523	2.90%
WR	901,125	918,499	946,181	5.00%

ACTION IC2				7
PERFORMANCE INDICATOR				
Total Dollars Collected ACS (000)				
DISTRICT	FY 93 BASELINE	FY 94 ACTUAL	FY 95 GOAL	% CHANGE FROM BASELINE
LN	282,957	293,812	267,000	-5.60%
SF	226,703	235,048	234,000	3.20%
Sea	255,463	268,608	302,379	18.40%
WR	765,123	797,468	803,379	5.00%

ACTION IC2				8
PERFORMANCE INDICATOR				
Total Dollars Collected SCCB (000)				
DISTRICT	FY 93 BASELINE	FY 94 ACTUAL	FY 95 GOAL	% CHANGE FROM BASELINE
FSC	216,426	324,599	227,247	5.00%
WR	216,426	324,599	227,247	5.00%

ACTION IP13				35
PERFORMANCE INDICATOR				
CPf Dollars Collected Per Staff-Year (000)				
DISTRICT	FY 93 BASELINE	FY 94 ACTUAL	FY 95 GOAL	% CHANGE FROM BASELINE
Ano	304	284	310	2.00%
Bol	280	347	370	32.10%
Hon	491	549	475	-3.30%
LN	301	338	378	25.60%
LV	396	437	378	-4.50%
LA	394	411	396	0.50%
Por	473	491	468	-1.10%
Sac	388	377	395	1.83%
SF	377	366	382	1.30%
SJ	352	352	334	-5.10%
Sea	424	432	440	3.80%
WR	368	383	378	2.70%

ACTION IP13				36
PERFORMANCE INDICATOR				
ACS Dollars Collected Per Staff-Year (000)				
DISTRICT	FY 93 BASELINE	FY 94 ACTUAL	FY 95 GOAL	% CHANGE FROM BASELINE
LN	1,281	1,484	1,450	13.20%
SF	1,324	1,496	1,443	9.00%
Sea	1,371	1,769	1,782	30.00%
WR	1,322	1,573	1,540	16.50%

ACTION IP13				34
PERFORMANCE INDICATOR				
SCCB Dollars Collected Per Staff-Year (000)				
DISTRICT	FY 93 BASELINE	FY 94 ACTUAL	FY 95 GOAL	% CHANGE FROM BASELINE
FSC	345	432	376	9.00%
WR	345	432	376	9.00%

Exhibit 20

Senior Executive's Performance Plan	Rating Period
	From 10-1- To 9-30-
Executive's Name	Position and Location
	District Director

Critical Elements and Performance Standards

The following critical elements apply to all Senior Executives. The uniform standards appearing with each element describe general requirements for fully successful performance in all organizational components and reflect the importance of successfully managing day-to-day operations. Beyond these uniform standards, additional standards *must* be prepared for each critical element. These additional specific standards or expectations should identify significant objectives for the rating period based on the organization's needs and the needs of the individual executive.

Organizational Initiative, Communications, Commitment and Impact

Objective: Determines and revises, when appropriate, goals and objectives. Directs a management system for integrating diverse organizational goals and evaluates its quality and progress. Establishes and maintains effective communications within and outside the agency. Recognizes personal potential to impact on Servicewide problems. Is willing to participate in study group and task force assignments and will accept positions of greater responsibility. Makes appropriate recommendations through proper channels to policy council relating to policy matters or to the Director, Legislative Affairs Division relating to legislative matters. (Note: When appraising performance, the evaluator should be able to describe fully the personal impact of the executive on the organization and his/her organizational commitment. As necessary, the evaluator may draw upon specific accomplishments under the next three critical elements to assess performance under this critical element.)

Uniform Standards: Sets long-term and short-term objectives that are responsive to agency priorities.

Develops effective and innovative approaches for meeting agency goals and problems.

Articulates and communicates agency goals within and outside the Service and gains others' commitment to organizational effectiveness.

Provides leadership and, by personal example, fosters the development of improved policies, programs and organizational commitment.

Effectively represents IRS in the community.

Establishes and maintains a positive working relationship with union officials without adverse impact on the achievement of agency goals and objectives.

Additional Standards:

1. Work within the Joint Quality Council to support teams so projects are properly identified, managed effectively and completed timely.

2. Provide Ethics training to all managers by March 31, 1991.

Program Management and Accomplishments

Objective: Seeks improvements in quality, efficiency and productivity of work or service. Plans, organizes, directs and controls assigned activities and projects to accomplish work objectives in compliance with procedural, administrative and technical requirements. Continually emphasizes the need for quality in all areas.

Uniform Standards: Meets National Office, Regional Office and local program directives within budgeted allocations on a timely basis.

Identifies problems and devises innovative solutions to problems.

Assures that the achievement of specific goals does not adversely impact the attainment of a broader organizational mission.

Maintains necessary technical and management skills.

Uses effective monitoring and evaluation procedures which ensure timely, high quality results.

Additional Standards:

1. Take management actions directed at achieving increased productivity goals as per Business Plans of individual functions.

Exhibit 21

DEPARTMENT OF THE TREASURY
INTERNAL REVENUE SERVICE
WASHINGTON, D.C. 20224

Regional Commissioner - Western Region			
TO:	FOR:	TO:	FOR:
C	A	REEO:	
CS		RCC	
S		RDA	
RC:C			
RC:C:RFA			
RQIM			
RPRO		DIRS	

SEP 19 1995

MEMORANDUM FOR ALL REGIONAL COMMISSIONERS

FROM:

Director, Analysis and Studies Division

SUBJECT: Revised Draft 1995 Field Office Performance Index

Attached is a revised draft of the 1995 Field Office Performance Index. Regional as well as district rankings are included in this draft.

We greatly appreciate all the hard work and time that was spent reviewing the draft index and 'straw' weighting scheme. The volume of responses was tenfold the number we received last year. Our fax machine is broken and my staff is exhausted! We have tried to address in Attachment 1 the most frequently occurring comments and recommendations raised in your responses.

Several changes to the index are incorporated in this draft. Attachments 2-3 display the revised index and weighting system used to calculate the latest rankings. Attachment 4 contains the rankings. On Thursday of this week, we will mail out a technical appendix that should allow your analysts to duplicate our calculations and identify our mistakes!

We continue to work to improve this product. Data for almost 20% of the measures we hope to include in this year's index has not yet been received. Several methodological changes proposed by you and your staffs are being tested (see Attachment 1). We expect additional comments from the field and national office. So once again, we publish this caution: the attached rankings are likely to change in the final draft of the index due out October 15th.

Please fax or phone your comments or recommendations on the revised draft by October 6th so they may be incorporated into the final draft.

I can be reached by phone at (   ), or your staff can reach 6412. Our fax number is

INTERNAL REVENUE SERVICE
RECEIVED

OCT 03 1995

DISTRICT DIRECTOR
LAGUNA NIGUEL DISTRICT

	A	C	I
DO			✓
ADD			✓
CTRL			
TOM			
COLL		✓	
EXAM	✓	✓	
TPS			✓
DORA			
CI			
ISD			
PRO			
EEO			
RETURN TO:			

REGIONAL RANKINGS BY GOAL

INCREASE VOLUNTARY COMPLIANCE

GOAL: COLLECT TAX DUE
(90% Weight)

Region	Rank	Score
Central	1	0.519
Mid-West	2	0.289
Mid-Atlantic	3	0.241
Southwest	4	-0.051
Southeast	5	-0.070
Western	6	-0.199
North-Atlantic	7	-0.728

GOAL: PUBLIC RECOGNITION
FOR ETHICAL CONDUCT
(10% Weight)

Region	Rank	Score
Central	1	1.003
Mid-West	2	0.352
Mid-Atlantic	3	0.195
Southwest	4	0.055
Southeast	5	-0.026
Western	6	-0.464
North-Atlantic	7	-1.124

MAXIMIZE CUSTOMER SATISFACTION AND REDUCE BURDEN

GOAL: RESOLVE TAXPAYER
INQUIRIES WITH ONLY
ONE CONTACT
(20% Weight)

DATA NOT YET
AVAILABLE

GOAL: REDUCE TAXPAYER
BURDEN
(80% Weight)

Region	Rank	Score
Mid-Atlantic	1	0.280
North-Atlantic	2	0.233
Southeast	3	0.086
Southwest	4	-0.045
Western	5	-0.121
Central	6	-0.163
Mid-West	7	-0.271

ACHIEVE QUALITY-DRIVEN PRODUCTIVITY

GOAL: REDUCE PAPER
PROCESSING
(10% Weight)

Region	Rank	Score
Southeast	1	1.602
Central	2	0.858
Southwest	3	0.595
Mid-West	4	0.254
Mid-Atlantic	5	-0.615
North-Atlantic	6	-1.033
Western	7	-1.462

GOAL: MEET DIVERSE
CUSTOMER NEEDS/
DIVERSE WORKFORCE
(5% Weight)

Region	Rank	Score
Southeast	1	0.748
Western	2	0.698
North-Atlantic	3	0.475
Southwest	4	0.364
Mid-Atlantic	5	-0.490
Mid-West	6	-0.701
Central	7	-1.004

GOAL: INCREASE THE
PRODUCTIVITY OF THE
SERVICE
(85% Weight)

Region	Rank	Score
Southeast	1	0.407
Southwest	2	0.104
Mid-West	3	-0.046
Western	4	-0.047
Mid-Atlantic	5	-0.103
Central	6	-0.113
North-Atlantic	7	-0.202

OVERALL REGION PERFORMANCE

Region	Rank	Score
Southeast	1	0.192
Mid-Atlantic	2	0.116
Central	3	0.101
Southwest	4	0.028
Mid-West	5	-0.006
Western	6	-0.156
North-Atlantic	7	-0.252

REGION PERFORMANCE BY MAJOR OBJECTIVE

INCREASE VOLUNTARY COMPLIANCE

Region	Rank	Score
Central	1	0.557
Mid-West	2	0.296
Mid-Atlantic	3	0.296
Southwest	4	-0.041
Southeast	5	-0.056
Western	6	-0.225
North-Atlantic	7	-0.765

MAXIMIZE CUSTOMER SATISFACTION/ REDUCE BURDEN

Region	Rank	Score
Mid-Atlantic	1	0.280
North-Atlantic	2	0.233
Southeast	3	0.096
Southwest	4	-0.043
Western	5	-0.121
Central	6	-0.183
Mid-West	7	-0.272

ACHIEVE QUALITY-DRIVEN PRODUCTIVITY

Region	Rank	Score
Southeast	1	0.544
Southwest	2	0.166
Mid-West	3	-0.049
Central	4	-0.081
Western	5	-0.151
Mid-Atlantic	6	-0.178
North-Atlantic	7	-0.252

OVERALL DISTRICT PERFORMANCE

District	Rank	Score
Aberdeen	1	0.693
Jackson	2	0.505
Albuquerque	3	0.438
Boise	4	0.400
Parkersburg	5	0.387
St Louis	6	0.258
Cheyenne	7	0.254
Buffalo	8	0.228
Columbia	9	0.227
Wilmington	10	0.227
Greensboro	11	0.211
Austin	12	0.191
Omaha	13	0.173
Atlanta	14	0.171
Seattle	15	0.169
Phoenix	16	0.167
Richmond	17	0.164
Pittsburgh	18	0.160
Indianapolis	19	0.148
New Orleans	20	0.130
Hartford	21	0.096
Springfield	22	0.089
Detroit	23	0.085
Albany	24	0.078
Ft Lauderdale	25	0.074
Providence	26	0.069
Jacksonville	27	0.053
Cincinnati	28	0.052
Louisville	29	0.024
Wichita	30	0.022
St Paul	31	0.019
Portsmouth	32	0.011
Denver	33	0.010
Oklahoma City	34	-0.011
Baltimore	35	-0.017
Portland	36	-0.018
Helena	37	-0.024
Salt Lake City	38	-0.025
Dallas	39	-0.043
Milwaukee	40	-0.071
Little Rock	41	-0.075
Nashville	42	-0.089
Des Moines	43	-0.092
Newark	44	-0.103
Augusta	45	-0.133
San Francisco	46	-0.134
Brooklyn	47	-0.140
Cleveland	48	-0.149
Los Angeles	49	-0.158
Sacramento	50	-0.172
Houston	51	-0.188
Las Vegas	52	-0.189
Philadelphia	53	-0.201
Burlington	54	-0.215
Anchorage	55	-0.253
Fargo	56	-0.254
Laguna Niguel	57	-0.279
Chicago	58	-0.282
Boston	59	-0.293
Birmingham	60	-0.305
Honolulu	61	-0.395
San Jose	62	-0.407
Manhattan	63	-0.417

Exhibit 22

Internal Revenue Service
memorandum
                                        1284

date: NOV 0 1 1995

to: Directors
Western Region (Simultaneous copies to Chiefs, Collection, Compliance, DORA,
Examination, and Quality Assurance Divisions)

from: Chief Compliance Officer C
Western Region

subject: Month-at-a-Glance: September FY 95

Attached is the report for September FY 95.

If there are any questions concerning Month-at-a-Glance, our point of contact is

Attachment

CHIEF COMPLIANCE OFFICER

WESTERN REGION

MONTH-AT-A-GLANCE

September FY95

Collection Data
(Pages 1-4 and 12)

Compliance Performance Indicators
September FY 95

RAOP PERFORMANCE INDICATOR 1C2	FY 93	FY 94	FY 95	PR %	Trend	% Chg.	Goal
DOLLARS COLLECTED CFf (000) - WR	$901,125	$1,047,529	$1,208,299	109%		15%	$1,107,829
Anchorage	$24,409	$23,209	$23,465	96%		1%	$24,545
Boise	$15,503	$19,477	$18,696	91%		(4%)	$20,598
Honolulu	$25,362	$29,745	$26,389	84%		(11%)	$31,457
Las Vegas	$40,428	$52,350	$55,160	100%		5%	$55,363
Portland	$57,730	$65,514	$62,520	90%		(5%)	$69,285
Sacramento	$101,267	$109,622	$116,417	100%		6%	$115,932
San Francisco	$77,009	$81,315	$100,645	117%		24%	$85,996
San Jose	$110,874	$126,097	$137,427	103%		9%	$133,356
Seattle	$95,704	$110,559	$114,875	98%		4%	$116,923
Laguna Niguel	$172,280	$226,794	$301,547	126%		33%	$239,849
Los Angeles	$180,559	$202,849	$251,166	117%		24%	$214,526
DOLLARS COLLECTED ACS (000) - WR	$765,123	$759,239	$746,859	93%		(2%)	$802,944
Laguna Niguel	$282,957	$278,861	$255,277	87%		(8%)	$294,913
San Francisco	$226,703	$227,881	$232,283	96%		2%	$240,999
Seattle	$255,463	$252,497	$259,298	97%		3%	$267,032
DOLLARS COLLECTED SCCB (000)	$216,426	$333,703	$439,696	125%		32%	$352,912
DOLLARS COLL. NOTICES (000) (Unallocated)	$1,531,326	$1,638,650	$1,570,334	90%		(4%)	$1,754,557
DOLLARS COLLECTED WR TOTAL (000)	$3,414,000	$3,779,121	$3,965,187	99%		5%	$4,018,243

RAOP PERFORMANCE INDICATOR IP13	FY 93	FY 94	FY 95	PR %	Trend	% Chg.	Goal
DOLLARS COLL. PER STAFF-YEAR CFf (000) - WR	$368	$383	$398		↑3	4%	$405
Anchorage	$304	$284	$294		↑1	3%	$300
Boise	$280	$347	$342		↑2	(1%)	$367
Honolulu	$491	$549	$378		↑1	(31%)	$581
Las Vegas	$396	$437	$404		↑4	(8%)	$462
Portland	$473	$491	$447	—	↓1	(9%)	$519
Sacramento	$388	$377	$358		↑3	(5%)	$399
San Francisco	$377	$366	$450	—	↓3	23%	$387
San Jose	$352	$352	$332		↑1	(6%)	$372
Seattle	$424	$432	$435	—	↑2	1%	$457
Laguna Niguel	$301	$338	$412	—	↑1	22%	$357
Los Angeles	$394	$411	$417	—	↑3	2%	$435
DOLLARS COLL. PER STAFF-YEAR ACS (000) - WR	$1,322	$1,498	$1,140		↑1	(24%)	$1,584
Laguna Niguel	$1,281	$1,409	$1,095		↑1	(22%)	$1,490
San Francisco	$1,324	$1,451	$1,107		↓9	(24%)	$1,535
Seattle	$1,371	$1,663	$1,223		↓1	(26%)	$1,759
DOLLARS COLL. PER STAFF-YEAR SCCB (000)	$345	$432	$613		↑1	42%	$457
DOLLARS COLL. PER STAFF-YEAR WR TOTAL (000)	$516	$543	$556		↑1	2%	$574

Exhibit 23

November 18, 1994

NTEU National President.
Washington, D.C.

Dear

I spoke with   early this morning concerning statements made by Laguna Niguel
Collection Division Chief Yvonne Wiley attributed to you. These statements were made
at an LMRC Collection Sub-Committee meeting held on November 15, 1994. NTEU
members present besides myself were: ·   · Ch. 106,   , - Ch. 117
and   Ch. 234. Present for management. were: Yvonne Wiley - Chief Collection
Division,   Assistant Chief Collection Division, Field Branch Chiefs
                          . Also present were to LR Specialists: ·
and .   another management official and the Assistant Chief's Secretary who was
to be taking minutes of the meeting.

During Wiley's opening statements of the meeting she was talking about the goal of the
division locally and across the country was to increase dollars collected. She stated,
"The number one priority is to increase dollars collected and productivity". She went on
to state that, "NTEU President Bob Tobias has joined in with Mike Dolan in supporting our
efforts to improve the dollars collected. A few months ago the was a video conference held
regarding policy statement P-120 with Mike Dolan and top executives to change the policy.
Dolan talked to the top executives and to Bob Tobias about changes in that policy."
Wiley stated that, "The Top Executives and Tobias have pledged their support for management's
efforts to increase dollars collected this year. Collection of dollars is a national problem.
If we don't increase dollars collected there will be contracting out of collection functions."

Wiley continued on in talking about a concern that "productivity is not at a level we want".
She stated further, "   met with -° ~and ·   concerning our efforts to increase dollars
collected and our program this year. They pledged to support our efforts." She went on
to discuss that in the interests of the partnership between NTEU and management that
this support is pledged.

  : have tried to list here those things she stated directly related to you. There were
several other disturbing statements she made concerning her belief as to the lack of
work being done in the District. Time does not presently permit me to expand on those
items at this time. I will work on a more detailed report on those this weekend and fax
those to you as well.

Since I will be in Laguna today, if you should need further clarification on the above quotes
please have Verna page me at (610)624-6458 or leave a message at my message center at
(800) 864-8444.

Exhibit 24

NEWS FROM

Prevent ~ Differentiate
Integrate ~ *Chief* ~
Compliance
Officer
Faster ~ Better ~ Cheaper

Western Region
November - December 1994

To My Compliance Colleagues:

As I talk to people throughout the Region about the need to improve our productivity, I sometimes hear the comeback, "Well it's okay to push for revenue but we will have to sacrifice voluntary compliance to do it." I don't see it that way.

The central reason for the existence of any tax system in all cultures and civilizations throughout history has been to raise the revenue needed to fuel the engine of government. Voluntary compliance is a means to that end. We try to increase voluntary compliance because it raises revenue at the least cost to the IRS and with the least intrusiveness on the taxpayer. In other words, it's the most efficient and effective way to raise revenue. While there are legitimate questions concerning short term vs long term focus, revenue is the objective. If this point needs reinforcement, note that one has only to come within hailing distance of a meeting of tax administrators from other jurisdictions — state tax commissioners, for instance — to see that for these tax officials, a laser-like focus on revenue is part of the air they breathe. Anything else is unthinkable.

The voluntary compliance level has been stable for a long time. We are experimenting with various techniques to boost it and we are also engaged in R & D (DORA and NORA) trying to learn more about what goes into voluntary compliance. At this stage, however, we know a lot less than we need to know. So

traditional enforcement, closing cases, dollars per hour continue to be our mainstay.

The search for voluntary compliance will often dictate the broad categories of work that management identifies. However, once a case is selected we are clearly looking for dollars, yield, return on investment. Our managers and examiners and collectors should have a crystal clear understanding of this. We must scrupulously observe taxpayer rights. We want to collect only the proper tax at the least cost. But revenue is our business. And since employee time is our largest expense, the phrase "at the least cost" must translate to a continuing and intense focus on the time to be expended in relation to the potential dollar yield — by every Compliance employee.

In these times when business has gone through a painful restructuring to become lean and mean, to restore the traditional American productivity advantage, citizens are demanding that public bureaucracies also deliver value, that they perform. In our case that means increased productivity, collecting more of the revenue that's due and owing, and assuring the compliant taxpayer that others are paying their fair share too.

Best,

Frank

Bob Tobias on Accountability
for Results
(from the fall 1994 Leader's Digest)

LD: There will be some managers who will be critical of this increasing involvement of the Union. Managers are responsible and accountable for meeting the annual business plan or performance expectations. But how is the Union accountable?

Tobias: On most TQO work groups, the "Union" will be bargaining unit employees selected by NTEU using criteria jointly determined by NTEU and management. They will be accountable, as all IRS employees are accountable, for doing their jobs and meeting performance expectations. Plus, a TQO critical element will be an added part of everyone's job.

As for accountability in the NTEU internal structure, as mentioned earlier, NTEU local and national officers are accountable to their members. If union members don't like what their elected leaders are doing, they can vote them out at the next election.

NTEU is also laying its credibility on the line with Congress. In testimony earlier this year, I made a pledge to Congress: Give IRS an additional $405 million for jobs and training and we, NTEU and IRS, will produce results--greater revenue collection and greater service to taxpayers. Partnership is the essential means for improving the Service and NTEU and IRS are both accountable to Congress for its success.

Two Regional FedState Teams Win
Significant Achievement Awards

Beverly Monaco, Acting Director, External Liaison Division, National Office, recently announced that two Western Region nominees for 1994 FedState awards have won their categories. They are the "California Collection FedState Steering Committee" which undertook the Business Masterfile Taxpayer Delinquency Investigation Queue, and the "Fact of Filing Team" which tackled Tax Currency Conditional Licensing.

Members of the first team include: Hank Aouate, Chief, Compliance Division (FSC); Stephen Barnes, FSC Programmatic Review Specialist; Gary Green Chief, Compliance 2000 (FSC); Delores Johnson Chief, Collection, Sacramento District; Kathy Jones, FedState Coordinator, Sacramento District; Catherine Lunderville, Asst. Chief, Collection, San Francisco District; John Pointer, Asst. Chief, Collection, Laguna Niguel District; Debbie Reed, Revenue Officer, Laguna Niguel District; Pete Stipek, former Asst. Chief, Collection, San Jose District; and Roy Tresaugue, Asst. Chief, Collection, Los Angeles District.

Winning the Data Exchange and Application category, this team analyzed the BMF-TDI process and achieved a breakthrough in systems improvement. Matching data from the State Employment Development Department (EDD), they learned that an extremely large percentage of the accounts had no match or were no longer in business. National Office subsequently approved the closure of 52,401 stand alone TDI cases containing 703,005 modules.

Members of the second team include: Hank Aouate, Chief, FSC Compliance Division; Mike Frates, Chief, Exam Branch III, San Jose District; Rilla Livingston, WR FedState Coordinator; Marlene McGuinness, FedState Coordinator, San Jose District; Barbara Spalinger, Taxpayer Education Coordinator, San Jose District; and John Sullivan, Chief, Examination Division, San Jose District.

Winning the Early Intervention and Education Category, this team executed an historic agreement with the California State Department of Industrial Relations, Division of Labor Standards Enforcement. Farm labor contractors seeking state licenses must now annually prove their compliance with Federal tax obligations. Significant sanctions will be imposed against farm labor contractor, operating without a valid license as well as those who employ them.

The annual FedState awards are presented to IRS managers and employees to recognize and encourage the development of joint FedState tax administration opportunities that improve compliance, reduce burden and enhance overall service to taxpayers.

Rilla Livingston (408) 494-8600

Collection FedState Success

The Collection FedState Steering Committee, fresh from the success of the California BMF TDI Project, has agreed to take on two new projects:

1. FTD Alerts - The Committee asked Fresno Service Center to analyze the FTD alert process to determine if it can be enhanced. Items of concern were:
   a. The feasibility of using State EDD data to enhance the process;
   b. How can Field Collection receive credit for working these accounts?

2. Accelerate Processing/Case Building for TDAs - The Inventory Delivery Subcommittee has been charged with:
   a. Using ARMIS, analyze the three largest contributors (source of assessment) for both IMF and BMF TDAs in each district;
   b. Determining if cases can be accelerated to the field at or prior to first notice;
   c. Determining what should be included in case building;
   d. Determining source of cases to be accelerated (ESB etc.);
   e. Determining if districts can receive credit for this type of work.

These projects will be coordinated through this Steering Committee and the results shared through future Newsletters.

Steve Barnes (209) 456-5262

FedState Breakthrough!
State Loans to Pay Delinquent Taxes

In 1994, the Alaska Legislature passed and Governor Hickle signed S.B. 251. The new law allows the state to loan up to $30,000 to salmon fishers for the payment of federal tax debts. State government officials say they have $14 million available in their revolving loan fund and do not anticipate loan demand

2

Exhibit 25

. . .and the NTEU Viewpoint

LD also interviewed NTEU National President Robert Tobias to get the NTEU viewpoint on the Partnership Agreement.

LD: What does the Partnership Agreement mean to the labor management philosophy of NTEU?

Tobias: NTEU's "philosophy" on labor-management relations can be summarized by the first point in NTEU's mission statement:

"We must create a workplace where employees are treated with dignity and respect, encouraged to reach their full potential and allowed to participate in the decision-making process at the job site on matters that affect them."

The Partnership Agreement very clearly brings the union closer to achieving this goal for IRS employees. We now have a formal instrument to improve labor relations that is less adversarial. Yet we retain the right to use our adversarial tools, if necessary.

LD: A significant portion of the leadership in the IRS is the front-line manager. Under this new partnership and changing labor environment, what's a manager going to have to do differently?

Tobias: The basic difference for managers will be to acknowledge fully that employees, through their union, have worthwhile knowledge and skills to contribute to improving processes. Then managers must act on that acknowledgement, asking for and respecting input from union leaders and union-designated bargaining unit representatives before decisions are made.

Managers will not be giving up their management prerogative. Final decisions will still be made by managers. They will just have to accept contribu-

tions from a hitherto untapped resource: the employees who actually do the work. And they will be required to act like work team coaches, not bosses.

The Partnership Agreement spells out specific actions for managers in terms of delegating, monitoring, and measuring work and performance. More detailed actions will be forthcoming from the IRS-NTEU National Partnership Council.

LD: What does NTEU view as the benefit of the Partnership?

Tobias: The overwhelming benefit is the opportunity for increased job satisfaction for employees. Employee job satisfaction comes first from more control over establishing work processes and procedures, and then from enhanced authority and responsibility to make decisions concerning work assigned. This is the meaning of employee empowerment.

Employees currently are under-utilized and underproductive, not because they're incompetent or unwilling, but because of the work structure. The research on this subject says that the most highly productive workplaces are those where unions are involved in the quality improvement process from the outset, not where management unilaterally has introduced quality into the workplace. So NTEU involvement will provide the greatest benefit for both IRS employees and management.

LD: What has NTEU given up to get that?

Tobias: Partnership means abandoning the safety of the status quo. By changing our primary role from management adversary to management partner, NTEU local and national leaders have made themselves vulnerable to charges of "sleeping with the enemy" from our membership. In effect, we have pledged that an IRS-NTEU partnership will improve employees' work lives. Now we will have to deliver on our promises or risk

losing membership, which is the power base for every union.

IRS and NTEU leaders understand that if the partnership fails, a return to a purely adversarial relationship is almost inevitable. That alternative would be extremely unfortunate. It's an incentive to all of us to make partnership work.

LD: What does the Service gain by more involvement of NTEU on the front end?

Tobias: Past conventional wisdom was that efficiency and productivity could be increased only by increasing pressure on employees to produce more. This assumed employees were at fault – if they would only work harder or smarter, productivity would increase.

Quality improvement guru W. Edwards Deming stated that 85 percent of an employee's productivity is linked to the work process. Working harder will not automatically improve productivity. And because those working in the system have knowledge of what must be done to improve system performance, it makes good management sense to include employees and their union on the front end.

LD: What do you think a front-line manager will see immediately as a result of this change?

Tobias: Already managers have seen a lot of confusion, from their employees and from fellow managers, about what the partnership means. That is why this article was written and why you will be receiving many future communications clarifying various aspects of the partnership.

Though few have yet been certified for TQO, enough units have implemented TQO-like processes for us to have learned from their experience. From their reports, front-line managers were surprised and pleased at the high levels of employee enthusiasm, diligence and commitment, both during the change process and after implementation. And, as hoped, the changes resulted in improved productivity and efficiency of the work process and product.

(continued on p. 25)

Exhibit 26

Internal Revenue Service
memorandum

date:

to: Regional Commissioner
     Western Region

from: District Director C
       Laguna Niguel District

subject: Letter from Robert Tobias

      I am in receipt of a letter from   of NTEU to the Deputy
Commissioner, Mike Dolan, dated November 21, 1994. Attached to that letter is a
copy of a letter from   to Mr.   dated November 18, 1994. After
reading both letters and discussing them with Mrs. Wiley, she has provided me
with a copy of a "Special Bulletin" from NTEU Chapter 92 stating in part some of
the very same words that are being quoted as coming from Mrs. Wiley. Attached
you will find a copy of the bulletin wherein it is stated that "NTEU acknowledges
the business decision to increase the dollars collected, and we support the
concept." In addition, attached find a copy of the newsletter from   'or
November-December 1994, wherein statements are taken from the fall 1994
Leader's Digest that are supposedly direct quotes from Robert Tobias on
Accountability For Results. Mr.   is saying in his own word what Mrs. Wiley
said in the sub committee meeting "In testimony earlier this year, I made a pledge
to Congress: Give IRS an additional $405 million for jobs and training and we,
NTEU and IRS, will produce results---greater revenue collection and greater
service to taxpayers. Partnership is the essential means for improving the Service
and NTEU and IRS are both accountable to Congress for its success."

      Mrs. Wiley denies making any specific quotes from Mr. Tobias or anyone
else. She does admit to giving a similar message to those in attendance at the
November 15, 1994, sub committee meeting. She does specifically deny saying
"if we don't increase dollars collected there will be contracting out of collection
functions." She has advised me she said something along the lines of finding it a
necessity to improve in the areas of dollars collected and overall productivity and
that in the not too distant past there had been discussions about contracting out
ACS work and that she wondered whether at some time in the future this might be
considered more efficient than the current collection efforts. Also, Mr.
indicated in his letter that "Mr.   failed to accurately quote me or Mrs. Wiley
failed to accurately quote Mr. .   During the sub committee meeting Mrs.
Wiley did not attribute any of her comments to me; rather her comments were
based on   newsletter.

-2-

Regional Commissioner
Western Region

    Mrs. Wiley and the Collection Division Managers are placing special emphasis on the need for restoring productivity within the Division. She is in complete agreement with   words in his newsletter wherein he discusses the need to "restore the traditional American productivity advantage" and further states, "In our case that means increased productivity, collecting more of the revenue that's due and owing, and assuring the compliant taxpayer that others are paying their fair share too."

    It appears from the letter from Mr.   that he finds fault with what Mrs. Wiley said at the sub committee meeting. Based on the contents of the letter and the partnership relationship we have entered into with NTEU I fail to see any problems that could have been created by Laguna Niguel management. A true partnership is based on accountability of both partners and as '   ' article says, "it is the essential means for improving the Service."

    If you have any addition questions please contact Mrs. Wiley, Chief, Collection Division, at (714) 643-4071.

Attachments

Exhibit 27

LAGUNA NIGUEL/SANTA ANA POD - ASSESSMENT REPORT

CONCLUSIONS

The following are a series of conclusions which the consultant drew from the answers given to the open ended structured interview questions and the numerically based questions.

1 - Parties recognize some fundamental strengths in their current union-management relationship: The strengths which both parties identified are basically strengths which rest with the union. Both parties also acknowledged the capability of union and management leaders as a strength of the current union-management relationship. Management also saw many other strengths in the current union-management relationship; many of these strengths rest with management. The strength of the parties separately and together could be very useful for improving and strengthening the union-management relationship further.

2 - No shared perspective on what the weaknesses of the current union-management relationship are: both parties identified some serious weaknesses in their current union-management relationship. However, the parties didn't have a common or shared perspective focused on one set of weaknesses. Such divergent views of the weaknesses is usually an indicator of misunderstanding and sometimes conflict in the current union-management relationship. Exactly what this means is not clear.

3 - Mutual respect and disrespect - Management believes that it respects the legitimate roles of the union, and the union concurs. Management rated the respect it gives the legitimate roles of the union an average rating of 4.9; the union rated the respect it receives from management for its legitimate roles an average rating of 6.

However, the union believes that its respects the legitimate roles of management, and management does not concur. The union rated the respect it gives the legitimate roles of management an average rating of 6.5. Management rated the respect it receives from the union for its legitimate roles an average rating of 2.3.

The rating scale is 1 to 7.

8 - Both parties have a vision of a wide range of potential areas for additional cooperation: what's important here is not only that the parties have thought about what else they could do in the cooperative arena but also that they are able to think of themselves in these terms.

9 - No real shared perspective about the forces which would work against successful cooperation: the parties didn't identify the same forces which would work against successful cooperative effort. However, both parties identified some significant forces which would work against cooperation. The union generally sees the forces against cooperation residing in management. Management sees some significant forces against cooperation relating to: egos and personalities on both sides; the conflicts among the four NTEU chapters; protracted negotiations which don'ts result in agreements, and lack of funding for agreements which are reached.

10 - No real shared perspective about the forces which would work in favor of successful cooperation: the parties also didn't identify the same forces which would work in favor of successful cooperative effort. To summarize these perspectives: the union sees the leadership of the two parties as the key force in favor of success with cooperation. Management sees mutual pride in working for IRS, resolution of issues at the first level, and more effective negotiations as the key positive forces.

11- Opportunity for success - both parties believe that there are many win-win opportunities in this workplace around which the union and management can cooperate. When asked to indicate the extent of such opportunities, the union rated an average of 7 on a scale of 1 to 7. Management rated an average of 5.5 on the same scale.

12 - Chances for success - the two parties have very different perspectives on the likelihood of success. When asked to rate the likelihood of success on a scale of 1 to 7, the union rated an average of 7 and management rated an average of 2.8. Please note that many managers indicated that they were factoring in the impact of the actions of the other NTEU chapters on what the Laguna Niguel POD could do. The disparity between the union's perspective on the likelihood for success and the management perspective can be attributed in large part of this.

13 - Similar and dissimilar perceptions of the current organizational climate in this POD: both parties were to indicate their agreement or disagreement with a series of thirteen statements describing the organization

LAGUNA NIGUEL/SANTA ANA POD - ASSESSMENT REPORT   Laguna Niguel 5
                                                         Santa Ana

m - Extent to which this is a good place to work (from 1 to 7) - union
average, 5.7; management average, 5.3

**14 - Clear and common perspective about the desirability of the a true
partnership:** both parties described three key characteristics they want to
achieve in their union-management relationship five years from now:

- Open and honest lines of communication up and down and across
the entire organization

- Leading together and working together with a focus on
accomplishing our goals so that a real partnership is achieved

- Respect each others rights and responsibilities, mutual
accountability, and being able to agree to disagree.

For the union this means that the leaders of Chapter 108 will work with
each other to:

    a - Specify the institutional interests the union has in having a
    constructive relationship with management in this POD and in
    cooperatively working with management here

    b - Define in behaviorally specific terms the kind of union-
    management relationship you want to have in this POD. You will find
    plenty of information about desirable and undesirable behaviors from
    the perspectives of both parties in this report.

    c - Specify unilateral actions you can and will take as the union to
    begin to move the union-management relationship in a new, more
    constructive direction. These are actions you will take regardless of
    what management does to demonstrate your good faith and your
    commitment to improving the union-management relationship

You must build a union consensus in this Chapter around these three
things.

You will need facilitation to accomplish this work. There are OD
professionals at the Region and within the District who could facilitate the
doing of this work. NTEU also has professionals who could facilitate the
doing of this. The three tasks are very straightforward. Don't make them
into something more than they are.

**Recommendation #3: Hold a joint session involving the top union
and top management leaders in Laguna Niguel to do the following:**

    **a - Share and compare your institutional interests in having a
    constructive union-management relationship and in working
    cooperatively. Identify your shared or common interests**

    **b - Develop in specific behavioral terms a description of the kind
    of union-management relationship you will pursue here. You'll
    use the descriptions you developed independently to do this.**

    **c - Explore exactly what your current union-management
    relationship is through dialogue and by giving face to face
    feedback to each other**

LAGUNA NIGUEL/SANTA ANA POD - ASSESSMENT REPORT   Laguna Niguel 9
                                                        Santa Ana

process. Ideally the parties would continuously strive to improve the grievance handling process so that it:

- Is effective, i.e. meets the goals and objectives for which it is intended

- Supports solving problems before they become grievances and supports grievance resolution at the lowest levels possible

- Enhances rather than damages the union-management relationship.

This group could apply some very basic quality tools such as basic cause and effect analysis, pareto analysis, process mapping, and process analysis to do this work. Quality resources within the District should be utilized.

B1b - Weaknesses of U-M relationship, cont.

UNION PERSPECTIVE	MANAGEMENT PERSPECTIVE
	U-M relationships are too personality based
	Union and management not working toward same goals - management focused on protecting employee rights
	Both parties are trying to protect their ground
	Union not accountable in way management is accountable and not fully committed to IRS goals
	Union will pursue grievances without substance or grounds
	Union communications with management are accusatory
	Union structure and leaders in it not representative of majority of employees - out of touch

B3 - What are the common grievances

Appraisals/evaluations and promotions.
Also some conduct grievances

B4 - Resolution levels

Both parties acknowledged that different kinds of grievances are commonly resolved at different levels. Both parties also acknowledged that the personalities involved and the extent to which they are oriented to problemsolving also influence significantly the resolution level.

B5 - Resolution/problem solving at 1st level

The union perceives that they do utilize the procedure called for in NORD 4 and have been extremely successful at solving problems and resolving grievances before or at 1st level.

LAGUNA NIGUEL/SANTA ANA POD - ASSESSMENT REPORT   Laguna Niguel 13
                                                         Santa Ana

B7 - Negative behaviors

UNION PERSPECTIVE	MANAGEMENT PERSPECTIVE
Management taking unilateral actions when required to work with the union	Union distorting the facts; selectively sharing information
Management being a stickler for following exact procedure when it is to their advantage and seeking flexibility from the union when they need it	Union adopting an "us vs. them" attitude; union accusing management continuously; character assassination
Don't experience negative behaviors	Union blindly advocating for any employee regardless of the merits of the case
	Union not really checking out what the majority of employees want and taking action on that
	Both parties crucifying each other when mistakes are made
	Both parties allowing their personal animosities to affect their relationships

C1 - Joint efforts

Both parties indicated that when they have focused on what their interests are and what their goals should be, joint activities have been successful. Some examples of successful joint activities are: AWS argument and the Awards agreement

C2 - Potential areas for cooperation

Both parties indicated that there are a variety of potential areas of cooperation which could be pursued at all organizational levels.

LAGUNA NIGUEL/SANTA ANA POD - ASSESSMENT REPORT   Laguna Niguel 15
                                                          Santa Ana

D1 - Future relationship 3 years from now

UNION PERSPECTIVE		MANAGEMENT PERSPECTIVE
Open lines of communication up and down and across the organization - are frank with each other	←→	Open and honest communication
Are a real partnership; lead together	←→	Work together and accomplish organizational goals together; have established partnership
Both have rights and responsibilities and are accountable; have mutual respect	←→	Agree to disagree; respect and treat each other professionally
Take pride in our ability to solve problems together; routinely resolve issues		Mutual trust
		Congruent goals
		Mutually supportive
		Agree on what is best for employees

Laguna Niguel/Santa Ana

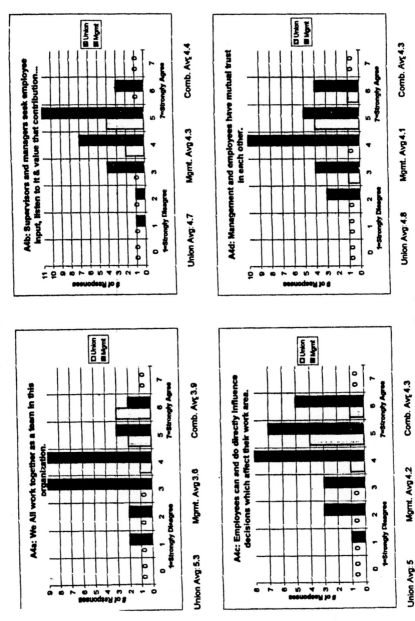

A4a: We All work together as a team in this organization.

Union Avg: 5.3   Mgmt. Avg 3.8   Comb. Avg 3.9

A4b: Supervisors and managers seek employee input, listen to it & value that contribution...

Union Avg: 4.7   Mgmt. Avg 4.3   Comb. Avg 4.4

A4c: Employees can and do directly influence decisions which affect their work area.

Union Avg: 5   Mgmt. Avg 4.2   Comb. Avg 4.3

A4d: Management and employees have mutual trust in each other.

Union Avg: 4.8   Mgmt. Avg 4.1   Comb. Avg 4.3

Laguna Niguel/Santa Ana

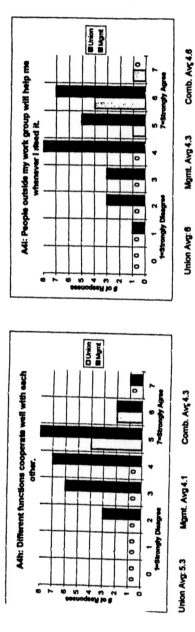

A4h: Different functions cooperate well with each other.

Union Avg: 5.3   Mgmt. Avg: 4.1   Comb. Avg: 4.3

A4i: People outside my work group will help me whenever I need it.

Union Avg: 8   Mgmt. Avg 4.3   Comb. Avg: 4.6

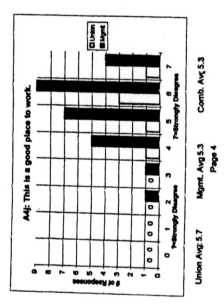

A4j: This is a good place to work.

Union Avg: 5.7   Mgmt. Avg 5.3   Comb. Avg 5.3

Page 4

Laguna Niguel/Santa Ana

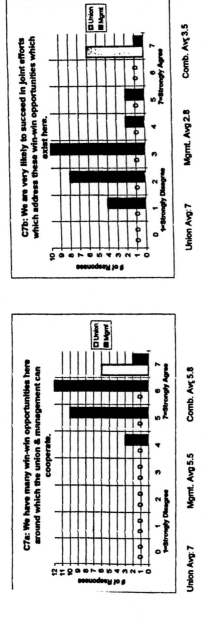

C7a: We have many win-win opportunities here around which the union & management can cooperate.

Union Avg: 7   Mgmt. Avg 5.5   Comb. Avg 5.8

C7b: We are very likely to succeed in joint efforts which address these win-win opportunities which exist here.

Union Avg: 7   Mgmt. Avg 2.8   Comb. Avg 3.5

Exhibit 28

Yvonne's copy

FORM EXEMPT UNDER 44 U.S.C. 3512

UNITED STATES OF AMERICA	FOR FLRA USE ONLY
FEDERAL LABOR RELATIONS AUTHORITY	Case No.
CHARGE AGAINST AN AGENCY	Date Filed

Complete instructions are on the back of this form.

1. Name and address of charged activity or agency	2. Name and address of charging labor organization or individual
Internal Revenue Service Laguna Niguel District 24000 Avila Road Laguna Niguel, CA 92677	National Treasury Employees Union (NTEU) Chapter P.O. Box 3482 Laguna Hills, CA 92654

3. Activity or agency contact information Name:	4. Labor organization or individual contact information Name:
Title: District Director Phone: ( )	Title: Chapter President, NTEU Phone: ( )

5. Which subsection(s) of 5 U.S.C. 7116(a) do you believe have been violated? [See reverse] (1) and __5__

6. Tell exactly WHAT the activity (or agency) did. Start with the DATE and LOCATION, state WHO was involved, including titles.

On April 24, 1995, a District Office Study (DOS-II) Memorandum of Understanding (MOU) was agreed to by National IRS and National NTEU. On May 2, 1995, a national tele-conference was held announcing the changes under DOS-II. The DOS-II MOU addressed the consolidation of IRS Districts and Regions. Also, it addressed significant NTEU internal changes. On May 3, 1995, a subsequent national teleconference was held. Under DOS-II, NTEU Chapters were not required to belong to a joint council where two or more union chapters existed within a district. Each chapter could decide to fashion a direct relationship with the district director, negotiate agreements with the district etc. This meant that a district, such as Laguna Niguel, could have a joint council and an independent chapter in the same district. Each body has equal represnetational and institutional standing in the district.
Pursuant to the DOS-II Agreement, and acting in total accordance with all of its provisions as reiterated on May 2, 1995 and May 3, 1995... NTEU Chapter 108 withdrew from the Southern California Joint Council on October 13, 1995. On October 17, 1995, NTEU Chapter 108 submitted a request to negotiate local district agreements. This request was submitted to   , District Director. On October 23, 1995, NTEU Chapter 108 submitted specific negotiation dates to the District Director. Mr. has failed to respond and there are no indicators that he plans to respond. The District Director is not acting in good faith. His blatant failure to even communicate with NTEU Chapter 108 since October 17, 1995 is a blatant violation of 5 U.S.C. 7116 (a) 1 & 5. This is ironic because the walking distance between our respective offices is less than one minute. Also, he has failed to respond to numerous voice mail messages.

7. Have you or anyone else raised this matter in any other procedure? ☒ No   ☐ Yes   If yes, where? [see reverse] _____

8. I DECLARE THAT I HAVE READ THIS CHARGE AND THAT THE STATEMENTS IN IT ARE TRUE TO THE BEST OF MY KNOWLEDGE AND BELIEF. I UNDERSTAND THAT MAKING WILLFULLY FALSE STATEMENTS ON THIS CHARGE CAN BE PUNISHED BY FINE AND IMPRISON-MENT. 18 U.S.C. 1001.

		November 21, 1995
Type or print your name	Your signature	Date

FLRA Form 22
(Rev 7-89)

Exhibit 29

MUST GO

Since   has become the President, Chief Steward, and
"Everything Else" in Chapter   .OUR CHAPTER HAS BEEN REDUCED
TO ZERO! However,   is Doing Well. She Works No Cases. She
Has An Office. She Travels. She Has a Private Phone.

Employees are being "fired" because she lacks the ability to
save their jobs. Accountability Reviews, Opportunity Letters,
Numerous Grievances...What does   , do? "ZERO".

We need a Chapter President with a certain degree of
sophistication. We do not intend to be cruel, however, our
Chapter President attends critical meetings, on behalf of our
membership, dressed in a worn out "sweat suit" and "truck driver
boots". On top of this, she displays a persona which turns
people off, to the detriment of our members. MEMBERS...WE CAN
DO BETTER!

Unfortunately, we cannot "reverse the clock". If we knew
then what we know now, we would have voted for   and he
would be our Chapter President. In 1996, Chapter . must run an
election for Chapter President.   , we hope you have not
become discouraged and will continue your involvement in Chapter
        Also,   our current Chapter Vice
President, would be a good choice for Chapter President. We have
the TALENT in our Chapter. LET'S USE IT OR WE WILL LOSE IT!!
Chapter   members are preparing to join other chapters in
disgust.

    , please set aside your ego and realize that you are
"OVER YOUR HEAD".   our members are losing their
jobs...Careers are being damaged...Please step aside so that our
Chapter can have competent leadership.

       if you do not remove yourself...the Membership Will
Remove You!!! Maybe We Should Abolish Chapter   and Merge With
Another Chapter!!!

       . Please do what is best for the Membership...NOT YOUR
EGO!!!

    *THE COMMITTEE TO RESTORE COMPETENCE TO OUR NTEU LEADERSHIP
IN CHAPTER   . LONG BEACH.

    *81 MEMBERS AND GROWING

Exhibit 30

October 17, 1995

Vice President
NTEU Chapter
P. O. Box 3482

Dear Mr.

In a letter dated August 10, 1995 (attached), I asked you to provide evidence concerning why I should not issue a cease and desist order pursuant to Article XVIII, Section 2 of the NTEU Constitution.

An anonymous letter was distributed to the members of Chapter   entitled "   Must Go." The letter challenges Ms.   as being "over her head" as Chapter President and asks her to resign, and suggests that the membership of Chapter   abolish itself and merge with another Chapter. Finally, the letter engages in an ad hominem attack of Ms.   criticizing her dress and demeanor.

Two separate handwriting analysis experts compared the handwritten addresses on the envelopes containing the anonymous flyer with handwritten letters signed by you. They each concluded without qualification that the handwriting on the envelopes was yours.

      made the following conclusions:

1. All of the envelopes were addressed by the same person.

2. The person's writing who was represented to me as matches the writing that is in dispute on all of the envelopes.

3. I highlighted some of the matching areas in yellow highlight ink. It is no exaggeration to say that I did not highlight all of the matches for the reason being that there would have been so much yellow highlight ink, the most profound matches could have been lost.

901 E Street. N.W. · Suite 600 · Washington, D.C. 20004-2037 · (202) 783-4444

was unequivocal in her conclusion it was you who
addressed the envelopes containing the anonymous letter.

Similarly,   , who conducted an independent
examination, concluded you addressed the envelopes:

> To perform this examination, I first
> determined there was sufficient writing to
> make an identification and that the writer
> made only a superficial attempt to disguise
> his writing. I also determined that the same
> person addressed each of the envelopes. I
> then compared the handwriting habits in the
> known writing to the handwriting habits of
> the 19 envelopes. As a result of this
> comparison, it is my opinion that the person
> whose handwriting you submitted as that of
>   is the same person who
> addressed the 19 envelopes.

In your response you denied that you had addressed the
envelopes and submitted an analysis of   Mr.
the analyst hired by you, failed to exonerate you. Rather, he
stated, "It is my professional opinion that the hand addressed
envelopes probably were not produced by the same person who
produced the exemplar writing."

In contrast to Ms.   and Ms.   Mr.   was not
definitive. He was unsure whether you addressed the envelopes
and concluded you "probably did not."

You argue that the technique used by Mr.   was a "more
comprehensive and professional examination" because he conducted
his examination "over transmitted light on a light table and
under a stereo microscope." In contrast to your conclusion, this
technique does not constitute a more "comprehensive examination"
because the documents examined by Mr.   were not original.
This technique is appropriate for the comparison of original
documents. And Mr.   did not have original documents. Even
if this technique is appropriate, however, Mr.   did not
absolve you of responsibility for addressing the envelopes.

You also argue that Mr.   "measured for the degree of
slant, size and spacing of words and letters alignment and
proportion." Measurements, however, are not significant because
the most common changes in an attempt to disguise a writing are
the slant and size of the letters. The crucial comparisons are
the handwriting characteristics, and Ms.   concluded,
without qualification, that the "handwriting characteristics are
still the same."

Finally, the veracity of Mr.   is certainly questionable. He has stated in numerous interviews and on national television that based on his handwriting analysis, Elvis Presley wrote his own autopsy report.

In evaluating all the evidence, it is my conclusion that you did in fact address the envelopes which contained the anonymous attack on Ms.   Such conduct clearly violates Article XVIII of the NTEU Constitution.

Pursuant to XVIII, Section 2 of the NTEU Constitution, I direct that you cease and desist from such conduct now and in the future. Failure to comply shall be reason for the immediate preferral of charges to the NTEU National Executive Board.

Sincerely,

National President

RMT:vg

Attachment

Exhibit 31

October 17, 1995

M E M O R A N D U M

To: Chapter   Members

Re: Anonymous Attack on Chapter   President

    An anonymous flyer was sent to all Chapter   members on or about August 2, 1995. It was an attack on the competence and character of Chapter President   written as though it was from a Chapter   member.

    I am also attaching a letter sent to Chapter President   in which I conclude there is insufficient evidence to link him to the writing and/or distribution of the flyer and a letter sent to   Vice President NTEU Chapter   in which I find that he addressed the envelopes containing the anonymous flyer. I direct   to cease and desist from all future similar activity.

    I am hopeful that this will put an end to the distribution of anonymous flyers.

National President

RMT:vg

Attachments (4)

Exhibit 32

Performance Management and Recognition System Appraisal	Period Covered

	From	To
Name of Employee	10/01/93	09/30/94

Organization Segment

Collection Division

Title of Present Position

Series and Grade

Rating of Critical Elements

Manager

1. Program Management and
   Accomplishments

        Exceeded
        Met
        ☐ Failed to meet

2. Managing Resources and
   Guiding Performance

        Exceeded
        Met
        ☐ Failed to meet

3. Implementing and Managing
   Equal Employment Opportunity

        Exceeded
        L. Met
        ☐ Failed to meet

NOTE: A rating of "Failed to meet" on any critical element shall result in a summary of Unacceptable

Reason for Appraisal (Check one)

☐ Annual Performance/Rating of Record

☐ Departure Appraisal/Rating of Critical Elements for Detail of 90 days or more (no summary rating assigned.

☐ Departure Appraisal and Summary Rating assigned due to position change (employee has served at least 90 days in the position)

☐ Departure Appraisal and Summary Rating assigned due to supervisor leaving (employee was supervised at least 90 days)

☐ Rating postponed until _____ (date) (employee has not served for at least 90 days)

Summary Rating

☐ Outstanding	☐ Minimally Successful
☒ Distinguished	☐ Unacceptable
☐ Fully Successful	☐ Unratable

Recommending Official's Signature/Title   Date

     Assistant District Director   9/12/94

Approving Official's Signature/Title   Date

     District Director   9/16/94

This appraisal has been discussed with me and I have been given a copy. I am aware that if I decide to request a reconsideration of my rating it must be submitted, in writing, to the Approving Official within fifteen workdays from receipt of my appraisal.

Employee Signature   *Yvonne Wiley*   Date   9/16/94

Exhibit 33

Introduction to Offers in Compromise

Introduction	In some cases, the Internal Revenue Service will accept less than full payment of an assessed or proposed liability to consider the liability fully satisfied. This is called an Offer in Compromise (OIC).
OIC is an alternative	Some taxpayers are unable to full pay their delinquencies. They may enter into a long term installment agreement, or their liabilities may be declared currently not collectible (CNC). An OIC may be a legitimate alternative to either of these solutions.
OIC gives the taxpayer a fresh start	An OIC is used to achieve collection of what could reasonably be collected, at the earliest possible time, with the least cost to the Government. It also gives the taxpayer a fresh start at voluntary compliance. The OIC policy and program of the Internal Revenue Service defines both OIC procedures and the Service's philosophy regarding offers.
Offer Policy	There are times when a taxpayer disputes the tax amount due and there is a reasonable doubt as to the liability. In other cases, the taxpayer may acknowledge that the tax is owed, but an analysis of their financial condition shows that the liability cannot realistically be collected in full. Policy Statement P-5-100 contains the Service's position on using OICs. It is on the next page.

Impact of OIC Policy for the IRS and Taxpayers

Impact	Policy Statement P-5-100 defines in general terms the goals of the offers program and the roles of the Government and taxpayer.
Goals of the OIC program	The goals of the OIC program are to achieve collection of: • what can reasonably be collected • at the earliest possible time • with the least cost to the government
An OIC provides alternatives to other measures	The acceptance of OIC is a legitimate alternative to: • closing a case currently not collectible, or • a protracted installment agreement.
An OIC can be in the best interest of both the Government and taxpayer	An OIC may be in the best interest of the taxpayer and Government by: • allowing the taxpayer to resolve the tax problem • providing the taxpayer with an opportunity for a fresh start at voluntary compliance • allowing the Government to resolve cases in a competent businesslike manner • collecting funds which may not be collectible through any other means